NINETEENTH EDITION

THE UK TEDDY BEAR GUIDE

GW00690594

PUBLISHING
Hugglets

Contents   3

THE UK
TEDDY BEAR
GUIDE 2006

Further copies
are available from the publisher
Hugglets, PO Box 290, Brighton, England, BN2 1DR
Single copies: UK £7.50, Europe £8.50, Rest of World £10.50 inc postage

ISBN 1 870880 33 1   ISSN 0952-8105

Cover Photo: Courtesy *Hermann Teddy Original* - see page 155

Published by: Hugglets, PO Box 290, Brighton, England, BN2 1DR
Tel: 01273 697974   Fax: 01273 626255   Email: info@hugglets.co.uk

Printed in Great Britain by Newman Thomson, Burgess Hill, England

The UK Teddy Bear Guide 2006 is compiled and published by
Glenn & Irene Jackman, Hugglets, October 2005.

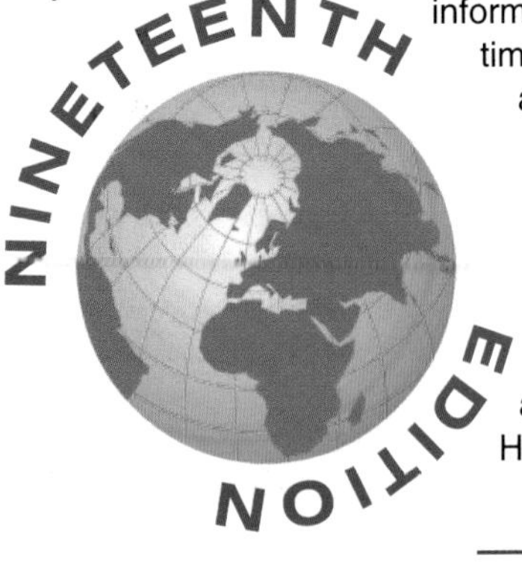

Great care has been taken to ensure the accuracy of information given and it is believed to be correct at the time of going to press. However, no liability can be accepted for loss or damage resulting from error or omission of any sort. Information is invited to ensure the future accuracy and comprehensive coverage of the Guide.

Readers are required to satisfy themselves on all matters concerning advertisers' standards, products and services, and no liability will be accepted by Hugglets in any way.

NINETEENTH EDITION

PUBLISHING

STEIFF CLUB

Exclusive
Limited Editions
for Club Members

Collectors' paradise

Free Gift
New members receive
a 7cm silver grey coloured
Teddy bear.
On renewal another
gift will also be yours.

A quarterly Club magazine
Including a UK
supplement with new
products, news and
Club event details for
collectors.

Valuable
Information about
Steiff and the Steiff
product range offering
a host of gift ideas and
a guide to collecting.

So many benefits for members!

Steiff BUTTON IN EAR

Annual membership £27
I would like to join the Steiff Club. Please send me an application form.

Send to:

**Leyla Maniera
Steiff UK
PO Box 158
Cranleigh
Surrey, GU6 8ZW**

First name
_____

Surname
_____

Address
_____

_____

Telephone
_____

Welcome to the Guide

THE UK
£5.95
TEDDY BEAR
GUIDE 2006

INCLUDES 2 free tickets for Hugglets Festivals worth £8

1001 sources for teddy bears and related collectables

The essential resource for all teddy bear lovers

● Welcome to the nineteenth annual edition of Hugglets' UK Teddy Bear Guide.

● This year we've added a new section called the *Bear Gallery* starting on page 109 which showcases the wonderful variety of styles available from bear artists represented in these pages. Pictures are captioned with the artist's businesss name which can be looked up in the *Bear Makers and Artists* section. UK artists start on page 121 and International artists start on page 181.

● 2005 was a landmark year for Hugglets - 20 years since we started making bears in 1985. The demands of a young and growing family meant that bear making soon had to give way to publishing the Guide and staging our Hugglets Teddy Bear Festivals. 20 years later and our children are almost grown up and the Guide and Festivals are still going strong. The first Guide was published in October 1987 and contained just 79 bear makers and 75 shops. This year we have 586 artists and 229 shops and sources for new and old bears. In October 2006 we'll publish the 20th annual edition - so if you want to appear in it or have idea for what you'd like to see - please get in touch.

● Don't forget that you can also download the 2006 Guide onto your computer from our website. Using Adobe Reader enables you to search the whole Guide in an instant on your PC or Mac. See our website at www.hugglets.co.uk

Glenn & Irene Jackman, Hugglets Publishing

Hugglets Festivals give you the chance to see many of the bears and artists found in these pages. The Winter BearFest and Teddies 2006 take place at Kensington Town Hall, London

Complimentary tickets for these two events (worth £8) have been included with this Guide! - see page 225

Exhibitor lists for Hugglets Festivals are available at

www.hugglets.co.uk

(International entries start page 48)

Many of the shops listed here are specialist teddy bear shops, but we also include toy and gift shops which have a range of bears on sale.

Readers are advised to telephone for stock details and opening times before travelling a distance. The *Teddy Bear Trail* section also gives location and stock information.

Some entries are 'mail order only' or dealers to visit by appointment.

• Collectors of old bears should turn to page 54.
• Many bear artists also sell directly - see page 121.

Open All Year
Tel: 01736 798586
71/73 Fore Street • St Ives
Cornwall • TR26 1HW

Steiff
Deans
Merrythought
Hermann
Russ
Boyd
Artist Bears

● **ABBEY BEARS**
71/73 Fore Street, St Ives, Cornwall, TR26 1HW
☎ 01736 798586
Please see display advertisement.

● **ABRACADABRA TEDDY BEARS**
8A Cross Street, Saffron Walden, Essex, CB10 1EX
☎ 01799 527222 Fax: As tel.
email: marsha@abracadabra-teddies.com
web: www.abracadabra-teddies.com
Please see display advertisement.

● **ALICE'S BEAR SHOP**
6 Bridge Street, Lyme Regis, Dorset, DT7 3QA
☎ 01297 444589
email: info@therealalicesbearshop.co.uk
web: www.therealalicesbearshop.co.uk
Artist Bear co-operative. Bearmaking classes, supplies and kits. Soft toys and traditional wooden toys. Open seven days a week.

● **ALL OCCASIONS**
57-59 Court Road, Malvern, Worcestershire, WR14 3BS
☎ 01684 566781
Collectors & Steiff teddy bears.

● **ALL YOU CAN BEAR**
Stand A25-B15, Grays Mews Antique Market, Davies Mews, London, W1 2LD
☎ 020 8368 5491 Fax: 020 8368 5776
email: sarah@allyoucanbear.com
web: www.allyoucanbear.com
Steiff, Dean's Club Store, Cotswold Bear Company, artists including Portobello, Bisson, Somethings Bruin, vintage items.

● **ALLSORTS OF BEARS**
Shop 4, Marine View, The Promenade, Cromer, Norfolk, NR27 9HE
☎ 01263 514111 email: info@allsortsofbears.com
web: www.allsortsofbears.com
Steiff, Dean's, Hermann Spielwaren, Robin Rive, Boyds, Merrythought plus many shop exclusive artist bears. Interest free layaway. Bears sent worldwide.

● AMBER, DOLLS, BEARS AND TRADITIONAL TOYS

at My Little World, 15 The Woolmead, East Street, Farnham, Surrey, GU9 7TX
☎ 01252 727722 Fax: 01252 725522
email: enquiries@mylittleworld.co.uk
Steiner, Hermann, Kosen and more!

● APPLE PIE HOUSE LTD

8 New Street, Ledbury, Herefordshire, HR8 2DX
☎ 01531 635290 Fax: 020 8662 0601
email: shop@applepiehouse.com
web: www.applepiehouse.com
Bear Heaven since 1997.

● ARCTOPHILIA

120 West Street, Faversham, Kent, ME13 7JB
☎ 01795 597770 Fax: As tel.
web: www.arctophilia.com
Teddy bears and beanies galore. Prices for all pockets. Mail order available. Open Tuesday to Saturday. See display advertisement.

● ARUNDEL TEDDY BEARS

21 High Street, Arundel, West Sussex, BN18 9AD
☎ 01903 884458
email: info@arundelteddybears.co.uk
web: www.arundelteddybears.co.uk
A leading specialist teddy bear shop since 1991, offering the latest Steiff, Dean's, Hermann limited editions, and much more.

● ASHBY BEARS & COLLECTABLES

Rushtons Yard, Off Market Street, Ashby-de-la Zouch, Leicestershire, LE65 1AL
☎ 01530 564444
email: sales@ashbybears.com
web: www.ashbybears.com
East Midlands largest selection. Club store for most leading manufacturers. Purchase securely on our hugely popular web site www.ashbybears.com

● ASQUITHS World Famous TEDDY BEAR SHOPS. ETON Berks and HENLEY Oxon

33 High Street, Eton by Windsor, Berkshire, SL4 6AX
☎ 01753 831200 & 2-4 New Street, Henley-on-Thames, Oxfordshire, RG9 2BT Tel: 01491 571978
email: asquithsbears@aol.com
web: www.asquiths.com
ASQUITHS 'World Famous' Teddy Bear Shops are located in the quintessentially English towns of Henley-on-Thames, and Eton by Windsor. The shops are open 7 days a week and are full of the World's finest bears from leading artists and top manufacturers. We are Club Stores for both Steiff and Hermann, and have our own Arctophiles Club for collectors to get the best in bears. Also in store for you are fabrics, prints, passports, stationery, and a comprehensive selection of teddy bear clothing. We repair and restore teddies back to health, and when Joan is not running the shops or talking about teddies on the local BBC radio, she designs ASQUITHS Luxury Teddy Bears which are in some of the country's most prestigious households. So bear in mind a visit to ASQUITHS and be in good company.

● BACTON BEARS

at Jeffries Country Clothing, Station Garage, Bacton, Stowmarket, Suffolk, IP14 4HP
☎ 01449 781087 Fax: 01449 780391
email: bactonbears@aol.com
web: www.bactonbears.co.uk
Literally hundreds of bears!

● BAR STREET BEARS

30 Bar Street, Scarborough, North Yorkshire, YO11 2HT
☎ 01723 353636
Please see display advertisement.

● BEAR BOTTOMS

12 Elvet Bridge, Durham, County Durham, DH1 3AA
☎ 0191 383 2922
email: enquiries@bearbottoms.co.uk
web: www.bearbottoms.co.uk and www.bearsupplies.co.uk
Steiff Club Store, Dean's Club Store, Merrythought Club Store, Hermann, Robin Rive, Russ, Boyds, gollies, old bears, bear making supplies.

BEAR CORNER

John Clare Cottage (rear of), 42 Church Street, Northborough, Peterborough, Cambridgeshire, PE6 9BN
☎ 01733 252408 Fax: As tel.
email: toni@bearcorner.co.uk
web: www.bearcorner.co.uk
Large selection of manufactured and artist bears. Steiff club store. Village location. On site parking. Open - please call.

THE BEAR CUPBOARD

24 Church Street, Coggeshall, Essex, CO6 1TX
☎ 01376 563739
email: bearcupboard@tiscali.co.uk
web: www.thebearcupboard.co.uk
Collectable bears, dolls and gifts. Visit our bears for a loving hug and a very warm welcome in historic Coggeshall.

THE BEAR EMPORIUM

Well View, Ridgeway Craft Centre, Ridgeway, Nr Sheffield, Derbyshire, S12 3XR
☎ 01142 482010
web: www.bear-emporium.com
For all your beary needs. Stockists of major leading makers. Bear gifts for all occasions. Teddy bear fairs and hospital.

THE BEAR FACTORY

London, W1F 7PA
☎ 0870 333 2458 Fax: 020 7479 7319
email: enquiries@bearfactory.co.uk
web: www.bearfactory.co.uk
Make your own furry friend.

BEAR GALLERY

61 The Promenade, Portstewart, Co. Londonderry, N/I, BT55 7AF
☎ 02870 831010
email: sales@beargallery.co.uk
web: www.beargallery.co.uk
Best of Steiff retailer. Superb range of classics, limited editions, country exclusives. Low prices, free UK delivery. Other major manufacturers.

THE BEAR GARDEN (GUILDFORD)

10 Jeffries Passage, Guildford, Surrey, GU1 4AP
☎ 01483 302581 Fax: 01483 457393
email: bears@beargarden.co.uk
web: www.beargarden.co.uk
Established 1992. Leading UK teddy bear specialist. Experts in Steiff, Deans and other quality teddy bear manufacturers and leading bear artists.

THE BEAR GARDEN (KINGSTON-UPON-THAMES)

1A Crown Arcade, Kingston upon Thames, Surrey, KT1 1JB
☎ 020 8974 6177 Fax: 020 8974 5332
email: bears@beargarden.co.uk
web: www.beargarden.co.uk
Includes Steiff mini-gallery.

THE BEAR HUGGERY

Tower House, Castle Street, Douglas, Isle of Man, IM1 2EZ
☎ 01624 676333/07624 490551
email: bearhuggery@manx.net
web: www.thebearhuggery.co.uk
Special bears & animals to love! Artist, vintage, teddy hospital, favourite manufacturers, one-offs and exclusives! Come and have a hug!

THE BEAR MUSEUM

38 Dragon Street, Petersfield, Hampshire, GU31 4JJ
☎ 01730 265108
web: www.bearmuseum.co.uk
Steiff main stockist.

THE BEAR PATCH

33 Market Place, Ashbourne, Derbyshire, DE6 1EU
☎ 01335 342391
Huge selection including Steiff, Dean's, Merrythought, Robin Rive, Steiner, Boyds, Deb Canham, Hermann, Gund, Kosen, artist bears and old bears.

BEAR SHOP BOLTON

14 St. Andrews Court, Bolton, Lancashire, BL1 1LD
☎ 01204 381937
web: www.bearshopbolton.co.uk
Stockists of:- Steiff, Boyds, Dean's, Cotswold, Hermann Teddy, Gund, Merrythought, limited editions, artist bears, gollys, rag dolls, and shop specials, etc.

Joan Bland
of Asquiths

meet the

Bacton Bears
at Jeffries Country Clothing

Station Garage, Bacton, Stowmarket, Suffolk. IP14 4HP

Tel: 01449 781087   Fax: 01449 780391

Steiff Club Store, stockists of Deans, Merrythought,
Robin Rive, Hermann & Russ bears

Visit our website: www.bactonbears.co.uk email: bactonbears@aol.com

---

● **THE BEAR SHOP**
3 Sir Isaacs Walk, Colchester, Essex, CO1 1JJ
☎ 01206 577345
email: enquiries@bearshops.co.uk
web: www.bearshops.co.uk
Cuddles and collectables, artist bears and limited editions. New bears always arriving. Visit or telephone for information. Open Mon-Sat 10am-5pm. See display advertisement.

● **THE BEAR SHOP**
18 Elm Hill, Norwich, Norfolk, NR3 1HN
☎ 01603 766866 Fax: 01603 618619
email: enquiries@bearshops.co.uk
web: www.bearshops.co.uk
Exclusive teddy bear shop in Norwich. All the famous makes plus many artist bears. Please send for your free catalogue or see our website.

● **THE BEAR SHOP (TOTNES)**
94 High Street, The Narrows, Totnes, Devon, TQ9 5SN
☎ 01803 866868/866086
email: james@bear-shop.co.uk
web: www.bearshop.co.uk
Please see display advertisement.

● **BEAR TODAY SHOP**
46 Hazel Drive, Wingerworth, Chesterfield, Derbyshire, S42 6NE
email: lara@beartoday.com
web: www.beartoday.com
Sell traditional and contemporary teddy bears including Gund, Steiff, Classic Pooh, Paddington. Are also specialists in quality licensed plush products.

● **BEARLY THERE YORKSHIRE**
PO Box 802, Bradford, BD10 9WX
☎ 08700 272825
email: teddy@bearlythere.co.uk
web: www.bearlythere.co.uk
Collectable teddy bears including limited editions. Books about teddy bears. Secure online ordering. Visit our site and adopt a bear!

● **BEARLY TRADING OF LONDON**
Bear Corner, 202 High Street, London, SE20 7QB
☎ 0208 466 6696 Fax: 0208 4603166
Steiff limited editions. Open Saturdays.

BEARS AND MODELS GALORE
50 Beach Road, Clacton-on-Sea, Essex, CO15 1UE
☎ 01255 436195 Fax: As tel.
email: mail@bearsandmodels.co.uk
web: www.bearsandmodels.co.uk
Steiff, Dean's, Merrythought, Anna Plush, Hermann, Kosen, Steiner, Noddy, Paddington, Pooh, Rupert, World of Miniatures, Artist's shop exclusives, Tedaway & Mail Order.

BEARS AT THE REAL MCCOY
5 Loan Road, Cullybackey, Ballymena, County Antrim, BT42 1ER, Northern Ireland, UK
☎ +44 (0)28 2588 2262 Fax: +44 (0)28 2588 0349
email: sales@realmccoy.freeserve.co.uk
web: www.bearsattherealmccoy.co.uk
Northern Ireland's leading bear specialists. Steiff (club store) and other major manufacturers. Old bears also available. Worldwide mail order.

BEARS AT WIRK
2A Market Place, Wirksworth, Derbyshire, DE4 4ET
☎ 01629 822898 Fax: 01629 822527
email: bears@wirk.freeserve.co.uk
web: www.bearsatwirk.co.uk
A warm and friendly welcome awaits you in this lovely Derbyshire heritage town. Please see display advertisement.

THE BEARS DEN
Craft Corner, 10 Imperial Buildings, Corporation Street, Rotherham, South Yorkshire, S60 1PA
☎ 01709 828619
Yorkshire's friendliest bear shop. Steiff and leading manufacturers. Unique artist bears. Shop exclusives. Layaway service. A shop well worth exploring.

BEARS GALORE
27 High Street, Rye, East Sussex, TN31 7JF
☎ 01797 223187 Fax: 01797 223676
email: info@bearsgalore.co.uk
web: www.bearsgalore.co.uk
Specialist bears below ground level.

● BEARS OF ROSEHILL

1-3 Griffin Street, Newport, Gwent, NP20 1GL, South Wales

☎ 01633 244554 Fax: As tel.
email: john@bearsofrosehill.fsnet.co.uk
web: www.bearsofrosehill.com
Layaway, mail order, repairs.

● BEARS ON THE SQUARE

2 The Square, Ironbridge, Shropshire, TF8 7AQ
☎ 01952 433924 Fax: 01952 433926
email: bernie@bearsonthesquare.com
web: www.bearsonthesquare.com
The Midland's largest selection of bears from major manufacturers and leading artists. Many shop exclusives. Worldwide mail order service.

● BEARS & STITCHES

4 Cumberland Street, Woodbridge, Suffolk, IP12 4AB
☎ 01394 388999 Fax: As tel.
Steiff, Robin Rive, Gund, Cambrian, Merrythought & Canterbury Bears. Unusual gifts for everyone.

● BEARS TO COLLECT

Tilbrook Mill, B645, Lower Dean, Nr Kimbolton, Huntingdon, Cambridgeshire, PE28 0LH
☎ 01480 860376 Fax: 01480 861025
email: shirley@bearstocollect.co.uk
web: www.bearstocollect.co.uk
Specialists in limited edition bears.

● BEARS4EVERYONE

2 Market Street, Otley, West Yorkshire, LS21 3AF
☎ 01943 468444
email: sales101@bears4everyone.com
web: www.bears4everyone.com
Visit bears4everyone in the delightful market town of Otley. Stockists of Dean's, Steiff, Hermann, Merrythought, Russ, Gund and many more.

WHICH STEIFF ARE YOU MISSING?
• Present • Indulgence • Birthday • Christening   Older Steiff Limited Editions
Tel: 01793 706662   www.bearsuwant.com

LIGHT UP YOUR LIFE!
SWITCH ON TO OUR DAZZLING ARRAY OF BEARS!

Canterbury
Clemens
Cotswold
Diddl
Grisly
Gund
Hansa
Halcyon days
Hermann
    Spielwaren
Russ
Steiner
Artist bears
Gollies
Pooh
Paddington

Layaways

Worldwide
    Mail order

Club store for....
Boyds
Dean's
Deb Canham
Hermann
Robin Rive
Steiff

Please note that no bears were harmed
in the making of this advertisement

Why not visit our 200 year old shop
in the delightful
Ironbridge Gorge World Heritage site
or buy securely on line from our
huge web site at...
www.bearsonthesquare.com

Bears on the Square

2 The Square, Ironbridge, Shropshire, TF8 7AQ

Tel: +44 (0)1952 433924 Fax: +44 (0)1952 433926

E-mail: teddies@bearsonthesquare.com

Open every day, 10.00am - 5.00pm

● BEL AIR - MEADOWHALL

7 Park Lane, Meadowhall Shopping Centre, Sheffield, South Yorkshire, S9 1EL
☎ 0114 256 9990 Fax: 0114 256 9935
email: belair@wilec.co.uk
web: www.belairgallery.co.uk
Steiff Club Store. A collector's paradise. Mail order, in person or online. See display advertisement.

● BROADWAY BEARS AT THE BINDERY

69 High Street, Broadway, Worcestershire, WR12 7DP
☎ 01386 854645 Fax: As tel.
email: cathy@broadwaybears.com
Artist and manufacturers' bears.

● CAMEO BEARS

228 Station Road, Bamber Bridge, Preston, Lancashire, PR5 6TQ
☎ 01772 627810 Fax: As tel.
email: claire@cameobears.co.uk
web: www.cameobears.co.uk
Showroom packed with hundreds of bears and gollies, manufacturers and artists. Efficient, friendly service. Colourful website with secure internet shopping.

● CAUSEWAY HOUSE CRAFTS AND CINNAMON BEAR COFFEE SHOP

Castleton, Hope Valley, Derbyshire, S33 8WE
☎ 01433 620343 Fax: 01433 620258
email: rog.vincent@virgin.net
Join us in our new coffee shop and find a new friend amongst Steiff, Robin Rive and Deb Canham bears.

● CE GIFTS & BEARS

5 Hebden Court, Matlock St, Bakewell, Derbyshire, DE45 1EE
☎ 01629 814811 Fax: 01629 814820
email: info@cegifts.co.uk
web: www.cegifts.co.uk
Collector & plush bears, gifts, more.

● CEJAIS COLLECTORS CORNER

169 Medieval Spon Street, Coventry, Warwickshire, CV1 3BB
☎ 024 76 633630
Dean's, Gund, Teddy Bear Orphanage, Steiff, Cotswold Bears, Robin Rive, Merrythought, 3 O'Clock Bears, Russ.

● CHARACTER BEARS

☎ 0870 241 3798
email: sales@characterbears.co.uk
web: www.characterbears.co.uk
Choose from over 50 different character bears for every interest and special occasion! To view the range, please visit www.characterbears.co.uk

● CHARLIE BEAR

Online shop
☎ 0870 760 7351
email: sales@charliebear.co.uk
web: www.charliebear.co.uk
Bears, clothing, accessories available online.

● THE CHOCOLATE BOX

Hollowgate, Holmfirth, West Yorkshire, HD9 2DG
☎ 01484 688222 Fax: 01484 685875
email: carolinejohn@btopenworld.com
Steiff, Merrythought, Cotswold, Gund teddybears. Large collection of collectors bears. Limited editions Steiff, Merrythought, Cotswold, Cliff Richard Gund teddybears.

● CHRISTMAS ANGELS

47 Low Petergate, York, North Yorkshire, YO1 7HT
☎ 01904 639908 Fax: 01904 613640
email: chris@mailbox01.freeserve.co.uk
web: www.christmasangels.co.uk
We stock dozens of makes both manufacturers and artist bears. Join our collectors' club and enjoy discounts on your purchases.

● DAWN CLARKE

Paramount, Hinckley Island Hotel, A5 Watling Street, Hinckley, Leicestershire, LE10 3JA
☎ 01455 230823 Fax: As tel.
email: dawn.clarke5@btinternet.com
For all your Steiff products.

Based on Pavarotti by Robin Rive

bears
to collect

Specialists in limited edition bears

Einstein by Robin Rive

Hero by Deb Canham

Extensive range in stock. Special orders taken.
Robin Rive, Deb Canham, Steiff, Deans, Merrythought,
Hermann Spielwaren, Teddy Hermann miniatures
Exclusive local artist bears and other beary items

Visit in person at:
Tilbrook Mill, Near Kimbolton, Lower Dean,
Huntingdon, Cambs, PE28 0LH
or telephone: 01480 860376
www.bearstocollect.co.uk
email: shirley@bearstocollect.co.uk

PUBLISHING

● DOLLY DOMAIN OF SOUTH SHIELDS

45 Henderson Road, Simonside, South Shields, Tyne & Wear, NE34 9QW
☎ 0191 42 40 400 Lo-call: 0845 6655 667
Fax: 0191 42 40 400
email: shop@dollydomain.com
web: www.dollydomain.com
Please see display advertisement. 'User friendly' website, free overnight mail orders, lo-call customer service line, best stocks and best prices.

● DOLLY LAND

864 Green Lanes, Winchmore Hill, London, N21 2RS
☎ 020 8360 1053 mob: 07940 205 928
Fax: 020 8364 1370
email: greta_dollyland@yahoo.co.uk
web: www.dolly-land.co.uk
We stock bears: old limited edition Steiff you are missing, Hermann, Merrythought, gollies, antique dolls, Annette Himstedt, trains, diecast, scalectric.

● DUCHESS COURT SHOPS LTD - BEAR ISLAND

Home Farm, Brodick, Isle of Arran, KA27 8DD
☎ 01770 302831 Fax: As tel.
email: duchesscourtshopsltd@tiscali.co.uk
web: www.bearisland.co.uk
A treasure island of collectable and huggable bears along with their friends all looking for loving homes. Please see advertisement.

● ELIZABETH BEARS

'Tudor Croft', 93 Eastwood Drive, Colchester, Essex, CO4 9EB
☎ 01206 844598
email: elizabethbears@aol.com
web: www.elizabethbears.com
Specialising in Portobello Bears and Gertie Wiggins including large range of other artist's bears. Tel: 01206 844598; www.elizabeth-bears.com.

Curiosity Corner

Bears, Dolls, Gifts and a whole lot more
Probably the best Bear and Doll shop in Suffolk
A STEIFF CLUB AND DEAN'S BEARS SPECIALISTS

With over 500 Bears and Dolls on display over 2 floors in our wonderful old shop in medieval Lavenham in Suffolk a great place to visit.

You will find one of the biggest displays of Steiff, Dean's, Merrythought, Robin Rive, and most manufacturers bears and a vast and varied range of artist bears including Janet Clark, Ellie Bears, Bells Bears and more.

Gifts such as Moorcroft, Gotz Dolls, Annette Himstedt and Mariquita Perez Dolls

1 Church Street, Lavenham, Sudbury, Suffolk, CO10 9QT
Tel/Fax 01787 248441
Email: i_george@lineone.net
Visit our website at
www.curiosity-corner.com

Picture: *Chuckles and Curios, Janet Clark shop exclusives*

● ESPECIALLY BEARS LTD

29 Royal Star Arcade, High Street, Maidstone, Kent, ME14 1JL
☎ 01622 690939 Fax: As tel.
email: winnieweb@talk21.com
web: www.especiallybears.com
Hundreds of teddy bears in all shapes and sizes. Gifts, cards and jewellery 'tedcetera'. 'Teddy Bear & Friends' magazine subscriptions.

● THE EXMOOR TEDDY BEAR CO LTD

The Steep, Dunster, Somerset, TA24 6SE
☎ 01643 821170
email: sales@exmoorteddybears.com
web: www.exmoorteddybears.com
Save money and join our Gold Club today! Beautiful bears and friends to collect, cuddle, give or simply love!

● THE EXMOOR TEDDY BEAR CO LTD

13 Guildhall Shopping Centre, Exeter, Devon, EX4 3HG
☎ 01392 499044
email: sales@exmoorteddybears.com
web: www.exmoorteddybears.com
Save money and join our Gold Club today! Beautiful bears and friends to collect, cuddle, give or simply love!

● THE EXMOOR TEDDY BEAR CO LTD

6-8 York Buildings, Cornhill, Bridgwater, Somerset, TA6 3BS
☎ 01278 450500
email: sales@exmoorteddybears.com
web: www.exmoorteddybears.com
Save money and join our Gold Club today! Beautiful bears and friends to collect, cuddle, give or simply love!

● THE EXMOOR TEDDY BEAR CO LTD
56b The Avenue, Minehead, Somerset, TA24 5BB
☎ 01643 702333
email: sales@exmoorteddybears.com
web: www.exmoorteddybears.com
Save money and join our Gold Club today! Beautiful bears and friends to collect, cuddle, give or simply love!

● FERNDOWN GALLERY
97 Victoria Road, Ferndown, Dorset, BH22 9HU
☎ 01202 861186
email: gallery@ferndowngallery.co.uk
web: www.ferndowngallery.co.uk
Big selection Steiff teddy bears.

● THE GEORGIAN WINDOW
85 Kington St Michael, Chippenham, Wiltshire, SN14 6HX
☎ 01249 750413
Steiff, Hermann, Cliff Richard Collection.

● GERALDINE'S OF EDINBURGH
133-135 Canongate, Edinburgh, Lothian, EH8 8BP, Scotland
☎ 0131 556 4295 Fax: As tel.
email: geraldine.e@virgin.net
web: www.dollsandteddies.com
Specialists of fine jointed mohair bears from childrens' heirlooms to collectors' limited editions. Mail orders of dolls and bears welcome.

● GIFT CONCEPTS LTD
29 Harley Street, London, W1G 9QR
☎ 020 7016 2713 Fax: 020 7182 7046
email: f.gild@gift-concepts.net
web: www.gift-concepts.net
Exclusive handmade limited edition bears.

● THE GIFT
5 Kirkgate, Newark, Nottinghamshire, NG24 1AD
☎ 01636 610075 Fax: 01636 704819
web: www.thegift-newarkbears.com
Over 400 different bears in stock. Steiff, Dean's, Steiner, Robin Rive, gollies, Hermann, Deb Canham Miniatures, Merrythought, and Cliff Richard Collection.

THE GIFT SHOP
@ LOCHLORIAN HOUSE HOTEL
13 Philip Street, Carnoustie, Angus, Scotland, DD7 6ED
☎ 01241 852182 Fax: 01241 855440
email: hotellochlorian@aol.com
web: www.lochlorian.co.uk
Lovely bears and quality gifts. Giftshop within 3 star hotel. Steiff, Boyds', Dean's, Ronnie Hek bears, Radley handbags and more.

GOLDILOCKS
4 The Mall, Ringwood Road, Burley, Ringwood, Hampshire, BH24 4BS
☎ 01425 403558 Fax: As tel.
email: carolinewaud@goldilocksbears.co.uk
web: www.goldilocksbears.co.uk
New Forest village. Good selection of bears at all prices including Steiff, Dean's, Hermann, Merrythought, Robin Rive, Cotswold.

DEAN'S CLUB STOCKIST

Goldilocks

**Enjoy a day in the Heart of the
NEW FOREST**
and visit GOLDILOCKS,
home for a wide range of Bears
incl. Steiff, Dean's, Hermann,
Merrythought, Robin Rive, Cotswold
and artists.

**4 The Mall, Ringwood Road,
BURLEY, Hampshire BH24 4BS**
(between Lyndhurst and Bournemouth)
www.goldilocksbears.co.uk

Also open Sundays
01425 403558
(Mail Order and
Lay-a-way Service Available)

DEAN'S Collectors Club

GORGE BEAR COMPANY
The Gorge, Cheddar, Somerset, BS27 3QE
☎ 01934 743333
email: bears@bear-world.com
web: www.bear-world.com
Secure on-line ordering.

GRETA MAY ANTIQUES
The New Curiosity Shop, 7 Tollgate Buildings, Hadlow Road, Tonbridge, Kent, TN9 1NX
☎ 01732 366730
email: gretamayantiques@hotmail.com
Artist bears and vintage bears.

GRIZZLY BUSINESS
'Candy Cottage', High Street, Alfriston, East Sussex, BN26 5JA ☎ 01323 870836
email: grizzly.business@virgin.net
web: www.grizzlybusiness.com
See an impressive collection from Steiff, Hermann, Dean's, Merrythought, Boyds, Ganz, Kosen, Robin Rive, Steiner, Cotswold Bears and many more.

GROWLIES OF SCOTLAND
15 Thorn Brae, Johnstone, Renfrewshire, PA5 8HF, Scotland
☎ 01505 336551 Fax: 01505 337373
email: teddies@growlies.co.uk
web: www.growlies.co.uk
The best bears in Scotland!

HALCYON OF ST. MARYCHURCH
42B Fore Street, St. Marychurch, Torquay, Devon, TQ1 4LX
☎ 01803 314958
email: dinahowell@btconnect.com
web: www.halcyonbears.com
An exciting range of bears.

HAMLEYS OF LONDON
188-196 Regent Street, London, W1R 6BT
☎ 020 7479 7308 Fax: 020 7479 7398
web: www.hamleys.com
Comprehensive range of collector bears.

PUBLISHING

HALCYON COLLECTIONS

TEDDIES
TO
TREASURE

- Dean's ● Merrythought,
- Cotswold ● Russ
- Local specialist makers
- Some discontinued bears
- Dolls Houses ● Pottery

42b Fore Street, St Marychurch,
Devon, TQ1 4LX Tel: 01803 314958

See our updated website
www.halcyonbears.com
Give Diana a ring

● HARLEQUIN COLLECTABLES
126 Northgate Street, Chester, Cheshire, CH1 2HT
☎ 01244 325767 Fax: As tel.
email: dolls@tinyworld.co.uk
web: www.buydollsandbears.co.uk
Please see display advertisement.

● HAUSSER MARKETING UK
☎ 01706 848670 Fax: 01706 841179
General agent for Steiner, Germany.

● THE HERITAGE BEAR COMPANY
Burnbrae Farm Cottage, Milton, Crocketford, Dumfries,
DG2 8QR
☎ 01556 690595 Fax: As tel.
email: nick.sandrarobson@btinternet.com
web: www.heritagebears.com
*Internet specialist in exclusive and limited
edition artist bears made in Scotland and
Merrythought bears from England. Callers by
appointment.*

● HOLDINGHAM BEARS
Unit 6, Navigation Yard, Carre Street, Sleaford,
Lincolnshire, NG34 7TR
☎ 01529 303266 Fax: 01529 307524
email: barbara@holdinghambears.com
web: www.holdinghambears.com
*Watch Barbara Daughtrey designing and
making quality collectors bears in her new
workshop situated in the HUB courtyard.
Commissions accepted.*

● IRONBRIDGE GORGE MUSEUM TEDDY BEAR SHOP
Ironbridge, Telford, Shropshire, TF8 7NJ
☎ 01952 433029
email: teddybears@ironbridge.org.uk
web: www.merrythought.co.uk
Merrythought specialists. Bear related gifts.

● JAC-Q-LYN'S LITTLE SHOP OF BEARS
60a St Edward St, Leek, Staffordshire
☎ 01538 388831
web: www.jacqlynbears.com
Stocking manufactured and artist bears.

● JARROLD DEPARTMENT STORE
London Street, Norwich, Norfolk, NR2 1JF
☎ 01603 697253 Fax: 01603 611295
email: info@jarroldthestore.co.uk
web: www.jarroldthestore.co.uk
Toys, soft toys, dolls, Steiff.

● JAYSART
5 Station Villas, Bredon, Tewkesbury, Gloucestershire,
GL20 7LU
☎ 01684 773333 Fax: As tel.
Please see display advertisement.

● JEANNE TOYS
544 Chorley Old Road, Bolton, Lancashire, BL1 6AB
☎ 01204 495583
Stockist of Steiff teddy bears.

Plan your trip to Somerset today and visit

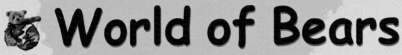

World of Bears

Three floors bursting with cuddles! Opposite Debenhams, behind Wimpy

World of Bears, 20 Lower Middle Street, Taunton, Somerset, TA1 1SF. Tel (01823) 332050

Welcome to my World of Teddy Bears and Friends. All the Bears and Friends are lovingly hand selected and cuddled. We have a tedtastic range of over 5000 different lines by all the major manufacturers. My World Beating range is all under one roof, such that when you come and visit us you can have a cup of tea, a cuddle and choose your favourite face!

Wow check out our Shop Exclusives from Deans, Hermann Spielwaren and Merrythought..

| Merrythought LE50 Cheeky Scrumpy Jack | Merrythought LE50 Cheeky Mouse | Merrythought LE50 Strawberries & Cream | Merrythought LE50 Cheeky Bee |

| Merrythought LE50 Cheeky Jack Frost | Deans Rag Book Co LE50 Currant Bun | Merrythought LE25 Traditional Bear | Hermann Spielwaren Morris LE50 |

If you cannot visit our shops, why not visit our extensive website with over 3,500 products on-line

www.bear-world.com or alternatively give us a call.

Check out our website for our 2006 events programme

The Gorge^ous Bear Co

The Gorge Bear Co, Queens Row, Cheddar Gorge, Somerset, BS27 3QE. Tel: (01934) 743333

Layaway service up to six months

Start collecting PawPrints™ today with every purchase, collect 500 PawPrints™ and save £5.00

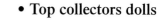

JENNY SCOTT'S BECKSIDE GALLERY

Church Avenue, Clapham, Via Lancaster, North Yorkshire, LA2 8EA
☎ 015242 51122 email: info@jennyscott.co.uk
web: www.jennyscott.co.uk
Extensive range of artist bears.

JU-BEARY BEARS

Studio 3, Barleylands Craft Village, Barleylands Road, Billericay, Essex, CM11 2UD
☎ 01268 525775
Come and visit the Ju-Beary Bears Studio. Open 11am til 4pm Wednesday to Sunday. Layaway service. Also Pooh, Cherished Teddies.

JUST BEARS

8 Bridge Street, Congleton, Cheshire, CW12 1AY
☎ 01260 291188
email: janbartlett3004@yahoo.co.uk
Specialist bear and gift shop.

JUST BEARS @ INSPIRATIONS

40-42 Princess Way, Swansea, West Glamorgan, SA1 5HE, Wales
☎ 01792 472737 Fax: As tel.
email: soo.harris@ntlworld.com
web: www.justbearsforless.com
Wales' stockist of Portobello and Barbara-Ann Bears. Mainstream bears and gollies. Flexible layaway. Mail order service. See display advertisement.

KIERON JAMES DESIGNS

79 High Street, Lindfield, West Sussex, RH16 2HN
☎ 01444 484870 Fax: 01444 484890
email: kieron.james@talk21.com
A shop in picturesque Lindfield village for fine teddy bears and gifts. Steiff, Hermann, Merrythought etc. Credit, debit cards accepted.

KIKISAMS

21 West Street, Oundle, Northamptonshire, PE8 4EJ
☎ 01832 275314
Stockists of Steiff, Boyds, Ty.

The Heritage Bear Company

Specialists in exclusive and limited
Edition artist bears made in Scotland
And Merrythought bears from England.
See website. Callers by appointment.

www.heritagebears.com tel/fax: 01556 690595 email: nick.sandrarobson@btinternet.com

KINGSTON BEARS

Ringwood Shopping Centre, 2 Market Place, Ringwood, Hampshire, BH24 1AW
☎ 01425 470422
email: kingstonbears@aol.com
web: www.kingstonbears.com
Workshop plus old bear selection.

KINGSWEAR BEARS AND FRIENDS

2A The Square, Kingswear, Dartmouth, Devon, TQ6 0AA
☎ 01803 752632
email: teddies@kingswearbears.com
web: www.kingswearbears.com
Free mail order. Riverside shop opposite steam train station. Steiff, Dean's, Merrythought, Hermann, Robin Rive, Steiner, Boyds & much more.

LATIMER OF BEWDLEY

2 Sandstone Road, Bewdley, Worcestershire, DY12 1BW
☎ 01299 404000 Fax: As tel.
email: latimerofbewdley@aol.com
web: www.latimerofbewdley.com
Teddy bear manufacturers and importers.

LEIGH TOY FAIR

45 Broadway West, Leigh-on-Sea, Essex, SS9 2BX
☎ 01702 473288 Fax: As tel.
email: info@leightoyfair.co.uk
web: www.leightoyfair.co.uk
Steiff Club 'best of' store, Dean's, Merrythought, Hermann, Deb Canham, Silver Cross prams, dolls houses, castles, forts, traditional wooden toys.

LET'S GO ROUND AGAIN!

2 Maypole Street, Wombourne, West Midlands, WV5 9JB
☎ 01902 324141
web: www.letsgoroundagain.co.uk
Please visit our village shop and meet the bears - including Cotswold, Boyds, Dean's, Steiff, Robin Rive, Merrythought. Mail order welcome.

LINCRAFTS

11 Torfrida Drive, Bourne, Lincolnshire, PE10 9QF
☎ 07050 245572
email: sales@lincrafts.com
web: www.lincrafts.com
Bearingtons, Ganz Cottage Collectibles, Boyds.

LITTLE BEARS

Stansted, Essex, CM24 8BX
☎ 01279 816022 Fax: As tel.
email: little.bears@btinternet.com
web: www.littlebears.co.uk
Bears & more by mail.

LODGE CORDELL

29 Earsham Street, Bungay, Suffolk, NR35 1AF
☎ 01986 894482
email: yvon@onetel.com
web: www.bungay-suffolk.co.uk
Steiff, Steiner, Cotswold collectors bears.

● MARY SHORTLE

9 Lord Mayors Walk, York, North Yorkshire, also at 9, 15 & 17 Queen's Arcade, Leeds.

☎ 01904 425168 / 631165 / 634045; Tel: 01132 456160 (Leeds) Fax: 01904 425168

email: mary@maryshortleofyork.com

web: www.maryshortleofyork.com

Antique and modern teddies. Limited editions, miniature teddies, leading artists. Teddy bear hospital. Hundreds of teddies to choose from.

● MAYFAIR CARDS & GIFTS

119 Connaught Avenue, Frinton-on-Sea, Essex

☎ 01255 674677

email: info@mayfairbears.co.uk

web: www.mayfairbears.co.uk

Bears from Merrythought, Dean's, Steiff, Robin Rive and Gund. Also some artist bears including many limited editions.

● MEMORY LANE

69 Wakefield Road, Sowerby Bridge, West Yorkshire, HX6 2UX

☎ 01422 833223 Fax: 01422 835230

web: www.memorylanebears.co.uk

Bears and friends. Sensible offers never refused. Some on website and more in stock. Ring within hours 12-4. Closed Thursday.

● MEMORY LANE

18 The Market, Wrythe Lane, Rose Hill, Carshalton, Surrey, SM5 1AG

☎ 0208 288 0820 Fax: 0208 288 0821

email: jane@memorylanebears.com

web: www.memorylanebears.com

Family run business. Extensive range for every Hug. Many Artist Bears. Club Store for Steiff, Deans, Merrythought, Hermann, Deb Canham.

● MEMORY LANE AT CORFE CASTLE DORSET

Bears & Bygones, 8 & 18A East Street, Corfe Castle, Wareham, Dorset, BH20 5ED

☎ 01929 480006 (shop) or 462168 (home)

Layaway and mail order available.

● MILFORD MODELS & HOBBIES

48 High Street, Milford-on-Sea, Hampshire, SO41 0QD
☎ 01590 642112 Fax: 01590 645029
email: mmh1@dsl.pipex.com
web: www.milfordmodels.co.uk
See display advertisement.

● MOHEART TEDDYBEARS

Tudor House, 58 High Street, Caergwrle, Nr Wrexham,
Flintshire, LL12 9LL, North Wales
☎ 01978 760700
*North Wales' largest teddy bear shop. Steiff,
Dean's, Merrythought, Kösen, Hermann,
Cotswold, Robin Rive, Gund. Artist & antique
bears. Bears restored.*

● JENNY MORGAN

11 Swincross Road, Stourbridge, West Midlands,
DY8 1NL
☎ 01384 397033 Fax: As tel.
Specialising in Steiff limited editions.

● NEW ENGLAND COUNTRY STORE

51 Broad Street, Worcester, WR1 3LR
☎ 01905 723463
web: www.newenglanddirect.co.uk
Boyds and Russ stockist.

● NO 9 PAWS FOR THOUGHT

9 Steep Hill, Lincoln, Lincolnshire, LN2 1LT
☎ 01522 510524
email: no9pawsforthought@btopenworld.com
web: www.no9pawsforthought.com
*Collectors bear and doll shop. Artist bears,
Dean's, Steiff, Merrythought, Robin Rive,
Steiner and Hermann. Layaway and mail order.*

● OCCASIONS UNLIMITED

The Lamb Arcade, 83 High Street, Wallingford,
Oxfordshire, OX10 0BX
☎ 01491 833800
email: dcbalchin@aol.com
web: www.occasions-unlimited.com
Lots of lovely bears.

● ORPHAN BEARS

92 Heath Street, Nutgrove, St Helens, Merseyside, WA9 5NJ

☎ 01744 812274 Fax: 01744 813334

email: info@orphanbears.co.uk

web: www.orphanbears.co.uk

Revolutionary new plush bears, designed by bear artists, from the Teddy Bear Orphanage, to give individuality back to plush bears.

● PARTY BEARS

The Antique Map Shop, 9/10 Pulteney Bridge, Bath, Avon, BA2 4AY

☎ **01225 446097**

email: sue@partybears.freeserve.co.uk

Collectors' limited edition & artist bears. Deb Canham (Collectors Club), Dean's, Boyds, Steiff, Steiner, Teddy Hermann, Hermann Spielwaren, Artist Bears.

● PAST & PRESENTS

Crag Brow, Bowness-on-Windermere, Cumbria, LA23 3BX

☎ 015394 45417

Steiff, Hermann, Steiner, Browne, Dean's, Robin Rive, Bukowski, Susan Jane, Gund, World of Miniature Bears, collectable and designer dolls.

● SUE PEARSON

18 Brighton Square, The Lanes, Brighton, East Sussex, BN1 1HD

☎ 01273 774851/329247 Fax: 01273 774851

email: sales@suepearson.co.uk

web: www.suepearson.co.uk

Please see advertisement page 7.

● PEGGOTTY – THE TEDDY HOUSE

The White Orchard, Back Lane, Bomere Heath, Shrewsbury, Shropshire, SY4 3PL
☎ 01939 291328
email: teddy@peggotty.force9.net
web: www.peggotty.f9.co.uk
We are moving. Watch our website for exciting new details and news. Until December 2005 our telephone number remains the same.

● POOH CORNER

High Street, Hartfield, East Sussex, TN7 4AE
☎ 01892 770456 Fax: 01892 770872
email: info@poohcorner.co.uk
web: www.pooh-country.co.uk
Pooh Corner for everything Pooh.

● POSTAL BEARS

6 Atherton Avenue, Mottram, Cheshire, SK14 6NJ
☎ 01457 766650 Fax: As tel.
email: elaine@postalbears.co.uk
web: www.postalbears.co.uk
Secure site, mail order, layaway.

● POTTERY PLUS

16 Seaside Road, Eastbourne, East Sussex, BN21 3PA
☎ 01323 727430
email: malcmar@aol.com
web: www.members.aol.com/pottplus/index.html
Deans, TY. Ceramic Pooh, Steiff.

● THE POTTING SHED

Ransoms Garden Centre, St. Martin, Jersey, JE3 6UD
☎ 01534 854203 Fax: As tel.
email: ransoms@localdial.com
Stockist of all major names. Also, own store limited edition Dean's Bear and Robin Rive Golly. Steiff club store.

● QVC

Marco Polo House, 346 Queenstown Road, London, SW8 4NQ
☎ 020 7705 5600 Fax: 020 7705 5601
email: webmasteruk@qvc.com
web: www.qvcuk.com
See ad for more details.

www.MemoryLaneBears.com

18 The Market,
Rosehill, Wrythe Lane
Carshalton, Surrey
SM5 1AG

Tel: 020 8288 0820
Fax: 020 8288 0821
jane@memorylanebears.com

Mail Order ¥ Layaway
¥ Collectable Dolls

All Modern Day Collectables

Second to none for Quality and Choice. Many Shop Exclusives

We are a family run
business and offer an
extensive range of Bears
for every type of Hug.

Along with our Artist Bears we are stockists and the Club Store for
Steiff, Hermann Original, Deans, Merrythought and Deb Canham

We are open Monday to
Saturday, 10am to 6pm

Please call to arrange out of
hours appointments

All major credit cards accepted

www.MemoryLaneBears.com

Visit our website or call in and see us, you will be amazed and delighted

Peggotty

For Exquisite Artist Bears

Portobello Bears Always in Stock

Peggotty is moving to America. We will continue to offer a superb range of Portobello bears plus many new and exciting American artists. Watch our website!

Email: teddy@peggotty.force9.net

www.peggotty.f9.co.uk

● **RAFFLES**
2 Curfew Yard, Thames Street, Windsor, Berkshire, SL4 1SN
☎ 01753 851325 Fax: 01753 831320
email: sv@rafflesgiftcollection.co.uk
web: www.rafflesgiftcollection.co.uk
Unique, special, Dean's and Boyds Bears.

● **RAZZLE DAZZLE**
119 Regent Street, Kingswood, Bristol, Avon, BS15 8LJ
☎ 01179 614141
The most enchanting shop in the southwest, stocking Steiff, Dean's, Hermann, Robin Rive, TBO, Boyds, Gund, Hansa, Hermann Spielwaren and unusual giftware.

● **ROUND ABOUT BEARS**
☎ 07785 788307
email: mille@roundaboutbears.co.uk
web: www.roundaboutbears.co.uk
Steiff club store specialising in new and old limited editions from all over the world. Premier stockist of Hovvig, Jill Baxter.

Milford Models & Hobbies

48 High Street, Milford-on-Sea, near Lymington, Hants, SO41 0QD   Tel: 01590 642112   Fax: 01590 645029
E.mail: mmh1@dsl.pipex.com
www.milfordmodels.co.uk

Steiff Limited Editions

Steiff, Merrythought, Dean's & Hermann Club Stores

Robin Rive, Gund, Schuco, Hantel, Numerous Artist Bears, Dolls house accessories and Bear related items.

Railways • Diecast • Kits
Britains • Schuco • Bassett-Lowke

STEIFF CLUB

● SELECTEDS
35 Queens Road, Southend-on-Sea, Essex, SS1 1LT
☎ 01702 390097
email: josee@selecteds.com
web: www.selecteds.com
Please see our display advertisement.

● SERENDIPITY
53 The Arcade, Piece Hall, Halifax, West Yorkshire, HX1 1RE
☎ 01422 340097
email: serendipityhalifax@hotmail.com
web: www.tedshop.com
Stockist of Steiff, Dean's, Hermann, Merrythought, Ty, Russ, Boyds and others. Also dolls and accessories, houses and twelfth scale miniatures.

● SHOWCASE
13 Montpellier Arcade, Cheltenham, Gloucestershire, GL50 1SU ☎ 01242 224144
web: www.showcaseonline.co.uk
Wide selection of unique and limited edition bears. All major names stocked. Also pictures, cards and gifts for all occasions.

● SIDMOUTH BEARS
Baskerville House, Old Fore Street, Sidmouth, Devon, EX10 8LP
☎ 01395 512888
email: shop@sidmouthbears.com
web: www.sidmouthbears.com
Bears to suit all tastes. Steiff, Dean's, Merrythought, Gund, Russ, Robin Rive. Artist bears, one-offs, limited editions and shop exclusives.

● SNUFF BOX (EST 1984)
51 Blackburn Road, Great Harwood, Lancashire, BB6 7DF
☎ 01254 888550 Fax: 01254 886889
email: naomi@snuffbox.fsnet.co.uk
web: www.snuffboxonline.co.uk
We stock Steiff, Deans, Hermann, Steiner, Merrythought & Rare Bears. Border Fine Arts, Enesco, Poole, Willow Tree & more....

● ST MARTIN'S GALLERY
The Old Church, Mockbeggar Lane, Ibsley, Hampshire, BH24 3PP
☎ 01425 489090
email: stmartins@ibsleyhants.freeserve.co.uk
web: www.stmartinsartandcraftcentre.com
Set in a 17th century church our bears and gollies are very well behaved. They include Robin Rive, Tailored Teddies, Steiner and many more.

● STEIFF GALLERY
The Glades, Bromley, Kent, BR1 1DN
☎ 0208 466 8444
email: london@steiff-gallery.co.uk
web: www.steiff-gallery.co.uk
Everything Steiff under one roof.

● STONEGATE TEDDY BEARS
13 Stonegate, York, North Yorkshire, YO1 8AN
☎ 01904 641074 Fax: As tel.
York's Only Steiff Club Store.

● THE SUFFOLK DOLL COMPANY
21 High Street, Hadleigh, Suffolk, IP7 5AG
☎ 01473 827600 Fax: As tel.
Steiff and other collectables. Layaway.

● TALENTS OF WINDSOR
12 Church Street, Windsor, Berkshire, SL4 1PE
☎ 01753 831459
email: info@talentsofwindsor.com
web: www.etalents.com
Steiff bears, animals store/online.

● TED'S PLACE
Unit 10, Blakemere Craft Centre, Chester Road, Sandiway, Cheshire, CW8 2EB
☎ 01606 888600 Fax: As tel.
email: tedsplace03@aol.com
web: www.tpcollectable.com
Teddy bears and things for all your special occasions. Limited editions, artist bears, plush, personalised teddy bears. Always something now.

● **TEDDEEZ BEAR CO**
3 Wenlock Way, High Street, Maldon, Essex, CM9 5AD
☎ 01621 842752
email: bears@hugsters.com
web: www.hugsters.com
Stockists of Diddl and friends, artist bears and dolls, French baby gifts, teddy bear hospital, Teddeez shop exclusives, beary gifts.

● **THE TEDDY BEAR CLUB**
'Exclusives', Great Baddow, Chelmsford, Essex
☎ 01245 478578 Fax: As tel.
email: teddybear@teddybearclub.co.uk
web: www.teddybearclub.co.uk
Buy Merrythought, Robin Rive, Cotswold, Artist, gift bears and gollies at the Teddy Bear Club. Not your average online store!

● **TEDDY BEAR HOUSE**
Trinity Street, Dorchester, Dorset, DT1 1TT
☎ 01305 263200 Fax: 01305 268885
email: info@teddybearhouse.co.uk
web: www.teddybearhouse.co.uk
Large selection of collectors' bears, limited editions and most leading makes. Steiff, Merrythought, Dean's Club. Something for all tastes.

● **THE TEDDY BEAR ORPHANAGE**
92 Heath Street, Nutgrove, St Helens, Merseyside, WA9 5NJ
☎ 01744 812274 Fax: 01744 813334
email: info@teddybearorphanage.co.uk
web: www.teddybearorphanage.co.uk
Artist, antique and discounted bears.

● **THE TEDDY BEAR SHOP**
6 Market Avenue, Huddersfield, W. Yorkshire, HD1 2BB
☎ 01484 420999 Fax: As tel.
email: sales@teddybearshuddersfield.co.uk
web: www.teddybearshuddersfield.co.uk
Boyd, Steiff, Robin Rive, Gund, Merrythought.

● TEDDY BEAR UK

95 Melton Road, West Bridgford, Nottingham, Nottinghamshire, NG2 6EN
☎ 0115 981 2013 Fax: 0115 953 4119
email: sales@teddy-bear-uk.com
web: www.teddy-bear-uk.com
Bears by Steiff, Boyds, Dean's, Merrythought, Hermann, Robin Rive, Gund, artist bears, plus bear giftware and needle-craft. See our display advertisement.

● TEDDY BEARS COTTAGE

Unit 4, White Hart Development, Off Market Place, Spalding, Lincolnshire, PE11 1SU
☎ 01775 722523
email: chris@teddybearscottage.co.uk
web: www.teddybearscottage.co.uk
Please see display advertisement.

● TEDDY BEARS & FRIENDS OF BOURNE

5a South Street, Bourne, Lincolnshire, PE10 9LY
☎ 01778 426898
email: info@bournebears.co.uk
web: www.bournebears.co.uk
Bears, bears and more bears.

● TEDDY BEARS OF WITNEY
99 High Street, Witney, Oxfordshire, OX28 6HY
☎ 01993 706616 Fax: 01993 702344
email: ordersonly@witneybears.co.uk
web: www.teddybears.co.uk
A haven for collectors with over one thousand new and old teddy bears to see. 2006 colour catalogue £5.

● TEDDY BEARSVILLE
28 High Street, Rowley Regis, West Midlands, B65 0DR
☎ 0121 559 9990 Fax: As tel.
email: sales@teddybearsville.net
web: www.teddybearsville.info
Wide range including Steiff USA exclusives, Dean's, Merrythought, Robin Rive, Gollies, Clemens, Hermann. 9ct gold teddy bear jewellery. Mail order.

● TEDDY 'N' FRIENDS
Jane Clayton, Trent House, Piddletrenthide, Dorset, DT2 7QX
☎ 01300 348483
Exceptional artist bears. Appointment only.

● THISTLEDOWN
On the net
☎ 023 9259 9932 email: mrsthistledown@aol.com
web: www.thistledowndollsandbears.co.uk
Collectors' bears and dolls.

● THUMBELINA'S
33 Harnet Street, Sandwich, Kent, CT13 9ES
☎ 01304 619802
Steiff, Robin Rive, Dean's, Hermann, Boyd and Cotswold Bear Company. Also $1/12$ dolls house miniatures and houses. Artist dolls.

● TOFFEE BEARS
Hailsham, East Sussex
☎ 01323 449748 email: carol@toffeebears.com
web: www.toffeebears.com
Specialising in top artists.

● THE TOY CHEST
1-2 Devonshire Arcade, Penrith, Cumbria, CA11 7SX
☎ 01768 891237 / 01768 774953
web: www.toychestpenrith.co.uk
Largest collection of bears in Cumbria and the Lake District. Two shops Penrith and Keswick. Not to be missed.

We are located at the heart of the picturesque market town of Beverley, East Riding of Yorkshire, in a Georgian grade II listed building

We stock all your favourite Teddy Bears!

Steiff, Teddy Hermann, Steiner, Robin Rive, Dean's, Merrythought, Gund, Clemens, Russ Berrie, Boyds, Deb Canham, Cotswold Bears, Cliff Richard Collection, Hildegard Gunzel, World of Miniatures, Heartfelt, Dormouse, Mister bears and various Artist bears.

We also have a number of older Steiff pieces just waiting to complete your collection.

In addition you can browse our beautiful range of traditional wooden toys and games, admire the world famous Stevensons rocking horses, reminisce over the classic metal pedal cars and then relax in our walled courtyard garden while you decide which of our lovable Teddy Bears will be joining your family.

Please visit our website to learn more about Beverley, view our store, browse our range and shop in the comfort of your own home.

www.toygalleryuk.com
Tel: 01482 864890
17 Ladygate, Beverley, East Yorks, HU17 8BH

THE TOY EMPORIUM
79 High Street, Bridgnorth, Shropshire, WV16 4DS
☎ 01746 765134 Fax: As tel.
email: thetoyemp@aol.com
web: www.thetoyemporium.co.uk
Steiff Club and specialist store.

TOY GALLERY
17 Ladygate, Beverley, East Yorkshire, HU17 8BH
☎ 01482 864890
email: enquiries@toygalleryuk.com
web: www.toygalleryuk.com
Large selection of fabulous bears.

TRADITIONAL TOYS LTD
6 Bull Ring, Llantrisant, Mid-Glamorgan, CF72 8EB
☎ 01443 222693 Fax: 01443 238436
A Victorian shop offering a large range of teddy bears as well as hand-made wooden toys and rocking horses.

TRAVELLING TEDDIES
Notwen Bower, Kirkpatrick Fleming, Dumfriesshire
☎ 01461 800587
email: hello@travellingteddies.com
web: www.travellingteddies.com
On-line teddy bear gift store.

TREASURED TEDDIES
at Farnborough Garden Centre, Southam Road, Farnborough, Banbury, Oxfordshire, OX17 7EL
☎ 01295 690479
Cuddly collectables and furry friends.

UNIQUE
23 Risbygate Street, Bury St Edmunds, Suffolk, IP33 3AA
☎ 01284 723116 Fax: 01284 702589
Bears from all leading makers.

WESTMEAD TEDDIES
The Tuck Shop, High Street, Godshill, Ventnor, Isle of Wight, PO38 3HH
☎ 01983 840643
Godshill's old tuck shop is home to teddies to suit all pockets from exclusive artist bears to pocket money teds.

WIGGINTONS
6/8 Old Cross, Hertford, Hertfordshire, SG14 1RB
☎ 01992 505695
Extensive collection of collector bears.

WORLD OF BEARS
Lower Middle Street, Taunton, Somerset, TA1 1SF
☎ 01823 332050
email: bears@bear-world.com
web: www.bear-world.com
Secure on-line ordering.

YORKSHIRE COLLECTABLES
9 Sheep Street, Skipton, North Yorkshire, BD23 1JH
☎ 01756 797453
email: sales@yorkshirecollectables.net
web: www.yorkshirecollectables.net
Please see our main advert for our great selection of bears. Shop located in the beautiful market town of Skipton.

International entries are included within each section and where the number is sufficient, as here, they are grouped after the UK entries. For information on telephoning abroad, please see page 219.

● BAMSERNES MAGASIN
Ringstedgade 15, 4000 Roskilde, Denmark
☎ +45 46 35 78 45
email: mail@bamsernesmagasin.dk
web: www.bamser.dk
Largest teddy bear shop in Denmark. Steiff clubstore, Boyds, Robin Rive, Hovvigs, Hermann Teddy, Hermann Spielwaren, Deb Canham, artist bears, Dean's.

● BÄRADIES
PO Box 1132, 82256 Fürstenfeldbruck, Germany
☎ +49 (0)8145 998 700 Fax: +49 (0)8145 998 702
email: birgit.gloeckler@baeradies.com
web: www.baeradies.com
Steiff specialist. See display advertisement.

● BÄRENBOUTIQUE
Sebastian-Kneipp-Str.2, 76476 Bischweier, Germany
☎ +49 (0)7222 50 60 15
email: info@baerenboutique.de
web: www.baerenboutique.de
Your online source for German teddy bears by Hermann Coburg, Teddy Hermann (club dealer), Martin Sonneberg, Grisly Spielwaren, Clemens Spieltiere.

● BEAR ESSENTIALS
PO Box 29102, Greenwoods Corner, Epsom, Auckland, 1003, New Zealand
☎ +64 (0)9 630 8479 Fax: +64 (0)9 630 8489
email: pooh@bearessentials.co.nz
web: www.bearessentials.co.nz
Bear Essentials: the complete on-line teddy bear store selling limited edition and artist bears, teddy making supplies plus cute cuddly bears.

● BEAR ESSENTIALS (IRELAND)
Anke Morgenroth, Tiernawannagh, Bawnboy, Co. Cavan, Ireland
☎ +353 (0)49 95 23461
email: anke@irishbears.com
web: www.irishbears.com
Workshop & showroom. Open 7 days all year around. Artist bears, Steiff, Russ, Gund, Teddy Bear Workshops for children/adults, Teddy Bear Hospital.

● BEAR GARDEN COMPANY
1Fl., No. 11-1, Alley 27, Lane 90, Deshing E. Rd Shrlin Chiu, Taipei, 11147 R.O.C., Taiwan
☎ +886 (0)2 8866 5587 Fax: +886 (0)2 2832 2605
email: service@bear-garden.com
web: www.bear-garden.com
Taiwan and overseas artist bears. Bear making supplies. Schulte mohair. Host of Taiwan Teddy Bear Association.

Bear Paths

2815 Jay Avenue
Cleveland, Ohio
44113, USA
Shop at
www.bearpaths.com

Visit our on-line
gallery filled with
more than 500
Artist Bears.

Register for our
exclusive
Plum Club.

It's the only way
to experience a
virtual Artist Bear
Show every week.

World Wide
Shipping Available

Tel 1-216-566-1519
Fax 1-216-566-7924
E-mail: bearpaths@aol.com

● THE BEAR NECESSITIES - KNARF-BEARS

Groeninge 23, 8000 Brugge, Belgium
☎ +32 (0)5034 1027 Fax: As tel.
email: info@thebearnecessities.be
web: www.thebearnecessities.be
Artist bears by Maria Devlieghere. Beautiful original artist collector's bears from around the world. Unique Knarf Bears - limited editions.

● BEAR PATHS

2815 Jay Avenue, Cleveland, OH 44113, USA
☎ +1 216 566 1519 Fax: +1 216 566 7924
email: bearpaths@aol.com
web: www.bearpaths.com
More than 500 artist bears online. Join Plum Club today ...it's free ... and an Internet show every Monday!

● FAIRYTALES INC

9 South Park Avenue, Lombard, IL 60148, USA
☎ +1 630 495 6909 Fax: +1 630 495 6553
email: rjtales@aol.com
web: www.fairy-tales-inc.com
FairyTales features the most desirable creations from Steiff, Deb Canham Artist Designs, Wee Forest Folk, Pam Holton, Boyds and more!

● GERMANBEARS.COM

USA
☎ +1 801 796 9888 Fax: +1 801 229 1123
email: ericb@tko.com web: www.germanbears.com
GermanBears.com is an authorized Steiff & Steiff Club dealer. All bears discounted, including US limited editions.

● THE HEN NEST

207 North Main Street, Columbia, AL 36319, USA
☎ +1 334 696 3480 Fax: +1 334 696 4390
email: hennest@aol.com web: www.hennest.com
Current and retired selections from R John Wright, Steiff, Deb Canham, Karl Gibbons Collection, Little Gems, Hermann, and Artist Bears.

Bed, Breakfast & Bears!

We carry over 10,000 teddy bears
from 80 sources in our 4-room shop

A magical place to visit and stay.

244 Main Street, Chester, Vermont 05143, USA
Tel: +1 802 875 2412 www.huggingbear.com

ITleem's

Dolls and Bears

Gae
Grose

Shop 45
London Court
Perth
WA 6000
Australia

Tel: +61 (0)8 9325 2897

Email: meemsbearsanddolls@msn.com

www.meems-bears-dolls.com

● **THE HUGGING BEAR INN &
SHOPPE**
244 Main Street, Chester, Vermont 05143, USA
☎ +1 802 875 2412
web: www.huggingbear.com
*Bed/Breakfast/Bears. We carry over 10,000
teddy bears and their friends in our 4-room
shop. Magical place to visit.*

● **KINDERTRUHE**
Satke Hellmuth, Kirchengasse 18, A-1070, Vienna,
Austria
☎ +43 (0)1 523 33 83 Fax: As tel.
email: office@kindertruhe.at
*Limited edition collectors' teddybears, spe-
cialist in Steiff replica bears, authorised
Steiff Club dealer. Many artists bears and
bearly components.*

● **L'OURS DU MARAIS**
18 Rue Pavée, 75004 Paris, France
☎ +33 (0)1 42 77 60 43 Fax: +33 (0)1 42 77 60 44
email: oursdumarais@wanadoo.fr
web: www.oursdumarais.com
*The first teddy bear shop in Paris. Many
bears by French and international artists.*

● **MEEM'S**
Shop: 45 London Court, Perth, Western Australia 6000,
Australia
☎ +61 (0)8 9325 2897 Fax: As tel.
email: meemsbearsanddolls@msn.com
web: www.meems-bears-dolls.com
*Unique to Australia. Hand crafted Australian
award winning bears and doll creations not
available in the UK or Europe.*

● **MEMORIES**
74 High Street, Killarney, Co. Kerry, Ireland
☎ +353 (0)64 34447 Fax: +353 (0)64 39990
*We stock Irish artist bears, antique and new
linens and lace. Also available Linen Chest
Dingle and White Room Kenmare.*

THE OLDE TEDDY BEAR SHOPPE

10449 Islington Avenue, Box 797, Kleinburg, Ontario, L0J 1C0, Canada
☎ +1 905 893 3590 Fax: +1 905 893 3605
email: info@theoldeteddybearshoppe.com
web: www.theoldeteddybearshoppe.com
North American Exclusive shop for Forget Me Not Bears, also Oz Matilda, Ro Lu, Ingrid Schmid and many other wonderful artists bears.

RUSSIAN TEDDY BEAR

Russia
☎ +7 095 219 7094
email: anna.kozlova@teddybear.ru
web: www.teddybear.ru
The site about teddy bears, teddy bear artists in Russia.

TEDDY BEARS DOWNSTAIRS

162 Swan Street, Morpeth, Hunter Valley, NSW 2321, Australia
☎ +61 (0)2 4933 1224 / +61 (0)2 4933 9794 Fax: +61 (0)2 4934 3778
email: aussiebear@kooee.com.au
Leading teddy bear and golly shop. With bear related items. The largest shop in Australia situated in historic village of Morpeth.

TEDDY BEARS' PICKNICK

PO Box 333, 3960 BH Wijk bij Duurstede, Netherlands
☎ +31 (0)343 577068 Fax: As tel.
email: picknick@xs4all.nl
web: www.teddybearspicknick.com
Visit our website to see Steiff, Kosen and Artist Bears and Cats, a.o. Forget me not bears. Worldwide mailorder.

TEDDY'S ROOM

Gewerbestr. 18, D 76327 Pfinztal-Berghausen (nr. Karlsruhe), Germany
☎ +49 (0)721 1517 809 mob: + 49 162 4321132
email: bears@teddysroom.com
web: www.teddysroom.com
Karlsruhe, Black Forest area, limited editions from Britain and Germany. Also shop exclusives from South Africa, Canada, USA and Holland.

THE TOY STORE / COLLECTORS GALLERY

Westgate Village, 3301 West Central Avenue, Toledo, OH 43606, USA
☎ +1 419 531 2839 Fax: +1 419 531 2730
email: info@toystorenet.com
web: www.toystorenet.com
We specialize in Steiff USA and International items, gollys, Merrythought USA. We accept all credit cards, paypal and money orders.

VILLAGE BEARS

2890 Hyde Park Street, Sarasota, Florida 34239, USA
☎ **+1 941 366 2667 Fax: +1 941 366 0334**
email: **villagebears@att.net**
web: **www.villagebears.com**
Specialising in R.John Wright, Steiff, Artist Bears, VanderBears, Golliwogs and Deb Canham. Worldwide shipping. Closed weekends and Mondays. Call for appointments.

END

Shops and Sources for Old Bears

Welcome to this section on sources for old bears. Many are dealers who operate on an appointment basis or sell through fairs and the internet. Some have shops, and auction houses are also included.

The numbers of old bears held in stock may range from under ten to over 100. Readers are advised to telephone regarding stock and viewing arrangements before travelling a distance.

● ABBEY BEARS
71/73 Fore Street, St Ives, Cornwall, TR26 1HW
☎ 01736 798586
For old bears and animals.

● ALL YOU CAN BEAR
Stand A25-B15, Grays Mews Antique Market, Davies Mews, London, W1 2LD
☎ 020 8368 5491   Fax: 020 8368 5776
email: sarah@allyoucanbear.com
web: www.allyoucanbear.com
Vintage items plus new Steiff, Dean's, Cotswold Bear Company, artists including Portobello, Bisson, Somethings Bruin. Please see display advertisement.

● ANTIQUE BEAR COLLECTOR
USA
☎ +1 770 834 9599
email: ellen.sotos@gmail.com
web: www.antiquebearcollector.com
A choice collection of antique Steiff, German, American and English teddy bears offered by Ellen Sotos, a long time collector.

Picture courtesy of the Puppenhausmuseum in Basel, Switzerland.

See ad page 103

● BABA BEARS
☎ 0845 257 6091
email: baba.bears@virgin.net
web: www.bababears.co.uk
Specializing in antique teddy bears and quality soft toys. At major bear and toy fairs, and mail order. Stocklist available.

● THE BEAR HUGGERY
Tower House, Castle Street, Douglas, Isle of Man, IM1 2EZ
☎ 01624 676333
email: bearhuggery@manx.net
web: www.thebearhuggery.co.uk
Genteel bearfolk awaiting suitable accommodation - references may be required. Sympathetic preservation undertaken for ailing bears. Artist, manufacturers, exclusives also available.

● THE BEAR PATCH
33 Market Place, Ashbourne, Derbyshire, DE6 1EU
☎ 01335 342391
Manufactured, artist and old bears.

● THE BEAR TRADING COMPANY
154 Princess Drive, Seaford, East Sussex, BN25 2TS
☎ 01323 491816 Fax: 01323 491370
email: beartrading@fsmail.net
web: www.beartradingcompany.co.uk
Please see our display advertisement.

● BEARABLE FRIENDS
65 Sarratt Avenue, Hemel Hempstead, Herts, HP2 7JF
☎ 01442 267328
email: info@bearablefriends.com
web: www.bearablefriends.com
Always good stocks available.

● BEARS OF WINDY HILL
PO Box 51, Shipley, West Yorkshire, BD18 2YH
☎ 01274 599175 Fax: As tel.
email: info@bearsofwindyhill.co.uk
web: www.bearsofwindyhill.co.uk
Old bears, animals and dolls.

● BONHAMS

Montpelier Street, Knightsbridge, London, SW7 1HH
☎ 08700 273627
email: rachel.gotch@bonhams.com
web: www.bonhams.com/toys
Auctioneers and valuers since 1793.

● BOURTON BEARS

☎ 01993 824756 Fax: As tel.
email: help@bourtonbears.com
web: www.bourtonbears.com
Antique teddy bears - over 350 in stock from Steiff, Chiltern, Farnell, Schuco, Bing, Merrythought and more. We also buy teddies.

● BOWDEN'S BEARS

20 Hawthorne Road, Stockton Heath, Warrington, Cheshire, WA4 6JP
☎ 01925 268533
email: geoffreybowden@tiscali.co.uk
Retired bears:- Merrythought, Dean's, Steiff.

● CHRISTIE'S

Daniel Agnew, 85 Old Brompton Road, London, SW7 3LD
☎ 020 7752 3335 Fax: 020 7930 6074
email: dagnew@christies.com
web: www.christies.com
Christie's holds regular auctions devoted to fine and rare Teddy Bears and soft toys including Steiff, Farnell, Bing, Schuco, etc.

● DOLLS, BEARS & BYGONES OF CORNWALL

☎ 01726 61392 Mobile: 078 8963 0051
email: dollsbearsbygone@aol.com
Fine quality antique dolls & bears.

● EVOLUTION BEARS

☎ 0151 678 9452
email: evobear04@aol.com
web: www.evolutionbears.com
Where the love of antique and vintage teddy bears comes to life

● GROWLERS TEDDYBEARS

23 Pamela Road, Exeter, Devon, EX1 2UF
☎ 01392 219917 Fax: 01392 670107
email: soo@growlers-teddybears.co.uk
web: www.growlers-teddybears.co.uk
The original teddy dating agency. Find your perfect partner. From a selection of single mature bears to suit you.

● LEANDA HARWOOD

☎ 01529 300737
email: leanda.harwood@virgin.net
Old teddy bears including Steiff.

● JEANNETTE - TEDDIES GALORE

☎ 0208 958 6101
email: amaz120@aol.com
Antique Bears, especially rare coloured.

● MARTIN KIDMAN

Ditchling, East Sussex, BN6 8UR
☎ 01273 842938 Fax: 01273 843002
email: info@martinkidman.com
web: www.martinkidman.com
Please see our display advertisement.

● LUCKY BEARS LIMITED

PO Box 2064, Hockley, Essex, SS5 5YB
☎ 01702 204182 Fax: 0870 705 3249
email: enquiries@luckybears.com
web: www.luckybears.com
Antique, vintage and collectable bears

● MARY SHORTLE

9 Lord Mayors Walk, York, North Yorkshire, also at 9, 15 & 17 Queen's Arcade, Leeds.
☎ 01904 425168 / 631165 / 634045; Tel: 01132 456160 (Leeds) Fax: 01904 425168
email: mary@maryshortleofyork.com
web: www.maryshortleofyork.com
Antique and modern teddies. Limited editions, miniature teddies, leading artists. Teddy bear hospital. Hundreds of teddies to choose from.

Bourton Bears

Give an old bear a home

One of the largest
selections of old bears.

Telephone: 01993 824756

www.bourtonbears.com

Viewing by Appointment

● MR PUNCH'S OLD TOYS
Admiral Vernon Arcade, 141-149 Portobello Road, London, W11
☎ 020 8878 0773 Fax: As tel.
email: mrpunch@oldtoys.freeserve.co.uk
web: www.mrpunchsoldtoys.com
Large stocks of vintage bears, soft toys, mechanical bears, dolls, gollies and related memorabilia, and all types of old toys.

● THE OLD BEAR COMPANY LTD
PO Box 29, Chesterfield, Derbyshire, S42 6ZE
☎ 01246 862387 Fax: 01246 863011
email: oldbears@oldbear.co.uk
web: www.oldbearcompany.com
Old teddies - please see display advertisement.

● OLD BEARS & FRIENDS
63 Sanderling Way, Iwade, Sittingbourne, Kent, ME9 8TE
☎ 01795 410314
email: oldteddysandme@aol.com
Old bears dolls bought sold.

● OLD BEARS NETWORK
Brown Cow Cottage, Godly Lane, Rishworth, Sowerby Bridge, West Yorkshire, HX6 4QR
☎ 01422 823079 Fax: As tel.
email: oldbears.network@zen.co.uk
web: www.oldbearsnetwork.co.uk
Vintage bears, clothing and accessories.

● THE OLD PLAYROOM
Unit 4, Mill Yard Craft Centre, Swan Street, West Malling, Kent, ME19 6LP
☎ 01732 845582
email: info@theoldplayroom.co.uk
web: www.dawnpotter.com
Old bears and collectable toys, artist bears (including Willow Bears), children's books (including Poems From The Playroom). Please see website.

● OLD TOYS VIENNA
☎ +43 (0)1 769 8901 email: indla17@gmx.net
web: www.oldtoys.info
Wide range early Steiff bears, famous German bears, Bing, Schuco, Craemer, Strunz, vintage Steiff animals, antique dolls, accessories. Reasonable prices!

A RARE HARWIN & CO.
'ALLY BEAR',
1st World War Highland Soldier
Teddy Bear
Sold for £7000,
3 July 2005, London

Auctions 2006
13 July
19 December

Enquiries
Daniel Agnew
dagnew@christies.com
+44 (0)20 7352 3335

Catalogues
+44 (0)20 7389 2820

South Kensington
85 Old Brompton Road
London, SW7 3LD

View catalogues and leave
bids online at christies.com

TEDDY BEARS
London, 2006

CHRISTIE'S
SINCE 1766

PAM PUDVINE
19 Stocks Lane, Boughton, Chester, Cheshire, CH3 5TE
☎ 01244 347900
email: pudvine@aol.com
Old teddies 1910 to 1960.

RAINEY DAYS OLD BEARS & FRIENDS
Lorraine Day
☎ 020 8647 6235
email: raineyrat@hotmail.com
web: www.raineydays.biz
Rare and unusual teddies/friends.

TEDDY BEARS AT HOME
North Tyneside
☎ 0191 2579541
email: shady100@blueyonder.co.uk
web: www.teddybearsathome.zoomshare.com
Teddy bear photos, vintage bears.

Rainey Days
Old Bears & Friends

Specialising in antique, rare and unusual teddy bears and friends

Tel 020 8647 6235
email: raineyrat@hotmail.com
www.raineydays.biz

● TEDDY BEARS OF WITNEY
99 High Street, Witney, Oxfordshire, OX28 6HY
☎ 01993 706616 Fax: 01993 702344
email: ordersonly@witneybears.co.uk
web: www.teddybears.co.uk
We pay fair prices for old teddy bears. We sell old bears in the shop, but not by mail order.

● TOYS OF YOUTH
PO Box 307, Bedford, Bedfordshire, MK43 8ZF
☎ 01234 841649 Fax: As tel.
email: info@toysofyouth.co.uk
web: www.toysofyouth.co.uk
Old bears and old toys for sale from our web-site, by mail order and at all major fairs. Bears purchased.

● VECTIS AUCTIONS
Fleck Way, Thornaby, Stockton on Tees, Cleveland, TS17 9JZ
☎ 01642 750616 Fax: 01642 769478
email: kathy@vectis.co.uk
web: www.vectis.co.uk
Largest toy auctioneer in world.

END

PUBLISHING

Teddy Bear Trail (shops index)

The Teddy Bear Trail has been compiled from the entries in our shops and sources sections which we understand to be retail outlets open during normal shop hours. Some are specialist teddy bear shops while others are general toy and gift shops which sell teddy bears. Please check opening times and stock details etc, before travelling a distance. See main listing in the shops section for more information. For your convenience, entries have been grouped into areas (see map opposite).

The codes which appear after the name of the business refer to the number of makers and different designs which you might expect to find there.

We asked the shops to indicate the bands they fall within. Our questions and the key for the codes appear below.

Question 1: How many different makers (bear artists or manufacturers) do you normally stock? A) 1-10   B) 11-25   C) 26-50   D) 51-100   E) over 100

Question 2 How many different designs/models of teddy bear do you normally have in stock? F) 1-25   G) 26-100)   H) 101-250   I) over 250

London & Southern Counties

Berkshire	Eton by Windsor	Asquiths	E/I
Berkshire	Windsor	Raffles	A/F
Berkshire	Windsor	Talents of Windsor	A/F
East Sussex	Alfriston	Grizzly Business	D/I
East Sussex	Brighton	Pearson, Sue	D/I
East Sussex	Eastbourne	Pottery Plus	A/G
East Sussex	Hartfield	Pooh Corner	
East Sussex	Hastings	Dolls House Plus	B/H
East Sussex	Rye	Bears Galore	C/I
Hampshire	Burley, Ringwood	Goldilocks	B/G
Hampshire	Ibsley	St Martin's Gallery	A/I
Hampshire	Milford-on-Sea	Milford Models & Hobbies	B/H
Hampshire	Petersfield	Bear Museum, The	A/H

Scotland

The North

Central England

Eastern Counties

Wales

London & South East

West Country

Hampshire	Ringwood	Kingston Bears	A/G
Isle of Wight	Ventnor	Westmead Teddies	C/I
Kent	Broadstairs	Bee Antiques and Collectables	A/G
Kent	Bromley	Steiff Gallery	A/I
Kent	Dover	Curiosity of Dover	A/G
Kent	Faversham	Arctophilia	C/I
Kent	Maidstone	Especially Bears Ltd	B/I
Kent	Sandwich	Thumbelina's	B/G
Kent	Tonbridge	Greta May	B/G
Kent	West Malling	Old Playroom, The	A/F
London		All You Can Bear	B/I
London		Bearly Trading of London	D/I
London		Dolly Land	C/I
London		Hamleys of London	D/I
Surrey	Carshalton	Memory Lane	C/G
Surrey	East Street, Farnham	Amber, Dolls, Bears and Traditional Toys	B/H
Surrey	Guildford	Bear Garden (Guildford), The	D/I
Surrey	Kingston upon Thames	Bear Garden (Kingston), The	D/I
West Sussex	Arundel	Arundel Teddy Bears	A/I
West Sussex	Lindfield	Kieron James Designs	B/H

Central England

Derbyshire	Ashbourne	Bear Patch	C/I
Derbyshire	Bakewell	Ce Gifts & Bears	B/H
Derbyshire	Chesterfield	Bear Today Shop	C/H
Derbyshire	Hope Valley	Causeway House Crafts	A/G
Derbyshire	Ridgeway, Nr Sheffield	Bear Emporium	B/H
Derbyshire	Wirksworth	Bears at Wirk	C/I
Gloucestershire	Cheltenham	Showcase	B/G
Gloucestershire	Tewkesbury	Jaysart	C/I
Herefordshire	Ledbury	Apple Pie House Ltd	C/I
Hertfordshire	Hertford	Wiggintons	B/H
Leicestershire	Ashby-de-la Zouch	Ashby Bears & Collectables	C/I
Leicestershire	Hinckley	Clarke, Dawn	A/G
Northamptonshire	Oundle	Kikisams	A/G
Nottinghamshire	Newark	Gift, The	A/I
Nottinghamshire	Nottingham	Teddy Bear UK	C/I
Oxfordshire	Farnborough, Banbury	Treasured Teddies	A/H
Oxfordshire	Henley on Thames	Asquiths	E/I
Oxfordshire	Wallingford	Occasions Unlimited	B/H

Oxfordshire	Witney	Teddy Bears of Witney	E/I
Shropshire	Bridgnorth	Toy Emporium	A/I
Shropshire	Ironbridge	Bears on the Square	E/I
Shropshire	Shrewsbury	Peggotty – The Teddy House	C/H
Shropshire	Telford	Ironbridge Gorge Museum Teddy Bear Shop	A/H
Staffordshire	Leek	Jac-q-Lyn's Little Shop of Bears	
Warwickshire	Coventry	Cejais Collectors Corner	A/H
Warwickshire	Stratford upon Avon	Curtis Brae of Stratford	B/I
West Midlands	Rowley Regis	Teddy Bearsville	B/H
West Midlands	Wombourne	Let's Go Round Again!	A/H
Worcestershire	Broadway	Broadway Dolls & Bears	B/I
Worcestershire	Malvern	All Occasions	B/H

The West Country

Avon	Bath	Party Bears	B/G
Avon	Bristol	Razzle Dazzle	D/H
Cornwall	East Looe	Cornwall Bear Shops	B/I
Cornwall	St Ives	Abbey Bears	B/I
Cornwall	Truro	Cornwall Bear Shops	B/I
Devon	Dartmouth	Kingswear Bears and Friends	B/I
Devon	Exeter	Exmoor Teddy Bear Co Ltd	C/I
Devon	Sidmouth	Sidmouth Bears	B/H
Devon	Torquay	Halcyon of St. Marychurch	A/G
Devon	Totnes	Bear Shop, Totnes	B/I
Dorset	Bournemouth	Bel Air - Bournemouth	A/I
Dorset	Dorchester	Teddy Bear House	C/I
Dorset	Ferndown	Ferndown Gallery	A/G
Dorset	Lyme Regis	Alice's Bear Shop	D/I
Somerset	Bridgwater	Exmoor Teddy Bear Co Ltd	C/I
Somerset	Cheddar	Gorge Bear Company	D/I
Somerset	Dunster	Exmoor Teddy Bear Co Ltd	C/I
Somerset	Minehead	Exmoor Teddy Bear Co Ltd	C/I
Somerset	Taunton	World of Bears	D/I
Wiltshire	Chippenham	Georgian Window	A/H

Wales

Flintshire	Caergwrle, Nr Wrexham	Moheart Teddybears	B/H
Gwent	Newport	Bears of Rosehill	C/I
Mid-Glamorgan	Llantrisant	Traditional Toys Ltd	B/I
West Glamorgan	Swansea	Just Bears @ Inspirations	B/H

Scotland

Isle of Arran	Brodick	Duchess Court Shops Ltd - Bear Island	
Lothian	Edinburgh	Geraldine's of Edinburgh	B/H
Renfrewshire	Johnstone	Growlies	B/H
Tayside	Angus	Gift Shop @ Lochlorian House Hotel	A/G

Eastern Counties

Cambridgeshire	Huntingdon	Bears To Collect	B/I
Cambridgeshire	Peterborough	Bear Corner	B/I
Essex	Clacton-on-Sea	Bears and Models Galore	C/I
Essex	Coggeshall	Bear Cupboard	B/H
Essex	Colchester	Bear Shop, Colchester, The	D/I
Essex	Frinton-on-Sea	Mayfair Cards & Gifts	A/G
Essex	Leigh-on-Sea	Leigh Toy Fair	B/H
Essex	Maldon	Teddeez Bear Co	C/H
Essex	Saffron Walden	Abracadabra Teddy Bears	D/I
Essex	Southend-on-Sea	SelecTeds	B/I
Lincolnshire	Bourne	Teddy Bears & Friends of Bourne	C/I
Lincolnshire	Lincoln	No 9 Paws for Thought	C/I
Lincolnshire	Spalding	Teddy Bears Cottage	B/I
Norfolk	Cromer	Allsorts of bears	C/I
Norfolk	Norwich	Bear Shop, Norwich, The	D/I
Norfolk	Norwich	Jarrold Department Store	A/I
North Lincolnshire	Barton-upon-Humber	Daisa Original Designs Ltd	A/F
Suffolk	Bacton, Stowmarket	Bacton Bears	A/I
Suffolk	Bungay	Lodge Cordell	A/G
Suffolk	Bury St Edmunds	Unique	A/I
Suffolk	Hadleigh	Suffolk Doll Company	B/H

Suffolk	Sudbury	Curiosity Corner	C/I
Suffolk	Woodbridge	Bears & Stitches	A/H
Cheshire	Chester	Harlequin Collectables	C/I
Cheshire	Congleton	Just Bears	B/G
Cheshire	Sandiway	Ted's Place	D/H

The North

County Durham	Durham	Bear Bottoms	E/I
Cumbria	Bowness-on-Windermere	Past & Presents	B/H
Cumbria	Penrith	Toy Chest	B/I
East Yorkshire	Beverley	Toy Gallery	B/H
Isle of Man	Douglas	Bear Huggery	C/I
Lancashire	Bolton	Bear Shop Bolton	B/I
Lancashire	Bolton	Jeanne Toys	A/F
Lancashire	Great Harwood	Snuff Box (est 1984)	A/H
Lancashire	Preston	Cameo Bears	C/I
North Yorkshire	Scarborough	Bar Street Bears	C/H
North Yorkshire	Skipton	Yorkshire Collectables	B/I
North Yorkshire	Via Lancaster	Jenny Scott's Beckside Gallery	B/H
North Yorkshire	York	Christmas Angels	C/I
North Yorkshire	York	Mary Shortle of York	E/I
North Yorkshire	York	Stonegate Teddy Bears	B/G
South Yorkshire	Rotherham	Bears Den	C/I
South Yorkshire	Sheffield	Bel Air - Meadowhall	A/I
Tyne & Wear	South Shields	Dolly Domain of South Shields	B/I
West Yorkshire	Halifax	Serendipity	B/H
West Yorkshire	Holmfirth	Chocolate Box	A/G
West Yorkshire	Huddersfield	Teddy Bear Shop	B/I
West Yorkshire	Leeds	Mary Shortle of York	E/I
West Yorkshire	Otley	bears4everyone	A/F
West Yorkshire	Sowerby Bridge	Memory Lane	A/I

Northern Ireland

Co. Londonderry	Portstewart	Bear Gallery	B/G
County Antrim	Ballymena	Bears at the Real McCoy	B/G

END

International entries start on page 78.

The products on offer by any individual or company are listed in the belief that they are suitable for bearmaking.

However, no responsibility can be accepted by the publisher and readers must satisfy themselves on all matters regarding safety.

● ADMIRAL BEARS SUPPLIES
16 Ormonde Avenue, Epsom, Surrey, KT19 9EP
☎ 01372 813558 Fax: As tel.
email: netty.paterson@ntlworld.com
web: www.admiral-bears.com
Please see display advertisement.

● BARBARA-ANN BEARS
42 Palmarsh Avenue, Hythe, Kent, CT21 6NR
☎ 01303 269038 Fax: 01303 266669
email: barbara-annbears@bigfoot.com
web: www.barbara-annbears.com
Bear-making workshops and one to one tuition, stunning range of colourful hand-dyed mohair and kits. Check website or call for details.

● BEAR BASICS
PO Box 6292, Sherborne, Dorset, DT9 9AN
☎ 01963 250116
email: enquiries@bearbasics.co.uk
web: www.bearbasics.co.uk
Please see display advertisement.

Bear Country

www.bearcountryuk.com

German Mohair
and Plush Fabrics plus
everything else for Bear making

Reasonable prices on a fully secure
website updated daily to ensure
everything listed is in stock

c/o 38 Eden grove, Swallownest,
Sheffield, S26 4TP.
Tel 0114 2879671
Email enquires@bearcountryuk.com

● **BEAR COUNTRY**
c/o 38 Eden Grove, Swallownest, Sheffield, S26 4TP
☎ 0114 287 9671 Fax: 0114 287 3037
email: enquiries@bearcountryuk.com
web: www.bearcountryuk.com
Please see display advertisement.

● **THE BEAR SUPPLIES COMPANY**
'Bear Bottoms', 12 Elvet Bridge, Durham, County Durham, DH1 3AA
☎ 0191 383 2922
email: enquiries@bearbottoms.co.uk
web: www.bearsupplies.co.uk
Eyes, joints, fillings, kits, patterns, mohair, felt, ultrasuede. Bear making courses beginners to professional. Free catalogue.

● **BEARS 4 HUGS**
Glasdrum Trust Cottages, Drimnin, Morvern, Argyll, PA34 5XZ
☎ 01967 421308
email: bears4hugs@tesco.net
web: www.bears4hugs.com
Exclusive weekend bear making courses for all abilities. Small numbers. Also winter bear making retreats. Please send sae for details.

● **BEARY SPECIAL SUPPLIES**
Woodland Teddies, Rita Harwood, 5 Mildenhall Road, Loughborough, Leicestershire, LE11 4SN
☎ 01509 267597 mob: 07973 821816 Fax: 01509 827389
email: supplies@woodlandteddies.com
web: www.woodlandteddies.co.uk
Mail order. See display advertisement.

● **BEDSPRING BEARS**
6 Nottingham Place, Lee-On-Solent, Hampshire, PO13 9LZ
☎ 023 9260 2075 Fax: As tel.
email: bedspringbears@btopenworld.com
web: www.bedspringbears.com
Bear and other animal kits in mohair, plush and cashmere. Mail order service available.

● **BRIDON BEARS & FRIENDS**
'Bears Cottage', 42 St Michael's Lane, Bridport, Dorset, DT6 3RD
☎ 01308 420796 Fax: As tel.
email: donna@bbears.fsnet.co.uk
web: www.bbears.fsnet.co.uk
Teddy kits, patterns, repairs, courses.

● **CHARLIE'S FURS AND FEATURES**
PO Box 814, Northwich, Cheshire, CW8 2WF
☎ 01606 888814 Fax: As tel.
email: charliesfursandfeatures@btopenworld.com
All bear making essentials - fabrics, fillings and features. Please phone for fair dates.

Emmary Bears

Emmary Bears is a small company based in Cornwall. We operate a mail order service and attend a number of shows each year.

We specialise in hand dyed mohair in a range of colours and qualities, including single colours and multi coloured pieces

Wholesale rates available

We also stock an extensive range of kits and patterns from leading bear artists including Kympatti Bears, Bearz by Ibé, Bearlissimo, Les Bears, Wellwood Bears, Gylls Bears - the list is almost endless!!!!

If you need components, bear making equipment, glasses, hats, clothing or even wings for your bear making we can supply you – just give us a ring.

For more information please ring 01208 872251 or write to 'Ridgeway', Bodmin Hill, Lostwithiel, Cornwall, PL22 0AJ, or visit our web-site at emmarybears.co.uk Callers by appointment only please.

TEDDY BEAR EYES

Premium quality glass collector teddy bear eyes.

Available in 24 different colours.

All eyes evenly sized & matching pupils.

Trade enquiries welcome.

Also available glass doll and animal eyes.

www.handglasscraft.co.uk

Hand Glass Craft

105 Dudley Rd, Brierley Hill,
West Midlands, DY5 1HD, England

Tel: 01384 573410 Fax: 01384 486467

● CHRISTIE BEARS LIMITED

Ref GD02, The Mount, Clevis Hill, Newton, Porthcawl, CF36 5NT
☎ 01656 789054 Fax: 01656 785044
email: enquiries@christiebears.co.uk
web: www.christiebears.co.uk
Suppliers of fabrics, components and tools to teddy bear makers around the world.

● COURSES WITH BEAR BITS

The Florins, Silver Street, Minting, Horncastle, Lincolnshire, LN9 5RP
☎ 01507 578360 Fax: As tel.
email: ashburner@bearbits.freeserve.co.uk
web: www.bearbits.com
Exclusive weekend bear making courses for beginners, improvers or advanced addicts! Very small numbers only. For information please send SAE.

● CUDDY LUGS

Willey Lane, Sticklepath, Okehampton, Devon, EX20 2NG
☎ 01837 840762
email: sheila@cuddylugs.com
web: www.cuddylugs.com
Knitting patterns for bears clothes including miniatures, yarns, needles, buttons etc. Send £3 for big catalogue or shop on line.

● DINKY-DO MINI SUPPLIES

Greenbanks, Molesworth, Cambridgeshire, PE28 0QD
email: vanessa@hbgcc.fsnet.co.uk
Everything to make small bears.

● EMMARY BEARS

'Ridgeway', Bodmin Hill, Lostwithiel, Cornwall, PL22 0AJ
☎ 01208 872251
web: www.emmarybears.co.uk
A large and varied selection of hand dyed mohair, components, patterns, kits and accessories. Wholesale rates also available.

G & T EVANS WOODWOOL

Dulas Mill, Ffordd Mochdre, Newtown, Powys, SY16 4JD
☎ 01686 622100 Fax: 01686 622220
email: gtevans1@aol.com
web: www.gtevans.co.uk
Manufacturers of superfine grades of wood wool. Samples available. For full details and list of stockists, call us today.

THE GLASS EYE CO.

School Bank Road, Llanrwst, Gwynedd, LL26 0HU
☎ 01492 642220 Fax: 01492 641643
email: sales@glasseyes.com
web: www.glasseyes.com
FREE! Full colour wall chart.

GOLD TEDDY

60 Mortimer Avenue, Batley, West Yorkshire, WF17 8BU
☎ 01924 420272 mob: 07950 329481
email: joan@goldteddy.co.uk
web: www.goldteddy.co.uk
Comprehensive selection of bear-making kits for beginners from exclusive designs. Free easy step-by-step instruction manual. Everything included to complete.

HAND GLASS CRAFT

105 Dudley Road, Brierley Hill, West Midlands, DY5 1HD
☎ 01384 573410 Fax: 01384 486467
web: www.handglasscraft.co.uk
Please see display advertisement.

HOLDINGHAM BEARS

Unit 6, Navigation Yard, Carre Street, Sleaford, Lincolnshire, NG34 7TR
☎ 01529 303266 Fax: 01529 307524
email: barbara@holdinghambears.com
web: www.holdinghambears.com
Watch Barbara Daughtrey designing and making quality collectors bears in her new workshop. Courses and kits available. SAE for details.

JANET CLARK ORIGINALS

61 Park Road, Hemel Hempstead, Hertfordshire, HP1 1JS
☎ 01442 265944 Fax: As tel.
email: JCTeddystyle@aol.com
web: www.janetclark.com
Please visit new website for bears, dolls, animals, patterns available. Classes online and hands on. Always new original characters.

REINHOLD LESCH GMBH

Ursula Clements, UK agent, Garden Flat, 4 Strathray Gardens, London, NW3 4NY
☎ 020 7794 2377 Fax: 020 7209 4799
email: ugmclements@yahoo.co.uk
German manufacturers of bear making components - quality glass and safety eyes, growlers, joints, etc. - catalogue available on request.

● LYRICAL BEARS

PO Box 111, Welwyn Garden City, Hertfordshire,
AL6 0XT
☎ 01438 351651 (evenings)
email: info@lyrical-bears.co.uk
web: www.lyrical-bears.co.uk
The largest range of miniature kits and supplies in the UK. Six first class stamps for catalogue and samples.

● NEW FOREST BEARS

38 South Street, Pennington, Lymington, Hampshire,
SO41 8DX
☎ 01590 673334
email: gilbears@aol.com
Bear-making workshops. SAE for details.

● NORBEARY FABRICS

14 Claymere Avenue, Norden, Rochdale, Lancs,
OL11 5WB
☎ 01706 659819 Fax: As tel.
email: norbeary@btinternet.com
web: www.norbeary.co.uk
Wide range of superb mohair fabrics at the very best value available - compare prices. For samples and pricelist send £5.

● OAKLEY FABRICS LTD

8 May Street, Luton, Bedfordshire, LU1 3QY
☎ 01582 424828/734733 Fax: 01582 455274
email: oakleyfabs@aol.com
web: www.oakleyfabrics.co.uk
Everything for bear making. Open 9.30am - 5.00pm Mondays - Fridays. 10.00am - 4.00pm Saturdays.

● PEACOCK FIBRES LTD

Gain Mill, Gain Lane, Bradford, W. Yorkshire, BD2 3LW
☎ 01274 633900 Fax: 01274 633910
email: info@noblecraft.co.uk
web: www.noblecraft.co.uk
English mohair, ultrasuede, polyester fillings (regular, heavy, super, lux). Recycled fibre, kapok, woodwool, shot, tendertouch baby fat. Next day delivery.

● R B BEAR SUPPLIES

Braeside, 3 Mineral Terrace, Foxdale, Isle of Man,
IM4 3EY
☎ 07624 482 403 Fax: 01624 801197
email: rbbearsupplies@yahoo.co.uk
web: www.bearsupplies.com
Exclusive mohair, kits, patterns, supplies.

RAINBOW DYES
20 West Head, Littlehampton, West Sussex,
BN17 6QP
☎ 01903 722078 Fax: As tel.
email: rainbowdyes@ukart.com
web: www.rainbowdyes.ukart.com
30 colours especially for mohair.

RECOLLECT - DOLLS & BEARS
17 Junction Road, Burgess Hill, West Sussex,
RH15 0HR
☎ 01444 871052 Fax: As tel.
email: dollshopuk@aol.com
web: www.dollshospital.co.uk
*Mohair bear kits, patterns, component packs
and mohair. Jointed porcelain bears. Bear
making supplies. Dolls hospital & supplies.*

TEDDY TRADERS
22 Holly Terrace, Heamoor, Penzance, Cornwall,
TR18 3EL
☎ 01736 363143/07919 802942
*German mohair, patterns, glass eyes, joints,
suede etc. Mail order. Catalogue on request.
Callers by appointment only please.*

TEDDYSMITHS
7 Friar Road, Brighton, East Sussex, BN1 6NG
☎ 07931 479736
email: teddysmiths@hotmail.com
*Miniature bearmaking supplies. Eyes, joints,
vintage longpile and other hand-dyed fabrics.
Send 6 x1st class stamps for catalogue.*

THE BEARS DEN
Craft Corner, 10 Imperial Buildings, Corporation Street,
Rotherham, South Yorkshire, S60 1PA
☎ 01709 828619
Bear making supplies and patterns.

V AND N BEAR SUPPLIES
3 Forewood Rise, Crowhurst, East Sussex, TN33 9AH
☎ 07971 213974
email: vandn.bearsupplies@btinternet.com
web: www.vandnbearsupplies.co.uk
Fabrics, components, patterns and tools.

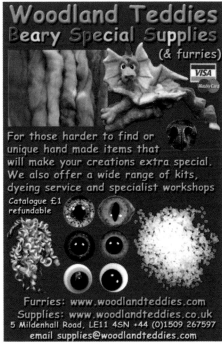

For information about telephoning abroad, please see page 219

● **BEARLAND EXPRESS/DEAR BEARS MARKET PLACE**
PO Box 26081, CRPO, Richmond, B.C., V6Y 3V3, Canada
☎ +1 604 872 2508 Fax: +1 604 872 2504
email: dearbears@dear-bears.com or bearlandexpress@gmail.com
web: www.dear-bears.com or www.bearlandexpress.com
Bear supplies & more - mohair, synthetics, patterns, kits... Artist bears, beaded purses, Crazy quilt patches. Store - Wed-Sat. Visa/Mastercard/Paypal.

● **BEARY CHEAP BEAR SUPPLIES**
PO Box 2465, Burleigh, Queensland 4220, Australia
☎ +61 (0)7 5520 3455 Fax: +61 (0)7 5520 3411
email: sales@bearycheap.com
web: www.bearycheap.com
Please see display advertisement.

● **BEARYWORKS**
2-1-6 Higashi-Yurigaoka, Asao-ku Kawasaki-shi, Kanagawa-ken, 215-0012, Japan
☎ Fax: +81 (0)44 966 1443
email: info@BearyWorks.com
web: www.BearyWorks.com
A web shop offering uniquely designed bear making supplies including stainless steel weights, lead-free; BearyShot. Planning to sell it overseas.

● **DER BÄR**
Peter Stock, Hauptstr. 23, D-40789 Monheim am Rhein, Germany
☎ +49 (0)2173 60428 Fax: +49 (0)2173 684210
email: der-baer.p.stock@gmx.de
web: www.der-baer-stock.com
Please see display advertisement.

When contacting advertisers please mention you saw their advertisement in the UK Teddy Bear Guide

● A HELMBOLD GMBH
Plüschweberei und Färberei, Hauptstr. 44, D-98634,
Oberweid, Germany
☎ +49 (0)36946 22009 Fax: +49 (0)36946 22020
email: Helmbold_GmbH@t-online.de
web: www.A-Helmbold.de
Please see display advertisement.

● PROBÄR GMBH
Heinrich Hertz Str 9, D48599 Gronau, Germany
☎ +49 (0)2562 7013 0 Fax: +49 (0)2562 7013 33
web: www.probear.com
Please see display advertisement.

● ROBERTA KASNICK RIPPERGER 4 CREATIVE DESIGN STUDIO
PO Box 1381, Elmhurst, Il 60126, USA
☎ email: rkr4cds@comcast.net
web: www.beyond-basic-bears.com
*Specializing in Needle Felted Realistic Bears
(especially Polars!). Kit line for beginner
through advanced: unique © 'Patch' tech-
niques taught!*

● TEDDYTECH
49 Florida Road, Durban 4001, South Africa
☎ +27 (0)31 312 7755 Fax: +27 (0)31 312 9564
email: ebeaton@global.co.za
web: www.teddytech.biz
*'Where the magic of bearmaking begins...'
SA distributor of Schulte mohairs, kits, patterns, bearmaking supplies.*

END

The largest supplier in Europe of "Schulte" mohair; cotton, viscose and synthetic plush

In our warehouse of almost 1000m² you will find one of the world's largest assortments of teddy bear making materials. We offer more than 400 different mohairs, plus other fabrics, plus everything needed to produce top quality bears: joints (wood and cardboard), fibre joints (for miniatures), safety-joints and eyes, glass eyes, growlers, T shape cotterpins, cotterkeys, scissors, patterns, kits, stuffing materials like fibrefill, sheepwool and cotton plus pellets in plastic, steel, glass, mineral and rubber etc.

Probear is situated in Germany, 10 minutes drive from the Dutch border. You can visit us during the week or on the internet

www.probear.com

Our mail order catalogue can be ordered free of charge. Our professional sample book with all our above mentioned fabrics plus paw materials like woolfelt, imitation leather (Suédine) and miniature fabrics can be purchased by transferring 35 Euros into our bank account

PROBÄR GmbH
Heinrich-Hertz-Str. 9 • D 48599 Gronau • Germany
Tel: 0049 2562 7013-0
Fax: 0049 2562 7013-33
www.probear.com • info@probeer.nl

PRO
Bär
GmbH

A list of the fair dates known at the time of publication can be found in the Fair Dates listing on page 89.

Dates can change so we recommend you confirm details with the organisers before travelling a distance.

● B.E.A.R. FAIRS

The Bear Emporium, Well View, Ridgeway Craft Centre, Ridgeway, Nr Sheffield, S12 3XR
☎ 07836 730719/ 01142 482010
web: www.bear-emporium.com
Sheffield Wednesday football ground, 8th July 2006. Wrexham Memorial Hall, 23rd September 2006. For all your beary needs.

● BEARS & DOLLS (MINIATURA)

41 Eastbourne Avenue, Hodge Hill, Birmingham, West Midlands, B34 6AR
☎ 0121 783 9922 Fax: As tel.
email: office@miniatura.co.uk
web: www.bearsdolls.com
Check website for 2006 dates.

● BLAKEMERE TEDDY BEAR FESTIVAL

PO Box 814, Northwich, Cheshire, CW8 2WF
☎ 01606 888814 Fax: As tel.
email: charliesfursandfeatures@btopenworld.com
Sunday May 14th 2006 at The Oaklands Hotel, Gorstage, Cheshire. 11 til 4pm. Third year running. Not to be missed!

● BRITISH BEAR FAIR

Tricia Leigh Expositions, Cheapside Lane, Denham Village, UB9 5AD
☎ 01895 834348
Sunday 11th December 2005, Hove.

● CORNWALL AND DEVON BEAR FAIRS

☎ 01208 872251
email: mary.saundry@btinternet.com
web: www.emmarybears.co.uk
Cornwall Bear Fair (at Lostwithiel): 27th November 2005 and 25th June 2006. Devon (at Exmouth): 21st May 2006. Over 45 stalls.

● DOLL & TEDDY FAIRS

Held at the National Motorcycle Museum
☎ 01530 274377 Fax: 024 7639 2284
Quality fairs with old, collectable, artist bears and dolls. Don't miss our all Vintage show 26th November 2006. See display advertisement.

● DOLLY'S DAYDREAMS

PO Box 1, Wisbech, Cambridgeshire, PE13 4QJ
☎ 01945 870160 Fax: 01945 870660
email: info@dollysdaydreams.com
web: www.dollysdaydreams.com
Organisers of established prestige fairs.

● EAST MIDLANDS DOLL FAIRS

5 Arran Close, Holmes Chapel, Cheshire, CW4 7QP
☎ 01477 534626 Fax: As tel.
Kelham Hall, Newark, Notts. (A617) Mansfield Road. Dolls, dollcraft, dolls houses, miniatures, teddies, juvenilia. Quality, friendly fairs. See display advertisement.

● THE ESSEX BEAR FAIR

Old Tithe Hall, Start Hill, Nr Bishops Stortford, Hertfordshire, CM22 7TF
☎ 01279 871110 Fax: 01279 870844
Long established popular annual event at the Brentwood Holiday Inn by Junction 28 of the M25 on Sunday 14th May.

FAIRYTALES INC
9 South Park Avenue, Lombard, IL 60148, USA
☎ +1 630 495 6909 Fax: +1 630 495 6553
email: rjtales@aol.com
web: www.fairy-tales-inc.com
Proud sponsor of Deb Canham Expo, May 5-7, 2006. Games, Prizes, Raffles, Auction and more!

FOUNTAIN FAYRES & EXHIBITIONS
7 Springfield, Thornbury, South Glos, BS35 2EL
☎ 01454 414671
Teddy bear and doll fayres at Winter Gardens, Weston-Super-Mare. The best in the West!

THE HAMPSHIRE TEDDY BEAR FAIR
Old Tithe Hall, Start Hill, Nr Bishops Stortford, Hertfordshire, CM22 7TF
☎ 01279 871110 Fax: 01279 870844
Extremely well established fairs at the prestigious Botleigh Grange Hotel, Hedge End, Southampton. Sunday 4th June and Sunday 19th November.

HUGGLETS
PO Box 290, Brighton, East Sussex, BN2 1DR
☎ 01273 697974 Fax: 01273 626255
email: info@hugglets.co.uk
web: www.hugglets.co.uk
Organisers of the Winter BearFest and Teddies 2006. Publishers of the UK Teddy Bear Guide.

DOLLY DOMAIN FAIRS
proudly present the
25th year
LEEDS
DOLL & TEDDY FAIR
Pudsey Civic Hall, New Pudsey
Saturday 25th March 2006
Saturday 14th October 2006
open 10.30 am to 4.00 pm
Held twice yearly since 1981, it is the longest established teddy and doll fair outside of London, and is fondly known as the 'Pudsey' fair.

All aspects of Teddy and Doll Collecting are covered in this 85 stand quality fair.

Fully signposted, large FREE car park. Excellent cafeteria facilities all day. 2 min walk from New Pudsey Station.

tel / fax: 0191 42 40 400
e-mail: fairs@dollydomain.com
web: www.dollydomain.com/fairs

Come to the
East Midlands
Doll Fair
with Dolls Houses & Teddies
'A MINIATURE WONDERLAND'

Bruce & Pam King present our BIG Show
THE KELHAM HALL DOUBLE
Kelham Hall, Notts
(A617 Newark to Mansfield)
The Dome Exhibition Hall & Conference Rooms
10.30am to 4pm
Sunday 30th October 2005
Sunday 19th February 2006
Sunday 2nd July 2006
Sunday 29th October 2006

Two full sized shows in one
100 Stands
Dolls House and Miniatures Show
plus
Dolls and Teddy Bear Show
• Advanced booking • Free parking • Refreshments
Enquiries: Bruce & Pam King 01477 534626

HUGGLETS

at Kensington Town Hall Hornton Street, London

Twice a year Hugglets Festivals offer you over 175 stands in five bear-packed halls. Choose from 10,000 bears and related collectables on sale at each event.

With 5 halls there's always something magical around the corner!

WINTER BEARFEST

Sunday 26th February 2006

(2007: Sunday 25th February)

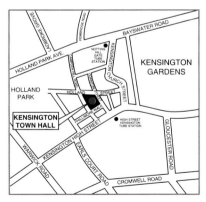

IN SEPTEMBER

TEDDIES 2006

Sunday 3rd September 2006

(2007: Sunday 2nd September)

Entry 11am - 4.30pm
Tickets at door: £4 adult, £2 child

Parking is only £4 for the day. 400 spaces.
Nearest Tube is High Street Kensington

Complimentary entry tickets on page 225

Hugglets, PO Box 290, Brighton, BN2 1DR Tel: +44 (0)1273 697974
Fax: +44 (0)1273 62 62 55 Email: info@hugglets.co.uk www.hugglets.co.uk

See you there!

FESTIVALS

IDEENWERKSTATT MACHL KEG

Polluxweg 22/25, 4030 Linz, Upper Austria, Austria
☎ +43 (0)732 946159 Fax: As tel.
email: agentur@machl.at
web: www.machl.at
Organiser of Austria's most successful Teddy Bear Shows: March 5 & October 15, 2006. Always in March: international contest: Crystal Teddy Award.

JAPAN TEDDY BEAR ASSOCIATION

#101, 1-21-3 Midorigaoka, Meguro-ku, Tokyo, 152-0034, Japan
☎ +81 (0)3 5726 4484 Fax: +81 (0)3 3723 7321
email: webmaster@jteddy.net
web: www.jteddy.net
The 14th Japan Teddy Bear Convention will be held 10th-11th June 2006 at Tokyo Trade Center.

LEEDS DOLL & TEDDY FAIR

Dolly Domain Fairs, 45 Henderson Road, South Shields, Tyne & Wear, NE34 9QW
☎ 0191 42 40 400 Fax: As tel.
email: fairs@dollydomain.com
web: www.dollydomain.com
25th year for 'Pudsey', Britain's oldest provincial teddy and doll fair. Free parking, see display advertisement for dates and details.

LINCOLN FAIRS

9 Steep Hill, Lincoln, Lincolnshire, LN2 1LT
☎ 01522 510524 Fax: As tel.
email: no9pawsforthought@btopenworld.com
web: www.no9pawsforthought.com
Lincolnshire premier collectable bear fair.

LLANGOLLEN TEDDY BEAR FAIR

Town Hall, Parade St, Llangollen, Wales
☎ 07885 710630
Sunday 25th June 2006.

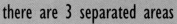

austria's most successful teddy bear show
organized by ideenwerkstatt

there are 3 separated areas
- the first only for the artist's, with max. 25 tables
- second for max. 3 tb shops
- third for one large supplier

international austrian teddy bear show

Show dates 2006:
March 5, with international Teddy Bear Contest - "Crystal Teddy Award" and October 15, both at Novotel, Linz-Upper Austria

ideenwerkstatt machl keg
Polluxweg 22/25
A-4030 Linz
tel+fax +43-732-94 61 59
e-mail: agentur@machl.at
www.machl.at

teddybear design:
Heather Lyell / New Zealand

PUBLISHING

The Rochester Teddy Bear Fair

Sunday 12th March & Sunday 8th October 2006

OVER 80 STALLS

CORN EXCHANGE,
Town Centre,
ROCHESTER, Kent

FREE VALUATIONS ON BEARS & TOYS
BY BONHAM'S THE AUCTIONEERS
open 10:00am - 4:00pm. Adm: £3; Child (4-16 years), £1
SIGNPOSTED   FREE PARKING NEARBY
ENQUIRIES 01 279 871 110

The Hampshire Teddy Bear Fair

BOTLEIGH GRANGE HOTEL

Hedge End, Southampton, Hampshire

Sunday 4th June and Sunday 19th November

OVER 60 STALLS

with everything for teddy collectors including
artist and designer bears; new, old and antique teddies;
limited edition bears; major manufacturer bears; materials;
soft and ceramic bears; kits and accessories
and lots more too. A TEDDY BEAR HOSPITAL and
FREE TEDDY VALUATIONS BY BONHAM'S AUCTIONEERS
PLUS A FREE PRIZE DRAW TO WIN A DESIGNER BEAR!
open: 10.30am - 4pm (last admission 3.45pm)
Admission: £2.50 Adults;
£2 Concessions
accompanied child 16 and younger FREE
CLEARLY SIGNPOSTED ❀ REFRESHMENTS

TOTALLY **TEDDIES**
TEDDY BEAR FAIRS

enquiries
01279
871110

TOTALLY **TEDDIES**
THE WONDERFUL WORLD OF TEDDIES

late 2005 and some 2006 dates

Sunday 20th November
SOUTHAMPTON BOTLEIGH GRANGE

Sunday 11th December
BASILDON HOLIDAY INN HOTEL

Tuesday 27th December
CHELMSFORD RIVERSIDE LEISURE CENTRE

and into 2006

Sunday 12th February
STRATFORD MOAT HOUSE HOTEL

Sunday 19th February
SOUTHEND CLIFF'S PAVILION

Sunday 12th March
ROCHESTER CORN EXCHANGE

Sunday 9th April
LOUGHBOROUGH TOWN HALL

Easter Monday 17th April
PORTSMOUTH MARRIOTT HOTEL

Sunday 14th May
BRENTWOOD HOLIDAY INN HOTEL

Bank Holiday Monday 29th May
CRAWLEY K2 LEISURE CENTRE

Sunday 4th June
SOUTHAMPTON BOTLEIGH GRANGE

Saturday 15th July
ILFRACOMBE LANDMARK THEATRE

Sunday 10th September
HATFIELD RED LION

Sunday 8th October
ROCHESTER CORN EXCHANGE

Sunday 15th October
BISHOP'S STORTFORD RHODES CENTRE

Sunday 22nd October
STRATFORD MOAT HOUSE HOTEL

Sunday 19th November
SOUTHAMPTON BOTLEIGH GRANGE

Fairs open 10.30am - 4pm
REFRESHMENTS ❀ CLEARLY SIGNPOSTED

Stallholders, FOR A FREE INFORMATION
and 05/2006 BOOKING PACK, telephone

TOTALLY **TEDDIES** 01279 871110

● THE LONDON TEDDY BEAR FAIR

Exhibition Dept, Warners Group Publications Plc, West Street, Bourne, Lincolnshire, PE10 9PH
☎ 01778 391123 Fax: 01778 392079
email: dolltedfairap@warnersgroup.co.uk
web: www.teddybearscene.co.uk
Sun 29th Oct 06, Alexandra Palace (West Hall), London. Huge range of British & International exhibitors - artist, manufactured & l/e bears, bear-a-bilia & materials.

● MIDLAND GOOD BEARS

40 Fairfax Road, Sutton Coldfield, West Midlands, B75 7JX
☎ 0121 311 1723 Fax: 0121 311 2870
email: tabbyevans@yahoo.co.uk
Organisers of hospitals displays events.

● THE MIDLAND TEDDY BEAR FESTIVAL

c/o 2 The Square, Ironbridge, Shropshire, TF8 7AQ
☎ 01952 433924 Fax: 01952 433926
email: bernie@bearsonthesquare.com
web: www.bearsonthesquare.com
Very popular 'bears only' fair for the discerning collector. 2006 date: 1st October at Telford Moat House.

● NOTTINGHAM BEAR FAIRS

Patchings Art Centre, Oxton Road, Calverton, Nottingham, NG14 6NU
☎ 0115 916 3731
email: maria@nottinghambearfair.co.uk
web: www.nottinghambearfair.co.uk
17th April and 28th August.

● ROCHESTER TEDDY BEAR FAIR

Old Tithe Hall, Start Hill, Nr Bishops Stortford, Hertfordshire, CM22 7TF
☎ 01279 871110 Fax: 01279 870844
One of the UK's major established teddy bear events. Two great fairs each year. Sundays 12th March and 8th October.

● SALON GUEULES DE MIEL

43 rue Cavendish, 75019 Paris, France
☎ +33 (0)1 42 00 64 27
email: gdmiel@agdm.org
web: www.salonagdm.com
AGDM Teddy Bear Show Paris 'Espace Reuilly' June 11th 2006 - 12 Rue Du Hénard - 75012 Paris - information: gdmiel@agdm.org - www.salonagdm.com

● STRATFORD-UPON-AVON TEDDY BEAR FAIR

Old Tithe Hall, Start Hill, Nr Bishops Stortford, Hertfordshire, CM22 7TF
☎ 01279 871110 Fax: 01279 870844
Important long established event at Stratford upon Avon Moat House Hotel twice yearly on Sundays 12th February and 22nd October.

TEDDIES 2006

Organisers: Hugglets, PO Box 290, Brighton, East Sussex, BN2 1DR
☎ 01273 697974 Fax: 01273 626255
email: info@hugglets.co.uk
web: www.hugglets.co.uk
Sunday 3rd September 2006 at Kensington Town Hall, London W8. Britain's longest established teddy event, 175 exhibitors. The original British Teddy Bear Festival. Thousands of bears, old and new, for sale.

● TOTALLY TEDDIES

Old Tithe Hall, Start Hill, Bishops Stortford, Hertfordshire, CM22 7TF
☎ 01279 871110 Fax: 01279 870844
Well established teddy bear fairs hosted annually around London in the Home Counties, Central and Southern England.

THE WINTER BEARFEST

Organisers: Hugglets, PO Box 290, Brighton, East Sussex, BN2 1DR
☎ 01273 697974 Fax: 01273 626255
email: info@hugglets.co.uk
web: www.hugglets.co.uk
Sunday 26th February 2006. Kensington Town Hall, Hornton Street, London W8. 175 exhibitors. Thousands of bears, old and new, for sale.

END

Key to Fair Organisers

BEAR	B.E.A.R. Events	07836 730719	EMDF	East Midlands Doll Fairs	01477 534626	
BL	Blakemere	01606 888814	FF	Fountain Fayres	01454 414671	
BOS	Bears on the Square	01952 433924	H	Hugglets	01273 697974	
CCF	Cherry Chums Fairs	07885 710630	LF	Lincoln Fairs	01522 510524	
DD	Dolly's Daydreams	01945 870160	N	Nottingham Bear Fairs	0115 9163731	
DDF	Dolly Domain Fairs	0191 424 0400	TLE	Tricia Leigh	01895 834348	
DTF	Doll & Teddy Fairs	01530 274377	TT	Totally Teddies	01279 871110	
EF	Emmary Fairs	01208 872251	WG	Warners Group	01778 391123	

This listing gives details of all the fairs known to us at the time of publication at which teddy bears are for sale. Please note that many of the events are not exclusively for bears. The figure given after the venue specifies, where known, the approximate number of stands, but at non-exclusive shows these are not all teddy bears. Dates and venues can change, so we recommend you confirm details with the organisers before travelling a distance. The list has been compiled from information supplied by the organisers. Some non-UK events are listed at the end.

October 2005

Sun	30th	The London Teddy Bear Fair	Alexandra Palace, London	150	WG
Sun	30th	The Kelham Hall Double	Kelham Hall, Kelham, Nr Newark, Notts	100	EMDF

November 2005

Sun	20th	Hampshire Teddy Bear Festival	Botleigh Grange Hotel, Hedge End, Southampton 70		TT
Sun	20th	Hinchingbrooke House Doll, Dolls House & Teddy Fair			
			Hinchingbrooke House, Brampton Rd, Huntingdon(A14,A1), Cambs	50	DD
Sun	27th	Vintage Bear, Doll & Toy Fair			
			National Motorcycle Museum, Bickenhill, Nr Birmingham	up to 90	DTF
Sun	27th	Cornwall Christmas Bear Fair			
			Lostwithiel Community Centre, Lostwithiel, Cornwall	45	EF

December 2005

Sun	11th	Basildon Bear Fair	Basildon, Holiday Inn Hotel	up to 45	TT
Sun	11th	The British Bear Fair 2005	Hove Town Hall, Norton Road, Hove	140	TLE
Tue	27th	Chelmsford Bear Fair			
			Chelmsford, Riverside Ice & Leisure Centre	up to 50	TT

February 2006

Sun	5th	Nostell Priory Doll, Dolls House & Teddy Fair			
			Old Riding School, Nostell Priory, nr Wakefield (A638), W. Yorkshire	50	DD
Sat	11th	Teddy Bear and Doll Fayre			
			The Winter Gardens Pavilion, Weston-S-Mare, Somerset	50	FF
Sun	12th	Stratford-upon-Avon Teddy Bear Fair			
			Stratford Upon Avon, Moat House Hotel	Up to 70	TT
Sun	19th	The Kelham Hall Double	Kelham Hall, Kelham, Nr Newark, Notts	100	EMDF
Sun	19th	Southend Teddy Bear Fair	Southend, Cliff's Pavilion	Up to 70	TT
Sun	26th	Winter BearFest '06	Kensington Town Hall, Hornton St, London	175	H

Winter BearFest
Sunday 26th February 2006
Kensington Town Hall, Hornton Street, London
The exhibitor list for the Winter BearFest is available at www.hugglets.co.uk

March 2006

Sun	12th	Rochester Teddy Bear Fair	Rochester, Corn Exchange	Up to 85	TT
Sun	19th	Great Spring Doll & Teddy Extravaganza			
			National Motorcycle Museum, Bickenhill, Nr Birmingham	up to 140	DTF
Sat	25th	Leeds Doll & Teddy Fair	Pudsey Civic Hall, Pudsey, Leeds	85	DDF

April 2006

Sun	9th	Loughborough Teddy Bear Fair	Loughborough Town Hall	Up to 70	TT
Sun	9th	North Wales Teddy Bear Festival			
			North Wales Theatre & Conference Centre, Llandudno	40	BEAR
Mon	17th	Nottingham Bear Fair	Patchings Art Centre, Nottingham		N
Mon	17th	Portsmouth Teddy Bear Fair	Portsmouth, Marriott Hotel	Up to 70	TT

PUBLISHING

May 2006

Sun	7th	A Collectors Teddy Bear Fair	Bishop Grosseteste College, Lincoln	50-60	LF
Sun	14th	Blakemere Teddy Bear Festival	The Oaklands Hotel, Gorstage, Cheshire	40	BL
Sun	14th	Essex Bear Fair			
		Brentwood, Holiday Inn Hotel, J28 of M25		Up to 41	TT
Sun	21st	Devon Bear Fair			
		Exmouth Pavilion, The Esplanade, Exmouth, nr Exeter		45	EF
Mon	29th	Crawley Bear Fair	Crawley, K2 Leisure Centre	Up to 41	TT

June 2006

Sun	4th	Hampshire Teddy Bear Festival	Botleigh Grange Hotel, Hedge End, Southampton	70	TT
Sun	25th	Cornwall Bear Fair			
		Lostwithiel Community Centre, Lostwithiel, Cornwall		45	EF
Sun	25th	Llangollen Teddy Bear Fair	Llangollen Town Hall		CCF

July 2006

Sun	2nd	The Kelham Hall Double	Kelham Hall, Kelham, Nr Newark, Notts	100	EMDF
Sat	8th	Sheffield Teddy Bear Fair	Sheffield Wednesday Football Ground	40	BEAR
Sat	15th	Ilfracombe Teddy Bear Fair	Landmark Theatre, Ilfracombe	up to 40	TT
Sun	30th	Dolly's Daydreams Annual Charity Event			
		Hilton East Midlands Airport, Castle Donington, Leicestershire (J24/M1).		50	DD

August 2006

Mon	28th	Nottingham Bear Fair	Patchings Art Centre, Nottingham		N

September 2006

Sun	3rd	Teddies 2006	Kensington Town Hall, Hornton St, London	175	H

FESTIVALS Hugglets

TEDDIES 2006
Sunday 3rd September 2006
Kensington Town Hall, Hornton Street, London
The exhibitor list for Teddies 2006 is available at www.hugglets.co.uk

Sun	10th	Hatfield Teddy Bear Fair	Red Lion, Hatfield	up to 40	TT

Sat	23rd	Wrexham Teddy Bear Fair	Memorial Hall,Wrexham	60	BEAR
Sun	24th	Great Autumn Doll & Teddy Extravaganza			
		National Motorcycle Museum, Bickenhill, Nr Birmingham		up to 140	DTF

October 2006

Sun	1st	Midland Teddy Bear Festival	The Moat House, Telford, Shropshire	85	BOS
Sun	8th	Rochester Teddy Bear Fair	Rochester, Corn Exchange	Up to 85	TT
Sun	15th	Bishop's Stortford Teddy Bear Fair			
		Bishop's Stortford, Rhodes Centre		Up to 70	TT
Sat	16th	Leeds Doll & Teddy Fair	Pudsey Civic Hall, Pudsey, Leeds	85	DDF
Sat	21st	Teddy Bear and Doll Fayre			
		The Winter Gardens Pavilion, Weston-S-Mare, Somerset		50	FF
Sun	22nd	Stratford-upon-Avon Teddy Bear Fair			
		Stratford Upon Avon, Moat House Hotel		Up to 70	TT
Sun	29th	The London Teddy Bear Fair	Alexandra Palace, London	150	WG
Sun	29th	The Kelham Hall Double	Kelham Hall, Kelham, Nr Newark, Notts	100	EMDF

International Fair Dates

AGM	Les Amis de Gueules de Miel	+33 (0)1 42 00 64 27
FT	Fairytales Inc	+1 630 495 6909
I	Ideenwerkstatt Machl Keg	+43 (0)732 946159
JTBA	Japan Teddy Bear Assn	+81 (0)3 5726 4484 8539

Sunday 5th March, International Teddy Bear Show, Linz, Austria, I
Fri-Sun, 5-7th May, Deb Canham Expo, Illinois, USA, FT
Sat/Sun, 10 - 11th June, Japan Teddy Bear Convention, Tokyo Trade Center, Japan, JTBA
Sun 11th June, AGDM 2005 Teddy Bear Show Espace Reuilly, Paris, 75, AGM
Sun 15th October, International Teddy Bear Show, Linz, Austria, I

END

Bear Repairers

The following list of repairers is given in the belief that they are capable and experienced in their work. However, no responsibility is accepted for work carried out and readers must satisfy themselves on all such matters.

● ALICE'S WONDERLAND
High Head Sculpture Valley, Ivesill, Carlisle, CA4 0PJ
☎ 01697 473025
Alice's Wonderland much improved site. Doll, teddy, doll's house museum. Open daily except Wednesday 10.30-5. Dolls and bears restored.

● ANGIEBEARS
27 Trubridge Road, Hoo St Werburgh, Rochester, Kent, ME3 9EN
☎ 01634 253165
email: angie@angiebears.net
web: www.angiebears.net
Repairer of old and antique bears, also a professional cleaning service is available.

● BA'S BEARS
5 Grove Street, Oxford, Oxfordshire, OX2 7JT
☎ 01865 435314
email: babruyn@hotmail.com
Mohair bear repairs April-Nov.

● THE BEAR EMPORIUM
Well View, Ridgeway Craft Centre, Ridgeway, Nr Sheffield, Derbyshire, S12 3XR
☎ **01142 482010**
web: www.bear-emporium.com
Plenty of love and care given to your special friend by expert restorers. No repair has defeated us yet.

● THE BEAR GARDEN
10 Jeffries Passage, Guildford, Surrey, GU1 4AP
☎ 01483 302581 Fax: 01483 457393
email: bears@beargarden.co.uk
web: www.beargarden.co.uk
Teddy bear and doll repairs. Patients also accepted at our Kingston-upon-Thames branch.

● BEAR LEE COTTAGE
Minto, Codmore Hill, Pulborough, West Sussex, RH20 1BQ
☎ **01798 872707**
Restoration of teddy bears and soft toys. Over 25 years experience. Visitors welcome by appointment or postal service.

● THE BEAR PATCH
33 Market Place, Ashbourne, Derbyshire, DE6 1EU
☎ 01335 342391
Well-loved bears expertly repaired by Pauline Johnson of Cubley Bears. Free quotation. Call at shop or phone for advice.

● BEARS BY SUSAN JANE KNOCK
6 Elizabeth Avenue, Witham, Essex, CM8 1JE
☎ 01376 521230
email: susan.k@tinyworld.co.uk
Bear artist offers careful and sympathetic repairs for old and invalid bears.

● BENEBEAR CLINIC
Pine House Cottage, Churt Road, Hindhead, Surrey, GU26 6HY
☎ 01428 605972
email: mary@benebears.com
web: www.benebears.com
Sick old bear? Don't despair!

● BORN AGAIN BEARS

Fareham, Hampshire
☎ 01329 313786 Fax: 01329 829875
email: sue@bornagainbears.co.uk
web: www.bornagainbears.co.uk
Exceptional quality restoration of treasured bears and soft toys. Highly recommended worldwide by Steiff, Harrods and top auctioneers. Postal service.

● BRACKEN BEARS

5 Hazelwood Cottages, High Street, Ticehurst, East Sussex, TN5 7AL
☎ 01580 200306 Fax: As tel.
Teddy doctor at the ready.

● BRIAN'S BEAR HEART HOSPITAL

76 Shortwood Avenue, Staines, Middlesex, TW18 4JL
Postal only.

● BRUINS ALL ROOND

email: teddyrepairer@btinternet.com
Twelve years experience. Please email.

● CREATIONS PAST

The Dolls House, Stonehall Common, Worcestershire, WR5 3QQ
☎ 01905 820792
email: mmbeardoll@aol.com
web: www.dollshousewallpaper.co.uk
Teddy bear clinic. Expert sympathetic restoration. Museum quality repairs to precious old Steiff, small Schuco, modern bears and dolls.

● CYNNAMAN RESTORATION SERVICES

48A Underhill Road, South Benfleet, Essex, SS7 1EP
☎ 01268 754184
Bears all ages lovingly restored.

● DAPHNE FRASER'S DOLL & BEAR HOSPITAL

'Glenbarry', 58 Victoria Road, Lenzie, Glasgow, Strathclyde, G66 5AP
☎ 0141 776 1281
Injured bears given loving care.

● DAY DREAM DOLLS & TEDDIES

142 - 144 Middlewich Road, Clive, Winsford, Cheshire, CW7 3NF
☎ 01606 592497
email: daydreamdolls@steggel.freeserve.co.uk
web: www.daydream-dolls.co.uk
Doll and teddy makers, hospital, courses. Stockists of Merrythought, Gund, Russ, Hansa. Plus own design bears, gollies, miniatures, limited editions.

● DEVON BEAR REPAIRS

Underhill, Broad Path, Stoke Gabriel, Devon, TQ9 6SQ
☎ 01803 782654
Bears of all ages restored with great care. Contact Jenny Williams.

● ANNA DICKERSON

Serenity, 17 Chapel Street, Barford, Norwich, Norfolk, NR9 4AB
☎ **01603 759647**
Loved bears repaired with care. Ailing bears received directly, by post or through 'The Bear Shop' at Norwich and Colchester.

● DOLLY MIXTURES

3 Holly Road, Oldbury, West Midlands
☎ 0121 422 6959
Bears, dolls, bought, sold, restored.

● DOT BIRD

4 Cavendish Terrace, Ripon, North Yorkshire, HG4 1PP
☎ 01765 607131
email: dotsbears@btinternet.com
Specialising in sympathetic restoration of vintage teddy bears. As seen in 'Teddy Bear Scene'. Meet me at the Hugglets fairs.

● FARNBOROUGH BEARS

78 West Heath Road, Farnborough, Hampshire, GU14 8QX
☎ 01252 543454
email: farnboroughbears@ntlworld.com
or janettruin@ntlworld.com
Bear artist Janet offers loving restoration for all types of bears. Write or phone or email first. Reasonable rates.

● FAUDS & GIBBLES

Glenesk, Coltfield, Forres, Moray, IV36 2UB
☎ 01343 850609
email: enquiry@faudsandgibbles.co.uk
web: www.faudsandgibbles.co.uk
Handmade unique and collectable miniature and nine-inch bears. Also doll and teddy hospital.

● FLYING HORSE ORIGINAL DESIGNS

Southsea, Hampshire
☎ 023 92 736634
Antique and modern bears professionally and sympathetically restored to a high standard. Sensible prices. Recommended by dealers, traders and collectors.

GERALDINE'S OF EDINBURGH

133-135 Canongate, Edinburgh, Lothian, EH8 8BP, Scotland
☎ 0131 556 4295 Fax: As tel.
email: geraldine.e@virgin.net
web: www.dollsandteddies.com
Doll & teddy restorers.

GUMDROP EDITIONS

Signals, Boswedden Terrace, St Just, Penzance, Cornwall, TR19 7NF
☎ 01736 787370
email: gail.edwards1@talk21.com
web: www.gumdrop-editions.com
Doctor Edwards of TBCI magazine offers sympathetic restorations, teds and friends. 20+ years professional/trade experience. Postal patients. Free estimates.

HANNA BRUCE BEARS & TEDDY HOSPITAL

120 E Main St., 1st Floor/Right, Lititz, PA 17543, USA
☎ Toll free in USA: 1-877-7BEARMD Fax: +1 717 626 1180
email: teddydoctor@hannabrucebears.com
web: www.hannabrucebears.com
Teddy bear/stuffed animal hospital specializing in restoration & reconstructions for over 8 years serving patients from the US, Canada & Europe.

MARY SHORTLE OF YORK

9 Lord Mayors Walk, York, North Yorkshire, also at 9, 15 & 17 Queen's Arcade, Leeds.
☎ 01904 425168 or 01132 456160 Fax: 01904 425168
email: mary@maryshortleofyork.com
web: www.maryshortleofyork.com
Expert teddy repairs. Over 20 years experience. Call for free estimates. Guaranteed satisfaction and personal service.

NEW FOREST DOLL MUSEUM

Bridge Street, Fordingbridge, Hants
☎ 012425 652450
email: alan.gordon13@btinternet.com
Teddies mended.

OLDENBEARS

40 Empress Avenue, Chingford, London, E4 8SR
☎ 020 8531 5061
email: info@oldenbears.co.uk
web: www.oldenbears.co.uk
Sympathetic, affordable teddy bear restoration.

RESTORATION

Bev McNab, Long Cottage, Egginton Road, Etwall, Derbyshire, DE65 6NB
☎ 01283 734147 Fax: As tel.
email: bevmcnab@aol.com
web: www.bear-hugs.co.uk
Superior restoration on yesterdays bears! Have your 'Teddy Bear' restored back to life!

ROBYN'S BEARS & BOUQUETS

Bear and Soft Toy Repair Service, 1 Grevillea Court, PO Box 73, Patterson Lakes 3197, Australia
☎ +61 (0)3 9772 8330 Fax: +61 (0)3 9776 2583
email: robyn@robyns-bears.com.au
web: www.robyns-bears.com.au/repairs/index.php
Expert repairs to all types of precious teddy bears and soft toys by experienced bear artist, Robyn Gladwin.

ROSEMARY'S DOLL'S HOSPITAL

Rosemary Nichols, Melita, 61 Vancouver Avenue, King's Lynn, Norfolk, PE30 5RD
☎ 01553 764474
Teddybears and Dolls lovingly restored.

ROYAL BERKSHIRE BEARS HOSPITAL

15 Delane Drive, Winnersh, Berkshire, RG41 5AT
☎ 0118 979 0228
email: leemoore@tinyworld.co.uk
Artist bears, Sasha dolls stockist.

SAD PADS

☎ 01622 754441
web: www.sadpadbears.com
Sad Pads. Sympathetic care for your dejected teddy bear. Vintage teddy bears and classic soft toys. Restoration and cleaning.

● ST ANN'S DOLLS HOSPITAL
14 Hildreth Road, Prestwood, Gt Missenden, Bucks,
HP16 0LU
☎ 01494 890220 Fax: As tel.
email: alan.ann@dollshospital.freeserve.co.uk
web: www.dollshospital.freeserve.co.uk
*Most repairs undertaken on old and modern
bears and dolls. Please ring for an appointment. Monday - Friday only.*

● TERRY'S TEDDY HOSPITAL
16 Lower Green, Tewin, Welwyn, Hertfordshire,
AL6 0LB
☎ 01438 718700 Fax: 01438 840411
email: tbrand@talk21.com
Repair, clean, tighten and stuff.

● ELIZABETH THOMPSON
12 Briar Thicket, Woodstock, Oxford, Oxfordshire,
OX20 1NT
☎ 01993 811915
*General care from geriatrics to new born:
from 'wear and tear' to sudden accidents and
attacks from dogs! Very reasonable rates.*

● TOBILANE DESIGNS
The Toy Works, Holly House, Askham, Penrith,
Cumbria, CA10 2PG
☎ 01931 712077
email: info@thetoyworks.co.uk
web: www.thetoyworks.co.uk
Teddy hospital and toy shop.

● WEAVERS BEARS
1 Elm Tree Cottage, The Common, Cranleigh, Surrey,
GU6 8NS
☎ 01483 273708
email: trishsunnucks@tiscali.co.uk
*Bears ancient & modern sympathetically
restored.*

● WELLFIELD BEARS
'Wellfields', Unit 7, The Globe Centre, Wellfield Road,
Cardiff, South Glamorgan, CF24 3PE
☎ 02920 453045
email: janice@wellfieldbears.co.uk
web: www.wellfieldbears.co.uk
*Steiff, artist bears, restorations, commis-
sions.*

● YESTERDAY'S CHILDREN
Mill House, Mill Lane, St. Ive's Cross, Sutton St. James,
Nr Spalding, Lincolnshire, PE12 0EJ
☎ 01945 440466
*All teddies, antique and modern dolls and
soft toys restored with care. Please write or
phone first.*

END

All Else That's Bruin incorporates a range of entries which are grouped as follows:

- Publications (mainly magazines and books)
- Illustrators and Portrait Artists (including greetings cards etc)
- Clubs
- Museums (we recommend you check details directly before travelling a distance)
- Internet Services
- Bear-related (including clothing, jewellery and other wares)

- PUBLICATIONS -

● AUSCRAFT PUBLICATIONS LTD
6 The Long Yard, Wickfield, Shefford Woodlands, Berks, RG17 7EH
☎ 01488 649955 Fax: 01488 649950
email: auscraft@auscraft.co.uk
web: www.auscraft.co.uk
Superb quality Australian craft magazines.

● BOATING BEARS
c/o Pam Chester-Browne, 23 Eden Avenue, Culcheth, Warrington, Cheshire, WA3 5HX
email: pam@chester-browne.freeserve.co.uk
Magazine/Newsletter for Boating Bears.

● GAZELLE
White Cross Mills, Hightown, Lancaster, LA1 4XS
☎ 01524 68765 Fax: 01524 63232
email: sales@gazellebooks.co.uk
web: www.gazellebooks.co.uk
Specialist teddy and doll books on making, buying, selling, identifying, valuing and collecting. FREE catalogue available upon request.

● GUERNSEY TEDDY PUBLICATIONS
Le Douit, St Peters, Guernsey, GY7 9EX
☎ 01481 266223
Guernsey Teddy Calendar. See Advertisement.

● HUGGLETS
PO Box 290, Brighton, East Sussex, BN2 1DR
☎ 01273 697974 Fax: 01273 626255
email: info@hugglets.co.uk
web: www.hugglets.co.uk
Publishers and Festival organisers. UK Teddy Bear Guide, Winter BearFest, Teddies 2006.

JUDY BEAR PRODUCTIONS

17 Melrose Crescent, Garswood, Wigan, Lancashire, WN4 0SL
☎ 01942 716367 Fax: As tel.
email: jane_e_donnelly@hotmail.com
Judy Bear's books and videos help prepare parents and children for a journey to theatre or visit to the dentist.

KAY TURMEAU BSC.HONS.LRPS

6 Hawkes Close, Wokingham, Berkshire, RG41 2SZ
☎ 0118 978 6267
email: kay.turmeau@btopenworld.com
Qualified freelance writer and photographer.

THE MULBERRY BUSH

Unit 4C, Huffwood Trading Estate, Partridge Green, Horsham, West Sussex, RH13 8AU
☎ 01273 493781 / 01403 711310 Fax: 01273 495138
email: mulberry@mulberrybush.com
web: www.mulberrybush.com
New/old books. Closing March 06.

N* COLLECTION

26 Kutuzovsky Prospekt, apart.20, Moscow, 121165, Russia
☎ +7 238 0073 Fax: As tel.
email: n-collection@rdm.ru
web: www.n-collection.ru
Magazine and books about artist/collectable dolls, teddy bears and miniatures (text Russian/English, colours pictures). On-line gallery/shop.

PAT RUSH

☎ 01732 361994/07715 704025
email: patrush@pavilion.co.uk
Writer specialising in teddy bears.

TEDDY BEAR CLUB INTERNATIONAL MAGAZINE

25 Phoenix Court, Hawkins Road, Colchester, Essex, CO2 8JY
☎ 01206 505961 Fax: 01206 505945
email: sharon@aceville.com
web: www.planet-teddybear.com
UK's best-selling bear magazine.

TEDDY BEAR SCENE MAGAZINE

Warners Group Publications Plc, West Street, Bourne, Lincolnshire, PE10 9PH
☎ 01778 391158 Fax: 01778 392079
email: teddybearscene@warnersgroup.co.uk
web: www.teddybearscene.co.uk
The UK's favourite Teddy Bear publication for both new and established collectors. Packed with interesting and informative editorial features. Available on the news stand or via subscription.

TEDDY BEAR TIMES

Ancient Lights, 19 River Road, Arundel, West Sussex, BN18 9EY
☎ 01903 884988 Fax: 01903 885514
email: jo@ashdown.co.uk
web: www.teddybeartimes.com
The magazine for you and your bear. Glossy publication covering everything in the bear world - especially limited edition artists' bears.

WEALDEN MANOR PRESS

2 Fircroft Close, Tilehurst, Reading, Berkshire, RG31 6LJ
☎ 0118 941 4000 Fax: As tel.
Discover Bearlight - unique hand crafted colourful books, full of real bears and teddies, story and myth. Send for colour brochure.

- ILLUSTRATORS AND PORTRAIT ARTISTS -

ART2HEART

112 Dawlish Crescent, Wyke Regis, Weymouth, Dorset, DT4 9JW
☎ 01305 775597
email: wendyart2heart@yahoo.co.uk
web: www.saa.co.uk/braden
Paintings, courses, greetings cards, stationery.

● AURORABEAREALIS
Kessock Post Office, North Kessock, Inverness, Highland, IV1 3XN
☎ 01463 731470 Fax: As tel.
email: susan@aurorabearealis.co.uk
web: www.aurorabearealis.co.uk
Bear portraits in pastels while he holidays in the Highlands or from quality photos. Other bear paintings too. SAE for details.

● BEAR PAWTRAITS
10 Chilham Avenue, Kent, CT8 8HD
☎ 0780 3780050
email: BearPawtraits@amserve.com
The final word in 'pawtrait'ure.

● BEAR-A-THOUGHT GREETINGS CARDS AND CALENDARS
PO Box 88, Newcastle-upon-Tyne, County Durham, NE17 7WY
☎ 01207 563220
email: michael@bear-a-thought.co.uk
web: www.bear-a-thought.co.uk
Unique greetings cards and calendars.

● CHESNEY DESIGNS
Greendales Hall, Mill Lane, Warton, Carnforth, Lancashire, LA5 9NW
☎ 01524 733152 Fax: As tel.
email: sarah.chesney@btinternet.com
Humorous teddy cards and gifts.

● JO JO CREATIONS LTD
Redcroft, Park Drive, Braintree, CM7 1AW
☎ 01376 339080 Fax: 01376 328633
email: jo@jojocreations.com
Handmade specialist teddy bear cards.

● LAZY DAYS AND BAGGY JUMPERS
☎ 07929 209233
email: info@lazydaysandbaggyjumpers.com
web: www.lazydaysandbaggyjumpers.com
Shaggy Knights lead 'Quest' to ignite imaginations, soothe weary souls and restore balance of 'Magic' to this world. See Advert.

● PRUE THEOBALDS

1 The Uplands, Maze Hill, St Leonards, East Sussex, TN38 0HL

☎ 01424 422306

email: pruet@dircon.co.uk

Teddy Bear illustrator. Mail order books, prints, greetings cards. For commissions and licences contact Christopher Maxwell-Stewart at above address.

● WEASELPIE PUBLISHING

9 New Road, Lake, Isle of Wight, PO36 9JN

☎ 01983 403224

email: info@weaselpie.com

web: www.weaselpie.com

Please see display advertisement.

- CLUBS -

● AVON BEARMAKERS

Elmbrook, Patch Elm Lane, Rangeworthy, South Gloucestershire, BS37 7LU

☎ 01454 228167

email: jayne@theoldchinashop.com

Bristol, South Glos, Somerset club.

● BRITISH TOYMAKERS GUILD

124 Walcot Street, Bath, Avon, BA1 5BG

☎ 01225 442440

email: info@toymakersguild.co.uk

web: www.toymakersguild.co.uk

SAE for membership information.

● DEAN'S RAG BOOK COMPANY LTD

PO Box 217, Hereford, HR1 9AB

☎ 01981 240966 Fax: 01981 241076

email: teddies@deansbears.com

web: www.deansbears.com

Membership includes free mohair bear and badge, competitions, colour magazine.

● GOOD BEARS OF THE WORLD (UK) TRUST

Brian Beacock, 76 Shortwood Avenue, Staines, Middlesex, TW18 4JL

email: alison-bob@amarsay.freeserve.co.uk

Charitable organisation distributing bears to comfort those in need. Annual membership £10, overseas £12. Three newsletters issued yearly. Postal only or email.

«Come on.

Thousands of my teddy brothers

are awaiting your visit.»

Puppenhausmuseum
Basel

Opening times:
MUSEUM/SHOP: Daily from
11 am to 5 pm, Thursdays until 8 pm
CAFE: Daily from 10 am to 6 pm,
Thursdays until 9 pm

Steinenvorstadt 1, CH-4051 Basel
Tel. +41 (0)61 225 95 95
Fax +41 (0)61 225 95 96
www.puppenhausmuseum.ch
The building has wheelchair access.

• world's greatest collection
of old **teddy bears**
• antique **toys**

● LES AMIS DE GUEULES DE MIEL

43 rue Cavendish, 75019 Paris, France
☎ +33 (0)1 42 00 64 27
email: gdmiel@agdm.org
web: www.agdm.org
French non-profit organisation for bear lovers (old, bear artists) - bears and therapies - quarterly magazine - website in French and in English.

● MERRYTHOUGHT INTERNATIONAL COLLECTOR'S CLUB

Ironbridge, Telford, Shropshire, TF8 7NJ
☎ 01952 433116 ext 21 Fax: 01952 432054
email: contact@merrythought.co.uk
Enjoy the magical world of Merrythought.

● ROBIN RIVE COLLECTORS CLUB

Countrylife New Zealand Ltd., PO Box 14391, Auckland 1006, New Zealand
☎ Fax: +64 9 5271 550
email: sales@robinrive.com
web: www.robinrive.com
Membership includes annual bear, catalogues, newsy Oakdale Farm Chronicle, exclusive member-only offers. Year runs from July. Join online.

● STEIFF CLUB UK

Ms Leyla Maniera, PO Box 158, Cranleigh, Surrey, GU6 8ZW
☎ 01932 568230 Fax: 01932 563427
web: www.steiff-club.de
Please see advertisement on Page 5.

● THE TEDDY BEAR ORPHANAGE

92 Heath Street, Nutgrove, St Helens, Merseyside, WA9 5NJ
☎ 01744 812274 Fax: 01744 813334
email: Info@teddybearorphanage.co.uk
web: www.teddybearorphanage.co.uk
Parents of Teddies Association. Membership £44.50 for free bear, termly newsletters, special offers, discount vouchers, Christmas and postcards.

● TEDI BACH HUG MINIATURES CLUB

Greenbanks, Molesworth, Cambridgeshire, PE28 0QD
email: vanessa@hbgcc.fsnet.co.uk
Quarterly newsletters, kits, supplies, UK/worldwide.

- MUSEUMS AND DISPLAYS -

● ALICE'S WONDERLAND

High Head Sculpture Valley, Ivesill, Carlisle, CA4 0PJ
☎ 01697 473025
Museum of dolls, teddies 1870-2005. Groups, schools welcomed. Open daily 10.30-5 closed Wednesday. Adults £2.50, Children £1. Family ticket £5.

● THE BRITISH BEAR COLLECTION

Banwell Castle, Banwell, Somerset, BS29 6NX
☎ 01934 822263
email: c_parsons@hotmail.co.uk
web: www.thebritishbearcollection.co.uk
Exciting new venue for 2006!

● THE DORSET TEDDY BEAR MUSEUM

Eastgate, Corner of High East St & Salisbury St, Dorchester, Dorset, DT1 1JU
☎ 01305 266040 Fax: 01305 268885
email: info@teddybearmuseum.co.uk
web: www.teddybearmuseum.co.uk
See Edward Bear and his family of people-sized bears, with teddies from throughout the last century in this enchanting museum.

● HAMILTON TOY COLLECTION

111 Main Street, Callander, Perthshire, FK17 8BQ
☎ 018773 30004
email: philip.hamilton1@btopenworld.com
150 teddies plus every toy imaginable at our friendly family museum (charge) & collectors' shop.

● MUSEUM OF CHILDHOOD
42 High Street (Royal Mile), Edinburgh
☎ 0131 529 4142 Fax: 0131 558 3103
email: admin@museumofchildhood.fsnet.co.uk
web: www.cac.org.uk
A storehouse of childhood memories.

● PUPPENHAUSMUSEUM
Steinenvorstadt 1, CH-4051 Basel, Switzerland
☎ +41 (0)61 225 95 95 Fax: +41 (0)61 225 95 96
web: www.puppenhausmuseum.ch
The collection, the only one of its kind in the world: teddy bears, doll's houses, shops, dolls and carrousels.

● THE TEDDY BEAR MUSEUM
19 Greenhill Street, Stratford-upon-Avon, Warwickshire, CV37 6LF
☎ 01789 293160
web: www.theteddybearmuseum.com
World famous BTA award winner.

● TEDDY BEARS OF BROMYARD
12 The Square, Bromyard, Herefordshire, HR7 4BP
☎ 01885 488329 Fax: As tel.
email: chris@bromyard57.freeserve.co.uk
Hundreds of rare bears.

● WOOKEY HOLE BEAR COLLECTION
Wookey Hole Caves Ltd, Wookey Hole, Wells, Somerset, BA5 1BB
☎ 01749 672243
web: www.wookey.co.uk
Please see display advertisement.

- INTERNET SERVICES -

● BEARARTISTSOFBRITAIN.ORG
Bear Artists of Britain, 26 Wheatsheaf Court, Sunderland, Tyne & Wear, SR6 0RF
☎ 07725 040179
email: john@bearartistsofbritain.org
web: www.bearartistsofbritain.org
Independent showcase for British bears.

● BRITISH BEARS ON THE NET
email: fiona@absolutelybear.com
or allbearbypaula@aol.com
web: www.britishbearsonthenet.co.uk
E-mail teddy bear chat group.

● DRAWING THE WEB, WEBSITE DESIGN
42 Palmarsh Avenue, Hythe, Kent, CT21 6NR
☎ 01303 269038 Fax: 01303 266669
email: andy@bears2000.freeserve.co.uk
web: www.drawingtheweb.com
Hand-drawn websites, stationery and logos. Designed to meet your needs and exceed your dreams. See website for details and examples.

● TEDDYNET.COM
TeddyNet, PO Box 23452, London, SE26 6GT
email: info@teddynet.com
web: www.teddynet.com
Teddy Directory and Web Design.

● TEDE-GUIDE
Hugglets, PO Box 290, Brighton, East Sussex, BN2 1DR
☎ 01273 697974 Fax: 01273 626255
email: info@hugglets.co.uk
web: www.hugglets.co.uk
Download the UK Teddy Bear Guide 2006 to your computer. Fully searchable using Acrobat Reader (available free).

- BEAR RELATED -

● ROSE ABDALLA
117 St. Pancras Way, Campden Town, London, NW1 0RD
☎ 020 7482 1911
Sailor/military costumes for teddies/dolls. Ladies & Gents in Victorian and Edwardian fashion. At home and Kensington doll/teddy fairs.

● ANN_KNITS 4 BEARS
14 Crete Lane, Dibden Purlieu, Southampton, Hampshire, SO45 4HW
☎ 02380 846987
email: ann@petri.fslife.co.uk
web: www.knits4bears.co.uk
Beautiful handknitted sweaters, cardi's and pullovers especially for bears, my individual designs. Also crochet collars, hats, tailor-made garments. Enquiries welcome.

● B&B WITH BEAR BITS
The Florins, Silver Street, Minting, Horncastle, Lincolnshire, LN9 5RP
☎ 01507 578360 Fax: As tel.
email: ashburner@bearbits.freeserve.co.uk
web: www.bearbits.com
B&B for bear lovers. Beautiful house, 15 miles from Lincoln; minutes from the Wolds. Two bedrooms with ensuites, warm welcome.

● COLLECT-TEDS
16 Ninelands Lane, Garforth, Leeds, West Yorkshire, LS25 2BY
☎ 0113 286 7372
email: collect.teds@dsl.pipex.com
Unique hand-modelled teddy teapots, clocks, mugs. Beautifully original one-off artist collector's bears. Wonderful vintage Steiff, Schuco, Hermann Bears and rarities.

● GALLERY FIFTY FIVE
The Jeanne Harris Group, PO Box 55, Barnet, Hertfordshire, EN4 0HF
☎ 020 8441 4920 Fax: 020 8449 2626
email: info@galleryfiftyfive.com
web: www.galleryfiftyfive.com
Keyrings, novelties, pencils, reflectors, sourcing.

● JUST BEARS RUBBER STAMPS
Sandhurst, 26 Alexandra Road, Harworth, Nr Doncaster, South Yorkshire, DN11 8EZ
☎ 01302 743811
email: sandhurst26@aol.com
120 designs. SAE free catalogue.

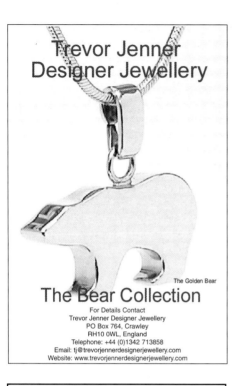

Trevor Jenner Designer Jewellery

The Golden Bear

The Bear Collection

For Details Contact
Trevor Jenner Designer Jewellery
PO Box 764, Crawley
RH10 0WL, England
Telephone: +44 (0)1342 713858
Email: tj@trevorjennerdesignerjewellery.com
Website: www.trevorjennerdesignerjewellery.com

● MERRY MAIDENS
23 Bowershott, Letchworth, Herts, SG6 2ET
☎ 01462 486734
email: merrymaidens@mbrackley.supanet.com
A huge range of clothes, shoes, accessories and novelty costumes all made to order. Send 6 x 1st class stamps for catalogue.

● STREETBROOKE BEAR
309F The Big Peg, 120 Vyse Street, Birmingham, B18 6ND
☎ 0121 236 6953 Fax: As tel.
email: info@streetbrookebear.co.uk
web: www.streetbrookebear.co.uk
High quality teddy bear jewellery. Hand made jewellery in precious metals. Pendants, brooches, earrings, rings. All hallmarked.

● TEDDY TRICOTTS
30 Letham Drive, Newlands, Glasgow, Strathclyde, G43 2SL ☎ 0141 637 6306
email: info@teddytricotts.co.uk
web: www.teddytricotts.co.uk
Give your teddy a treat and get him or her a made to measure handknitted jumper or cardigan.

● TRAFFORD PRINT & DESIGN
69 John Gray Road, Great Doddington, Wellingborough, Northants, NN29 7TX
☎ 01933 229366 Fax: As tel.
email: info@tpdprinting.com
Printed ribbon labels, swing tags, business cards, stamps, t-shirts etc. Please send four 1st class stamps for brochure and samples.

● TREVOR JENNER DESIGNER JEWELLERY
PO Box 764, Crawley, West Sussex, RH10 0WL
☎ 01342 713858
email: tj@trevorjennerdesignerjewellery.com
web: www.trevorjennerdesignerjewellery.com
Please see display advertisement.

● WILD DESIGNS
14 Spital Walk, Chester, Cheshire, CH3 5DB
☎ 01244 401856/01829 271873
email: wilddesigns@cheshire-uk.com
web: www.cheshire-uk.com
Elegant hand crafted bear jewellery exquisitely designed in silver with precious stones.

END

Bear Gallery

Welcome to this new section showcasing the wide variety of teddy bear styles available.

Please see the *Bear Makers and Artists* section for contact details (starting page 121).

Bärenhäusl Ositos Baren

A Hitchcock Bear

Ann Made Bears

Beani Bears

Baggies Bears

Bear Bits

Barnwell Bears

BearCraft

Bedspring Bears

Bearitz

Barbara-Ann Bears

PUBLISHING
Hugglets

Bisson Bears

Bees Knees Bears

Bears 4 Hugs

Beatrix Bears

Bell Bears

Bears by Susan Jane

PUBLISHING Hugglets

Benthall Bears

Billy Buff Bears

Bunky Bears

Bradgate Bears

Burlington Bears

BowJangle Bears

Burlington Bearties

Canterbury Bears

Butlers Bears

DoDo Bears

Dari Laut

Charlie Bears

E. J. Bears

Deb Canham

Hovvigs

Ellie-Bears

Folies D'Ours

Hartrick Bears

PUBLISHING

Hazelwood Bears

Hugs Unlimited

Hermann Teddy

Jan's Tiddy Bears

H M Bears

J C W Bears

PUBLISHING
Hugglets

Kingston Bears

Jabelow Bears

Karin Kronsteiner

Lea Bears

Madabout Bears

Love is in the Bear

PUBLISHING

Merry Bears

Lyndee-Lou

Meister Bear

Melissa Jayne

Oz Matilda

Sue Quinn

Scruffie Bears

Pennbeary

Pipedream Bears

Paw Lines

Portobello Bears

Pamela Ann Designs

PUBLISHING
Hugglets

Pywacket

Sally B Bears

Stine-Teddies

Teachers Pets

Studio 44

Robin Rive

PUBLISHING
Hugglets

Three O'Clock Bears

Toys Stuffed and Handmade by Susan

Whisty Bears

Whittle-Le-Woods

Woodville Bears

Woodland Teddies

Westie Bears

END

Bear Makers & Artists

For international artists please see page 181

A BETTER CLASS OF BEAR
Hillside, Hatch Lane, Chapel Row, Bucklebury, Berkshire, RG7 6NX
☎ 01189 713182
email: pam@hillier-brook.freeserve.co.uk
Limited edition quality collectors bears.

A.C. BEARS
25 McKinlay Crescent, Irvine, Ayrshire, KA12 8DP, Scotland
☎ 01294 271389 eve
email: ac-bears@tiscali.co.uk
Lovable handcrafted quality mohair bears.

A HITCHCOCK BEAR
2 Church Hill Road, Oxford, OX4 3SE
☎ 07773 296740
email: ahitchcockbear@yahoo.co.uk
Personalised bears made to order.

A LANIE BEARS UK
14 Kingfisher Way, Telford, Shropshire, TF1 6FW
☎ 01952 641643
email: info@mohairbears.co.uk
web: www.mohairbears.co.uk
Beary nice exclusive OOAK designs.

ABELIA BEARS
21 Rochford Close, Turnford, Broxbourne, Herts, EN10 6DL
☎ 01992 478229
email: info@abeliabears.com
web: www.abeliabears.com
Beautiful handcrafted artist bears.

ABSOLUTELY BEAR BY FIONA SMITH
124 Kingsley Road, Maidstone, Kent, ME15 7UL
☎ 01622 691760 Fax: As tel.
email: fiona@absolutelybear.com
web: www.absolutelybear.com
Designer teddies with big personalities waiting for a hug! See for yourself, visit my website at: www.absolutelybear.com

ACTUALLY BEARS BY JACKIE ™
Hunnypot House, 18 Lowry Way, Stowmarket, Suffolk, IP14 1UF
☎ 01449 675951
web: www.actuallybearsbyjackie.co.uk
Handsewn miniature and full-size bears.

ALDERSON BEARS
Narrow Lane House, Coasthill Crich, Nr Matlock, Derbyshire, DE4 5DS
☎ 01773 850078
Traditional hand crafted mohair bears.

ALEXANDER BEARS
Bexleyheath, Kent
☎ 01322 337797 or 07932 735123
email: alexbearuk@aol.com
Beautiful mohair bears for discerning collectors. 5"-30". One-offs and small LEs. Email for further details.

● ALICIA'S ZIZBEARS
24 Locke King Road, Weybridge, Surrey, KT13 0SY
☎ 01932 854499
email: alicia@zizbears.co.uk
web: www.zizbears.co.uk
Quality mohair bears hand sewn in small limited editions and one off creations by Alicia.

● ALL BEAR BY PAULA CARTER
One Underwood Close, Maidstone, Kent, ME15 6SR
☎ 01622 686970 Fax: As tel.
email: allbearbypaula@aol.com
web: www.allbear.co.uk
See full range on website!

● ALL THINGS ANGELIC
37 Queens Road, Aldershot, Hampshire, GU11 3JE
☎ 01252 690073
email: sales@chillandbrowse.co.uk
web: www.chillandbrowse.co.uk
Designer bears at affordable prices.

● ALL THINGS BEARY
33 Pentland View, Edinburgh, Lothian, EH10 6PY, Scotland
☎ 0131 477 6970
email: hugs@allbeary.com
web: www.allbeary.com
Bears for all, many miniatures, themed bears, T-shirts, china, cards, much more. Original handcrafted designs. New exciting website. Mail order.

● ALWAYS BEARING IN MIND
Margaret Ann Coltman, 50 Baronsmead Road, High Wycombe, Buckinghamshire, HP12 3PG
☎ 01494 437238
email: teddies@alwaysbearinginmind.co.uk
web: www.alwaysbearinginmind.co.uk
Happy hugs and beary bits.

● ANGIEBEARS
27 Trubridge Road, Hoo St Werburgh, Rochester, Kent, ME3 9EN
☎ 01634 253165
email: angie@angiebears.net
web: www.angiebears.net
Bear artist making quality bears.

● ANN MADE BEARS
60 Layfield Road, Hendon, London, NW4 3UG
☎ 020 8202 3165
email: ann@ann-made-bears.co.uk
web: www.ann-made-bears.co.uk
Original handcrafted artist bears designed and made by Ann Reed available at bear fairs and by mail order. Commissions taken.

● ANNIE DAVIS
(Malvern Bears), 'Delmar', Fairfields Road, Ledbury, Herefordshire, HR8 2EH
☎ 01531 634548
email: davisannie@easy.com
One-off designs 130mm(5") and larger.

● APIS BEARS
Hillside, 3 Dovedale Road, New Brighton, Merseyside, CH45 0LP
☎ 0151 638 8079
email: bears@apisbears.co.uk
web: www.apisbears.co.uk
Collectors bears in small sizes.

● APPLES 'N' BEARS
9 Adam Close, King's Lynn, Norfolk, PE30 4UD
☎ 01553 765559
email: applesnbearsuk@aol.com
web: www.applesnbears.co.uk
Artist bears for discerning collectors.

● APPLETREE BEARS
9 Hilltop Road, Stockton Heath, Warrington, Cheshire,
WA4 2DP
☎ 01925 263456
Individual handcrafted artist bears.

● ARBURY BEARS
1 Fair Isle Drive, Nuneaton, Warwickshire, CV10 7LJ
☎ 024 7674 1453
email: claire@arburybears.com
web: www.arburybears.com
Miniature bears with knitted accessories.

● ARCTURUS BEARS
2 Dovedale Road, Wallasey, Wirral, Cheshire,
CH45 0LP
☎ 0151 691 1297
email: rhianntaylor@yahoo.com
web: www.bearfacedchic.bravehost.com
One of a kind bears.

● ASHWAY BEARS
100 The Ashway, Brixworth, Northampton, NN6 9UZ
☎ 01604 889150
email: jane@ashwaybears.co.uk
web: www.ashwaybears.co.uk
Hand crafted traditional collector bears.

● ATLANTIC BEARS
5 Braeside, Gairloch, Ross-shire, IV21 2BG, Scotland
☎ 01445 712179
email: info@atlanticbears.com
web: www.atlanticbears.com
Callers welcome by appointment.

● B. A. BEARS
110 Waverton Road, Bentilee, Stoke-on-Trent, Staffs,
ST2 0QY
☎ 01782 318043 Fax: As tel.
email: babearsharg@aol.com
web: www.b.a.bears.s5.com
Quality bears with character. Original designs, one offs, limited editions, open editions. Award winning British bear artist.

As seen on ITV Central

Exclusively designed and handcrafted
by Janette Osman
- Crafting bears since 1994 -

www.beanibears.com

All enquiries welcome
Tel: 01543 444 784 or 07976 890 497
E-mail: janette@beanibears.com

● BACKSTAGE BEARS
232 Wellgate, Rotherham, South Yorkshire, S60 2PB
email: jayne.globe@virgin.net
web: www.backstagebears.com
Award-winning miniature bears.

● BAGGALEY BEARS
6 Boundary Road, Beeston, Nottingham,
Nottinghamshire, NG9 2RF
☎ 0115 8757 031
email: v.fletcher-baggaley@talk21.com
Quality, traditional hand-crafted bears.

● BAGGIES BEARS
299 Clockhouse Road, Beckenham, Kent, BR3 4LE
☎ 020 8658 4093
email: BaggiesBears@hills459.fsworld.co.uk
Quality Bears made with love.

● BAGSTER BEARS
by Caz, c/o 37 Marion Road, Norwich, Norfolk,
NR1 4BN
☎ 01603 632085
email: bagsterbears@ntlworld.com

Bears courses and B&B for bear lovers
by Jean & Bill Ashburner
to receive the full colour catalogue
of the bears we make and course details
please send
10 x 1st class stamps (refundable if you order)

and a few Rare Bits!

www.bearbits.com

Bear Bits, The Florins, Silver Street, Minting, Lincolnshire LN9 5RP Tel/Fax: 01507 578360

● BALFOUR BEARS
96 Dunholm Road, Dundee, DD2 4RW
☎ 01382 624605
email: trishabalfour@blueyonder.co.uk
web: www.balfourbears.co.uk
Award winning one of a kind creations. Bears, cats and bunnies created in the Scottish Highlands. Trade enquiries welcome.

● BARBARA-ANN BEARS
42 Palmarsh Avenue, Hythe, Kent, CT21 6NR
☎ 01303 269038 Fax: 01303 266669
email: barbara-annbears@bigfoot.com
web: www.barbara-annbears.com
Wild but gorgeous bears, dragons, hand-dyed mohair, kits, workshops and websites. Call, email or see the website and have fun!

● BARE BEARS
☎ 01506 834233
email: lorraine@barebears.co.uk
web: www.barebears.co.uk
Miniature bears handcrafted in Scotland.

● BARLING BEARS
13 Pear Tree Avenue, Ditton, Aylesford, Kent, ME20 6EB
☎ 01732 845059 Fax: As tel.
email: marilyn@barlingbears.co.uk
web: www.barlingbears.co.uk
Beautiful quality mohair collectors' bears, individually designed and hand-made exclusively by Marilyn. Fully jointed, traditionally made. Commissions welcome. See website.

● BARNEY BEARS
67 Cranleigh Drive, Leigh-on-Sea, Essex, SS9 1SX
☎ 01702 472636
email: jennifer@cunningham5097.freeserve.co.uk
web: http://mysite.freeserve.com/barneybears
Special bears to cherish forever.

● BARNWELL BEARS
Trenance, 57 Mill Lane, Upton, Chester, Cheshire, CH2 1BS
☎ 01244 380422
email:
melaniesmith@broadenyourhorizons.fsnet.co.uk
Award winning bears. See Gallery.

● BARRICANE BEARS
61 Langleigh Park, Ilfracombe, Devon, EX34 8RB
☎ 01271 866871
email: rachel@barricanebears.co.uk
web: www.barricanebears.co.uk
Artist bears of distinction.

● BARTON BEARS
Pear Trees, 61 Mount Road, Wallasey, Wirral, CH45 0NA
☎ 0151 639 1236
Individually made for quality and collectability.

● BAY BEARS
Bolton Lodge, 107 Main Road, Bolton-le-Sands, nr. Carforth, Lancashire, LA5 8EQ
☎ 01524 824537
email: doreenbark@aol.com
Traditional handmade mohair collectors' bears.

● BAY BEARS OF HERNE BAY
3 Elizabeth Way, Herne Bay, Kent
☎ 01227 374034
email: trblyth@lineone.net
See my bears on ebay.

by Janice Davidson

Tel: 01828 670561
Email: janice @bearitz.com

Fleur'

Fiore'

www.bearitz.com

Bears 4 Hugs

hand dyed and hand stitched
character bears and
bears on the fur
by Tina-Maria Layton

all dyes and materials are
natural products from local sources

www.bears4hugs.com
bears4hugs@tesco.net

● BAZIL BEARS
10 Brecon Close, Worcester Park, Surrey, KT4 8JW
☎ 0208 3301193
email: pauline@bazilbears.co.uk
web: www.bazilbears.co.uk
Handcrafted bears sewn with love.

● BEANI BEARS OF LICHFIELD
5 Fletcher Drive, Fradley, Staffordshire, WS13 8TH
☎ 01543 444784 / 07976 890497
email: janette@beanibears.com
web: www.beanibears.com
Handcrafted bears by Janette Osman.

● BEAR BAHOOCHIE
40 Morven Drive, Polmont, Falkirk, FK2 0XD, Scotland
☎ 01324 411823
email: kateri@bearbahoochie.co.uk
web: www.bearbahoochie.co.uk
Unique personalised miniature bears.

● BEAR BITS
The Florins, Silver Street, Minting, Horncastle, Lincolnshire, LN9 5RP
☎ 01507 578360 Fax: As tel.
email: ashburner@bearbits.freeserve.co.uk
web: www.bearbits.com
Wonderful bears. See display advertisement.

● BEAR CRAZEE
37 Willow Drive, Havercroft, Wakefield, West Yorkshire, WF4 2QA
☎ 01226 725390 mobile: 0798 607 2712
email: bears@bearcrazee.com
web: www.bearcrazee.com
Artist bears all delightfully different!

● BEAR FACED CHEEK!®
181 Courtenay Avenue, Harrow, Middlesex, HA3 6PT
☎ 020 8421 6507 or 079 5600 9193
email: lisa@bearfacedcheek.co.uk
web: www.bearfacedcheek.co.uk
Award winning artist bears.

● BEAR FRIENDS
Field End, Brigsteer, Cumbria, LA8 8AN
☎ 015395 68570
email: mb.mansbridge@btinternet.com
Traditional quality teddy bears.

BEAR IN MIND
360 London Road, Deal, Kent, CT14 9PS
☎ 01304 366234
email: bearinmind@btinternet.com
One-offs and special commission bears for the discerning collector. Handmade in the traditional way but full of modern character.

BEAR LEIGH MADE IT©
PO Box 73, Ludlow, Shropshire, SY8 4WP
email: bearleighmadeit@aol.com
web: www.bearleigh.com
One offs designed and hand crafted by Tracey Madden.

BEAR-FACED LIES
1 Rose Cottages, Exebridge, TA22 9BB
☎ 01398 324688 Fax: As tel.
email: charlotte@bear-faced-lies.com
web: www.bear-faced-lies.com
Hand-stitched miniature toys. BTG member.

BEARABILITY BY KIM
23 Burns Way, Clifford, Wetherby, West Yorkshire, LS23 6TA
☎ 01937 844030 Fax: 01937 843125
email: info@bearability.co.uk
web: www.bearability.co.uk
Handmade traditional and unique bears.

BEARBURY OF LONDON
27 Church Avenue, London, SW14 8NW
☎ 020 8392 2625
Beautiful bears by Turid Christensen.

THE BEARCRAFT BEAR COMPANY
2 Oak Terrace, Holmside Village, Durham, DH7 6ET
☎ 0191 3711162
email: aujc69@dsl.pipex.com
Traditional bears - see display advertisement. Bear making classes and supplies now at Biddick Arts Centre, Washington. Please phone for details.

BEARGORRAH!
38 Margaret Road, Colchester, Essex, CO1 1RZ
☎ 01206 564472
Bears and cats made from our own designs in finest quality mohair or alpaca. One offs or small limited editions.

BEARHUNT BEARS
4 Litchen Close, Ilkeston, Derbyshire, DE7 8HJ
☎ 07764 759703
email: bears@bearhuntbears.co.uk
web: www.bearhuntbears.co.uk
Handmade, collectable mohair teddy bears.

BEARITZ
Iona, Whitelea Road, Burrelton, By Blairgowrie, PH13 9NY
☎ 01828 670561 Fax: 01828 670766
email: janice@bearitz.com
web: www.bearitz.com
Handcrafted bears designed and created with finest mohairs, zany to soulful characters by Janice Davidson. Secure online shopping.

BEARLY SANE BEARS
107 Plymstock Road, Oreston, Plymouth, Devon, PL9 7PQ
☎ 01752 403515
email: bearlysanebears@aol.com
web: www.bearlysanebears.com
Collectors bears by Sharon Aish.

Bedspring Bears by Anne Thomas

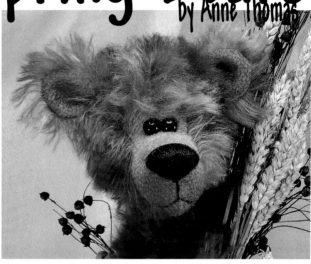

Award winning bears, animals and kits by Anne Thomas.
6 Nottingham Place
Lee-On-Solent
Hampshire
PO13 9LZ
Tel/Fax:
023 92 602075

www.bedspringbears.com   email:bedspringbears@btopenworld.com

● **BEARLY THERE**
5 Park Road, Netherton, Dudley, West Midlands, DY2 9BY
☎ 01384 236532 Fax: As tel.
email: lorraine@bearlythere.com
web: www.bearlythere.com
Miniature bears 1" to 5". Handsewn in uphol-stery fabric and mohair by Lorraine Jones. One off and limited editions.

● **BEARNARD BEARS**
65 Truslove Road, London, SE27 0QG
☎ 0208 655 7176
email: bearnardbears@yahoo.co.uk
Specializing in individual hand made bears from mohair or recycled fur, also hand dye to your choice of colour.

● **BEARS 4 HUGS**
Glasdrum Trust Cottages, Drimnin, Morvern, Argyll, PA34 5XZ
☎ 01967 421308
email: bears4hugs@tesco.net
web: www.bears4hugs.com
Please see display advertisement.

● **BEARS BY BOBBI**
1/2, 77 Walter Street, Dennistoun, Glasgow, G31 3PU
☎ 0141 554 7917
email: roberta.stevenson@tesco.net
Collectable handcrafted bears and friends.

● **BEARS BY DESIGN**
99 Alexander Close, Abingdon, Oxfordshire, OX14 1XD
☎ 01235 534536
email: info@bears-by-design.com
web: www.bears-by-design.com
Miniature bears to original designs.

● **BEARS BY EUNICE**
219 Salmon Street, London, NW9 8ND
☎ 020 8205 6308 Fax: As tel.
email: euniceedwards@freenet.co.uk
Lovable handcrafted mohair bears.

● **BEARS BY HAND**
41 Thetford Close, Danesholme, Corby, Northamptonshire, NN18 9PH ☎ 01536 461159
Traditional and collectors bears in mohair and other fine fabrics. Limited editions and special commissions. Large SAE for photographs, etc.

● BEARS BY HEATHER JAYNE
The Old Chapel, 50 High Street, Billinghay, Lincoln, LN4 4AU
☎ 01526 860321
email: heather.hocking@ntlworld.com
web: www.bearsbyheatherjayne.co.uk
One-off and limited editions.

● BEARS BY JANET STEWARD
Cops Bungalow, Monk Soham, Suffollk, IP13 7EJ
☎ 01728 685743
email: js@janetsteward.co.uk
web: www.janetsteward.co.uk
Collectors bears made at home.

● BEARS BY JULIA
3 Suffolk Avenue, West Mersea, Colchester, Essex, CO5 8ER   ☎ 01206 386654
Individually hand stitched collectors bears.

● BEARS BY MARYKE
Portland House, 265 Stockton Road, Hartlepool, Cleveland, TS25 5AU
☎ 077 0224 4922 / 01429 291538 Fax: 01429 291539
email: jagryk@aol.com
web: www.bearsbymaryke.co.uk
E.V.A. and B.B.A.A. winner 2001.

● BEARS BY SUSAN GAM
5 Pemberton Avenue, Gidea Park, Romford, Essex, RM2 6EX
☎ 01708 760021 Fax: As tel.
email: susan@bearsbysusangam.com
web: www.bearsbysusangam.com
Handcrafted miniature bears with personality!

● BEARS BY SUSAN JANE KNOCK
6 Elizabeth Avenue, Witham, Essex, CM8 1JE
☎ 01376 521230
email: susan.k@tinyworld.co.uk
Handmade artist bears to my own designs from 1"-16". Traditional and modern styles in mohair and antique velvets.

● BEARS EXTRAORDINAIRE
'Dragon House', 54 Station Road, Nailsea, North Somerset, BS48 4PA
☎ 01275 851999
email: jmprideaux@aol.com
Artist bears of some distinction.

● BEARS FOR TEA
PO Box 4711, Earley, Reading, Berkshire, RG6 4XN
☎ Fax: 0709 236 3700
email: mary@bears4t.com
web: www.bears4t.com
Artist made bears for you.

● BEARS IN THE BRAMBLES
The Brambles, Meadow Lane, Maltby, S Yorks, S66 7LD
☎ 01709 815733
email: bearsintheb@aol.com
Designer limited editions. Special commissions.

● BEARS OF GRACE
7 Howitts Gardens, Eynesbury, St Neots, Cambridgeshire, PE19 2PD
☎ 01480 385445
email: mickvernalls@yahoo.co.uk
Beautiful traditional bears aged with care. Original vintage clothes. Commissions taken. Enquiries welcome. Mail order.

Bees Knees Bears by Jo
www.beeskneesbears.co.uk
bkbears@btinternet.com
01902 843124

BEARS OF MY HEART

Tigh mo Cridhe, Skeabost Bridge, Isle of Skye, IV51 9NP, Scotland
☎ 01786 823344
email: sue@bearsofmyheart.com
web: www.bearsofmyheart.com
Artist bears from the heart.

BEARS PAW COLLECTABLES

The Retreat, 60 Naseby Road, Leicester, Leicestershire, LE4 9FH
☎ 0116 274 1441 Fax: As tel.
email: keith.w.freeman@btinternet.com
Small limited edition collector's bears using fine quality mohair, beautiful teddy china, silver plated teaspoons and handbags, etc.

BEARS UNLIMITED

14 Clausen Way, Pennington, Lymington, Hants, SO41 8BJ
☎ 01590 670536
email: jwallbearsunltd@aol.com
Handmade mohair collectors bears. Stitched with love. Lead or steel weighted. Individually hand-dyed and small limited editions. Selected fairs attended.

BEARS UPON SOAR

5 Hickling Drive, Sileby, Loughborough, Leicestershire, LE12 7PA
☎ 01509 813203 or 078666 16799
email: lisa@bearsuponsoar.co.uk
web: www.bearsuponsoar.co.uk
Handcrafted realistic bears.

BEARS UPON THE RIVER NIDD

67 Grimbald Road, Knaresborough, North Yorkshire, HG5 8HD
☎ 01423 541366
email: debbie_moloney@talk21.com
web: http://myweb.tiscali.co.uk/bearsuponrivernidd
Quality handcrafted bears. Great prices.

BEARS WITH ATTITUDE

83 Spinney Hill, Melbourne, Derbyshire, DE73 1LX
☎ 01332 865846 Fax: As tel.
email: suehargar@aol.com
Collectable bears, kits and supplies.

BEARSMITH

12 Woodlands, Winthorpe, Newark, Notts, NG24 2NL
Hand made bears.

BEARTIFACTS

Hideaway, 6 Avocet Drive, Altrincham, Cheshire, WA14 5NR
☎ 07816 185707
email: margaret_hatton@ryder.com
BeArtifacts Handmade Teddy Bears. Traditional fabric commissions or 'fur coat' conversions into family heirlooms accepted. Prices negotiable. Brochure available on request.

BEARZONE

15 Hasted Drive, Alresford, Hampshire, SO24 9PX
☎ 01962 734524
Individual bears to love forever.

BEATRIX BEARS

283 Monkmoor Road, Shrewsbury, Shropshire, SY2 5TF
☎ 01743 340276
email: beatrix.bears@virgin.net
web: www.beatrixbears.co.uk
Traditional and character artist bears. Worldwide delivery. All major credit cards accepted. Trade enquiries welcomed.

BEAU BEAR

195 Felsham Road, Putney, London, SW15 1BB
☎ 0208 7881052
Miniatures, silver character beau bears.

BEBBIN BEARS

by Yvonne Andrew, 7 Middle Road, Aylesbury, Buckinghamshire, HP21 7AD
☎ 01296 423755
email: yvonne@bebbinbears.co.uk
web: www.bebbinbears.co.uk
Exquisite, unique, award winning artist bears, designed and created for collectors. Each having their own special character, personality, and charm!

BECKSIDE BEARS

Beckside Cottage, Scargate Lane, Kirkby Green, Lincoln, LN4 3PG
☎ 01526 323312
email: becksidebears@hotmail.co.uk
web: www.becksidebears.co.uk
Unique designed hand sewn bears.

● BEDFORD BEARS

The Tithe Barn, Church Farm, Eyeworth, Sandy, Bedfordshire, SG19 2HH

☎ 01767 318626 Fax: 01767 631131

email: ann@bedfordbears.wanadoo.co.uk

web: www.bedfordbears.co.uk

Traditional bear makers since 1985.

● BEDRAGGLE BEARS™

36 North Road, St Andrews, Bristol, BS6 5AF

☎ 0117 9497389

email: suehoskins@hoskinsuk.co.uk

Old souls stitched with love into unique little bears with big hearts and a story to tell of past times.

● BEDSPRING BEARS

6 Nottingham Place, Lee-On-Solent, Hampshire, PO13 9LZ

☎ 023 9260 2075 Fax: As tel.

email: bedspringbears@btopenworld.com

web: www.bedspringbears.com

Handcrafted artist bears, cats, gollies etc.

● BEES KNEES BEARS

7 Madeira Avenue, Codsall, Wolverhampton, West Midlands, WV8 2DS

☎ 01902 843124 Fax: As tel.

email: bkbears@btinternet.com

web: www.beeskneesbears.co.uk

Original designs by Jo Matthews. Beautiful artist bears using the finest mohair and alpaca. Member of the British Toymakers Guild.

● BELL BEARS

The Workshop, 55 Tannsfeld Road, Sydenham, London, SE26 5DL

☎ 020 8778 0217 Fax: 020 8659 2278

email: bellbears@btinternet.com

Please see display advertisement.

● BELLY BUTTON BEARS

Fox Hollow, Greenfields, Earith, Huntingdon, Cambridgeshire, PE28 3QZ

☎ 01487 842538

email: bellybuttonbears@kipps.worldonline.co.uk

Exclusive hand crafted finest mohair bears. Unique one-offs and small limited editions. Created by Pat Kipps. Big Hug!

BEN DESIGN

Church Cottage, Church Lane, Bramshall, Uttoxeter, Staffordshire, ST14 5BQ
☎ 01889 560195 Fax: As tel.
email: friesian@btopenworld.com
Bears for every occasion.

BENEBEARS

Pine House Cottage, Churt Road, Hindhead, Surrey, GU26 6HY
☎ 01428 605972
email: mary@benebears.com
web: www.benebears.com
Bear artist Mary Tornabene's traditional handcrafted, quality mohair bears. Commissions any size a speciality. Repairs and restoration also undertaken.

BENJAMIN BEARS

61 Diana Road, Chatham, Kent, ME4 5PW
☎ 01634 832523
email: benjaminbears@btinternet.com
web: www.benjaminbears.org
Unique adorable bears, see website.

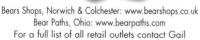
BENJI'S BEARS

13 Amberfield Close, Stoke-on-Trent, Staffordshire, ST3 1TZ
☎ 01782 320913
email: mtecap@ntlworld.com
Handmade miniature bears.

BENTHALL BEARS

Clematis Cottage, 15 Benthall Lane, Benthall, Shropshire, TF12 5RR
☎ 01952 883779
email: benthallbears@btopenworld.com
web: www.benthallbears.co.uk
Limited edition quality character bears.

BERTIE BEAR AND FRIENDS

Porth-Y-Pentre, Llanover, Abergavenny, Monmouthshire, S. Wales, NP7 9EY
☎ 01873 880076 Fax: As tel.
email: orders@bertiebear.co.uk
web: www.bertiebear.co.uk
Artist bears handmade with love!

BESSY BEARS

Strickland Hall, Little Strickland, Penrith, Cumbria, CA10 3EG
☎ 01931 716262 Fax: As tel.
Hand made mohair artist bears. Limited editions of one to five. Filled with cotton fibre, steel shot, attitude and courage.

BEST FRIENDS

23 Rodway Close, Brierley Hill, West Midlands, DY5 2NA
☎ 01384 897699
Bears handmade by Angela Michelle.

BEVERLEY MCKENZIE ORIGINALS

8 Hockliffe Brae, Walnut Tree, Milton Keynes, Buckinghamshire, MK7 7BQ
☎ 01908 695430 Fax: As tel.
email: mail@beverleymckenzie.com
web: www.beverleymckenzie.com
Bears of distinction

BEXI BEARS

Hazel Street Bee Farm, South Green, Sittingbourne, Kent, ME9 7SB
☎ 01622 884218
Small hand-made bears. We can be found at the 'Old Surgery', Clun, Shropshire.

BIG SOFTIES
by Val Lyle ☎ 01943 600997
Traditional teddies handmade in England.

BIG TREE BEARS
101 Howbeck Road, Arnold, Nottingham, Nottinghamshire, NG5 8QA
☎ 0115 952 4022
email: cm.holbrook@ntlworld.com
Christine Holbrook's beautiful collectors bears, hand crafted in the finest quality mohairs and alpacas. One-offs and small limited editions.

BILBO BEARS
3 Outwood Avenue, Clifton, Greater Manchester, M27 6NP ☎ 0161 794 7931
Quality mohair bears designed and lovingly made by Audrey Edwards for national and international collectors.

BILLY BUFF BEARS
Round Hill Farm, Cragg Vale, Hebden Bridge, West Yorkshire, HX7 5TS
☎ 01422 885059 Fax: As tel.
web: www.billybuffbears.com
Traditional bears fully jointed, original designs in mohair with stringed puppets being a speciality. Trade enquiries welcome. See display ad.

BILLY BUMPKIN BEARS
10 Watson Close, Broughton, Chester, CH4 0SS
☎ 01244 534857 Fax: As tel.
email: suecobden@onetel.com
Adorable bears of all sizes.

BISSON BEARS
Rock Cottage, 121 Main Street, Warton, Nr Carnforth, Lancashire, LA5 9PN
☎ 01524 735014 / 07788 501435
email: bissonbears@hotmail.com
web: www.bissonbears.com
Please see display advertisement.

BJ BEARS
48 Salisbury Road, Gloucester, GL1 4JQ
☎ 01452 547562
email: bjbears_uk@hotmail.com
We have moved hug. Too cute to describe bears. Lots of new ideas especially for you. Love Julie xx.

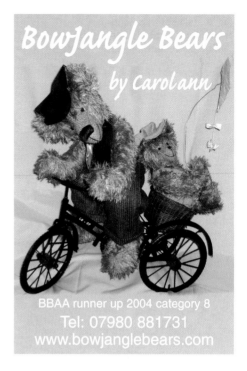

BLOSSOM TEDDIES
Ruach, 5 Springfields, Liscolman, Nr Ballymoney, Co. Antrim, BT53 8EX, Northern Ireland
☎ 028 207 42927
email: blossomteddies@aol.com
web: www.blossomteddies.com
Bears, cats, rabbits, pandas, koalas.

BLUEBEARY BEARS
40 Symes Road, Hamworthy, Poole, Dorset, BH15 4PT
☎ 01202 675735 email: bluebearybears@aol.com
web: www.bluebearybears.co.uk
Handmade mohair collector's bears.

BLUEMOON BEARS
65 Pendle Way, Pendlebury, Salford, M27 8QS
☎ 0161 727 8170
email: blue_moon@onetel.com
web: www.bluemoonbear-uk.com
Limited edition handmade mohair bears.

● BOBBYS BEARS
The Poplars, Orchard Close, Euxton, nr. Chorley, Lancashire, PR7 6LU
☎ 01257 232636
email: bobbys.bears@virgin.net
web: www.bobbysbears.com
Hand crafted traditional teddy bears.

● BODKIN BEARS
36 Cherry Orchard, Wotton-Under-Edge, Glos, GL12 7HT
☎ 01453 844551
Traditional handmade mohair collectors' bears.

● BOLEBRIDGE BEARS
48 Rosemary Road, Amington, Tamworth, Staffs, B77 3HF
☎ 01827 59097
email: vina.hollis@ukonline.co.uk
Bears with soul, lovingly made.

Bradgate Bears
by Judy Follows

'Attic Babies and Friends'
Tel: 0116 2870897
www.bradgatebears.co.uk

● BOWJANGLE BEARS
45 Blount Terrace, Kidderminster, Worcestershire, DY11 7AE
☎ 01562 862892 mob: 07980 881731
email: carolann@bowjanglebears.com
web: www.bowjanglebears.com
Cheeky little characters made with love (and mohair). Designed by Carol Ann for you.

● BOX BEARS
Top Floor, 208 Fernhead Road, London, W9 3EJ
☎ 07956 555230 Fax: 0208 962 0797
email: sharon@boxbears.co.uk
web: www.boxbears.co.uk
Bears, hares & friends. Handcrafted original designs using the finest materials. Member British Toymakers Guild. Visit new website.

● BOX YOUR BEARS
PO Box 19, Hitchin, Hertfordshire, SG4 9ZR
☎ 01462 626567
email: info@boxyourbears.co.uk
web: www.boxyourbears.co.uk
Call for a free colour brochure showing our range of boxed mohair bears in frames! More than just a bear!

● BRADGATE BEARS
24 Greys Drive, The Spinney, Groby, Leicester, LE6 0YW
☎ 0116 287 0897
email: judy@bradgatebears.co.uk
web: www.bradgatebears.co.uk
Nostalgic Attic Babies and Friends.

● BRADLEY BEARS
11 St Marys Close, Weston, Spalding, Lincs, PE12 6JL
☎ 01406 373073
email: michele-partridge@lineone.net
web: www.bradleybears.co.uk
Award Winning Bears - mostly one offs made from finest mohair and alpaca. Please come and visit my bears on www.bradley-bears.co.uk

● BRAMBLY BEARS
17 Old Mill Place, Tattenhall, Chester, Cheshire, CH3 9RJ
☎ 01829 770881 or 07921 336558
email: lm@bramblybears.co.uk
web: www.bramblybears.co.uk
Lovingly hand crafted bears.

● BRAMLEY BEARS
Bramley Cottage, 2 Waterlane Cottages, Ulcombe, Maidstone, Kent, ME17 1DL
☎ 01622 843556
email: julia.clarke@bramleybears.co.uk
web: www.bramleybears.co.uk
Sweet little bears to collect.

● BRAURONIA BEARS
'Robins Patch', 52 Church Road, Locks Heath, Southampton, Hampshire, SO31 6LQ
☎ 01489 559318
email: lynn.eaton@ntlworld.com
Bears to love and cherish.

● BRAVEHEART BEARS
3 The Oaks, Thorndon, Nr Eye, Suffolk, IP23 7JR
☎ 01379 678704
email: cheryl@braveheartbears.co.uk
web: www.braveheartbears.co.uk
Exclusively handmade traditional collector bears.

● BRIDGET'S BEARS
Bridget Singer, 68 Warwick Road, Thornton Heath, Surrey, CR7 7NE
☎ 020 8689 4091
email: bridgetsbears@ukgateway.net
web: www.bridgetsbears.ukgateway.net
Exquisite Unique Handmodelled Pottery Bears.

● BRIDGWATER BEARS
100 Bridgwater Road, Ipswich, Suffolk, IP2 9QF
☎ 01473 412066
email: lm.dye@ntlworld.com
Lots of new bears and old favourites all in super mohair including many one offs.

● BRODIE BEARS
Ali Morton, 23 Hill Place, Ardrossan, Ayrshire, KA22 8HY, Scotland
☎ 01294 468532
email: alimorton1@aol.com
web: www.brodiebears.co.uk

● BROOKLYN BEARS
Combe Acre, Whiston, Northampton, NN7 1NN
☎ 01604 891585
email: lilymay6@aol.com
Handmade bears cute cuddly lovable.

● BROTHERWOOD BEARS
47 Poynder Place, Hilmarton, Calne, Wiltshire, SN11 8SQ
☎ 01249 760284 Fax: 01249 760530
email: suebrotherwood@aol.com
web: www.brotherwoodbears.com
Original bears and gollies hand crafted with love and a little flair!

● BROW BEARS
9 Ireleth Brow, Askam in Furness, Cumbria, LA16 7HB
☎ 01229 467861
Traditional handmade mohair collectors bears.

● BRYONY BEARS
51 St Fabians Drive, Chelmsford, Essex, CM1 2PU
☎ 01245 264651
email: karen@bryonybears.com
web: www.bryonybears.com
Adorable mohair, crocheted, needlefelted bears.

● BRYS BRUINS BEARS
93 High Street, Gosberton, Spalding, Lincolnshire, PE11 4NA
☎ 01775 840916
email: brysbruin@aol.com web: www.brysbruins.com
Contemporary, wacky, fun artist bears.

● BUCKIE BEARS
18 Reidhaven Street, Ianstown, Buckie, Morayshire,
AB56 1SB, Scotland
☎ 01542 835639 Fax: As tel.
email: niki@buckiebears.co.uk
web: www.buckiebears.co.uk
Hand made mohair artist bears.

● BUFF 'N' CO. BEARS
2 Harewood Road, Holymoorside, Chesterfield,
Derbyshire, S42 7HT
☎ 01246 569393
email: buff@buff-n-co.com
web: www.buff-n-co.com
Dressed miniature bears 2 inches.

● BUMBLE BEARS
17 Adur Close, West End, Southampton, Hampshire,
SO18 3NH
☎ 023 80 326663
email: anthony.wells73@ntlworld.com
Limited editions and special commissions.

● BUNKY BEARS
104B Northgate, Newark, Nottinghamshire, NG24 1HF
☎ 01636 678724
email: enquiries@bunkybears.co.uk
web: www.BunkyBears.co.uk
Traditional and contemporary artist bears.

● BUNTY BEARS
Meadow View Cottage, Newton-St-Cyres, Exeter,
Devon, EX5 5AX
☎ 01392 851448
*Traditional handmade collectors' bears in
mohair. Also bears lovingly repaired.*

● BURL'S BEARS
PO Box 814, Northwich, Cheshire, CW8 2WF
☎ 01606 888814 Fax: As tel.
email: charliesfursandfeatures@btopenworld.com
Individual hand made mohair bears.

● BURLEY BEARS
23 Meadow View Road, Bearwood, Bournemouth,
Dorset, BH11 9RD
☎ 01202 571867 Fax: 01202 253738
email: burleybears@hotmail.com
Crafted with love by Sharon.

● BURLINGTON BEARTIES
2 Ambergate Drive, Kingswinford, West Midlands, DY6 7HZ
☎ 01384 279731
email: bridgemark@bearties.freeserve.co.uk
Collectors bears, cats and rabbits.

● BURLINGTONBEARS.COM
28 Burlington Gardens, Selsey, West Sussex, PO20 0DP
☎ 01243 602654 Fax: As tel.
email: tania@burlingtonbears.com
web: www.burlingtonbears.com
*Exclusively designed wild and wacky
bears and other creatures lovingly handcrafted. Commissions welcomed.*

● BURTONIAN BEARS
18 Briar Close, Newhall, Swadlincote, Derbyshire,
DE11 0RX
☎ 01283 550074
email: bearsales@burtonianbears.co.uk
web: www.burtonianbears.co.uk
*Traditional and individual bruins lovingly cre-
ated by Sharon Mellor using finest quality
materials. Trade enquiries and commissions
welcome. Photographs available.*

BUTLERS BEARS

Pool House, Pool Drive, Hadnall, Shrewsbury, Shropshire, SY4 4BQ
☎ 01939 210672
email: butlers-bears@tiscali.co.uk
Please see display advertisement.

C & M'S BEARHUGS

Patchings Art Centre, Oxton Road, Calverton, Nottingham, NG14 6NU
☎ 0115 916 3731
email: maria@bearhugs.co.uk
web: www.bearhugs.co.uk
Unique and limited edition artist teddy bears. Packed full of personality. Sold exclusively from the studio and on the web.

CANDI BEARS

Steffi McIntyre, 43 Brewlands Crescent, Symington, KA1 5RN
☎ 01563 830729 or 07769 574274
email: candibearsbysteffi@yahoo.co.uk
web: www.candibears.bravehost.com
Collectors bears. Traditional and character styles. All bears one of a kind. Commissions undertaken. See web site for more details.

CANTERBURY BEARS

1 Builders Square, Littlebourne, Nr Canterbury, Kent, CT3 1XU
☎ 01227 728630 Fax: 01227 710118
email: enquiries@canterburybears.co.uk
web: www.canterburybears.co.uk
Established 1979. Original English bears of distinction. Made in England. Our quality is legendary our designs unique.

CARIAD BEARS

11 Plastirion Avenue, Prestatyn, Denbighshire, LL19 9DY
☎ 01745 859487
Exclusive hand made one-off bears.

CARMICHAEL BEARS

54 Limekiln Row, Castlefields, Runcorn, Cheshire, WA7 2LT
☎ 01928 563874
email: karen@carmichaelbears.co.uk
web: www.carmichaelbears.co.uk
Handcrafted mohair teddy bears.

CEES BEARS

56 Hawthorn Road, Reepham, Lincoln, Lincolnshire, LN3 4DU
☎ 01522 800942
email: gracee@ntlworld.com
web: www.ceesbears.com
Artist bears made for charity. Handmade using high quality mohair. All sewn with love. Proceeds go to terminal cancer care.

CELTIC COMPANIONS

PO Box 8525, Saltcoats, Ayrshire, KA21 5WJ
☎ 01294 471760
email: norma@celtic-companions.co.uk
web: www.celtic-companions.co.uk
Teddies of quality and character. Handmade in Scotland. Secure online ordering. Worldwide delivery. Layaway available. All major credit cards accepted.

CHAMBEARS

26 Barleycorn Way, Hornchurch, Essex, RM11 3JJ
☎ 01708 449370
Bears handmade with love.

● CHANNEL ISLAND TOYS

25/27 Victoria Road, St Peter Port, Guernsey, GY1 1HU
☎ 01481 723871 Fax: 01481 711625
email: sales@channel-teddy.co.uk
web: www.channel-teddy.co.uk
Teddy bears with embroidered clothing.

● CHAPPLE BEARS

Belvedere, 43 Trelissick Road, Hayle, Cornwall, TR27 4HY
☎ 01736 755577
Bears of distinction wearing hallmarked silver collars. Individually designed. Unique and beautifully made by the artist Beryl Chapple. Details £2.

● CHARLIE BEARS LTD

The Willows, None Go Bye Farm, Otley Old Road, Leeds, W. Yorkshire, LS18 5HZ
☎ 0113 2842742 mob:07966 104276 Fax: 0113 2842742
email: sales@charliebears.com
web: www.charliebears.com
Please see display advertisement.

● CHARNWOOD BEARS

15 Amis Close, Loughborough, Leicestershire, LE11 5AA
☎ 01509 844002 Fax: As tel.
email: fnwebster@aol.com
web: www.thehouseofbruin.co.uk
Hand made traditional and artist bears by Frank Webster since 1988. Commissions accepted, trade enquiries welcomed.

● CHELTENHAM BEARS

7 Edendale Road, Golden Valley Park, Cheltenham, Gloucestershire
☎ 07905 307859 email: suerowe@ip3.co.uk
web: www.cheltenhambears.co.uk
Beautiful individual bears and dogs, also rabbits and cats. Handmade with love and awaiting adoption.

● CHERRY'S CHUMS

1 Piper Close, Perton, Wolverhampton, West Midlands, WV6 7NS
☎ 07885 710630
email: cherry@chums65.freeserve.co.uk
Traditional pellet filled mohair bears in a range of sizes, styles, colours, prices. Lovingly handmade for collectors by Cherry Swinnerton.

● CHESTER BEARS
40 Meadows View, Marford, Wrexham, Clwyd, LL12 8LS
☎ 01978 855604
email: chesterbears@moviebus.com
Traditional hand made bears using top quality materials. Small limited editions.

● CHRISTINE PIKE BEARS
9 New Road, Lake, Sandown, Isle of Wight, PO36 9JN
☎ 01983 403224 Fax: As tel.
email: christine@christinepike.com
web: www.christinepike.com
Character and traditional artist bears. Award winning artist bears. Also freelance journalism and illustration: bears and dolls my speciality.

● CHUBBY CUBS
28 Maunleigh, Forest Town, Mansfield, Nottinghamshire, NG19 0PP
☎ 01623 407988
email: chubbycubbears@hotmail.com
Makers of modern and traditional teddy bears, various limited editions. Details £2 for catalogue and photos, refundable on first order.

1 Builders Square, Court Hill, Littlebourne, Canterbury, Kent, CT3 1XU
Tel: 01227 728630 Fax: 01227 710118
Email: enquiries@canterburybears.co.uk
Web: www.canterburybears.co.uk

● CLAYTON BEARS
58 Whitcliffe Lane, Ripon, North Yorkshire, HG4 2JN
☎ 01765 608797
email: claytonbears@aol.com
web: www.claytonbears.co.uk
Original designs by Sue Newlands.

● CLEMENS BEARS OF GERMANY
c/o A M International Agencies Ltd., Digital House, Peak Business Park, Foxwood Rd, Chesterfield, Derbyshire, S41 9RF
☎ 01246 269723 Fax: 01246 269724
email: enquiries@AM-International-Agencies.com
web: www.clemens.de
Famous traditional and artists bears.

● COLLECT-TEDS
16 Ninelands Lane, Garforth, Leeds, West Yorkshire, LS25 2BY
☎ 0113 286 7372
email: collect.teds@dsl.pipex.com
Beautifully original artist collector's bears - one-offs, commissions. Unique hand-modelled teddy teapots, clocks, mugs. Vintage Steiff, Schuco, Hermann Bears and rarities.

● COMPANION BEARS
6 Claremont Drive, Timperley, Altrincham, Cheshire, WA14 5ND
☎ 0161 976 1877
email: elaine@elainelonsdale.com
web: www.elainelonsdale.com
Unique range of bears/animals.

● CONRADI CREATIONS
21 Telford Avenue, Streatham Hill, London, SW2 4XL
☎ 020 8671 2794
email: karin_conradi@hotmail.com
web: www.conradicreations.com
Beautiful quality handstitched traditional bears with handpainted faces. Commissions undertaken.

● THE COTSWOLD BEAR COMPANY
Unit 2, Howsell Rd Ind Est., Howsell Road, Malvern Link, Worcestershire, WR14 1UJ
☎ 01684 564310 Fax: 01684 891796
email: post@thecotswoldbearco.com
web: www.thecotswoldbearco.com
Please call for more details.

● LIZZIE COVE
7 Neves Close, Lingwood, Norwich, Norfolk, NR13 4AW
☎ 01603 717050
Old/unusual fabrics. Character one-offs.

● COVENTRY BEARS
c/o 2 Warriston Avenue, Edinburgh, EH3 5ND
☎ 07947 066675
email: lauracoventry@yahoo.co.uk
Laura's miniature bears and friends.

● COWSLIP BEAR COMPANY
2 Warren Avenue, Mudeford, Christchurch, Dorset, BH23 3JX
☎ 01202 382073 or 07776 108528
email: cowslipbears@ntlworld.com
web: www.cowslipbears.co.uk
Hand made mohair and alpaca bears 6" to 8" and 22" to 31" all one of a kind original Cowslip smiley bears.

● CROSSFOOT BEARS
Greenfields, Allengrove, Heads Nook, Brampton, Cumbria, CA8 9AP
☎ 01228 561892
email: donna@alderman-dixon.fsnet.co.uk
web: www.crossfootbears.co.uk
Handmade, jointed, collectable, mohair, loveable.

● CROTCHETY BEARS
4 Spring Grove Crescent, Kidderminster, Worcestershire, DY11 7JB
☎ 01562 752289
Hand made collectors teddy bears.

● CURIO BEARS BY DEBBIE ROBINSON
Woodburyside, Bere Regis, Wareham, Dorset, BH20 7LX
☎ 01929 471225 Fax: 01929 472584
email: debs@wside.fslife.co.uk
web: www.curiobears.com
Individualistic hand-crafted miniature character bears.

● CYMRUTED COLLECTABLE BEARS
2 Penisaf Avenue, Towyn, Abergele, North Wales, LL22 9LL
☎ 01745 336844
email: contact@cymruted.com
web: www.cymruted.com
Handmade collectable teddy bears.

● CYNNAMAN TRADITIONAL BEARS
48A Underhill Road, South Benfleet, Essex, SS7 1EP
☎ 01268 754184
National and international classic collector bears and limited editions. All jointed, made lovingly from the finest mohairs and traditional materials.

● DAISA ORIGINAL DESIGNS LTD
Appletree Lodge, Westfield Lakes, Barton-upon-Humber, North Lincolnshire, DN18 5RG
☎ 01652 661881 Fax: 01652 661882
email: sales@itsadodl.com
web: www.theoriginalreikibear.com and www.itsadodl.com
The original Reikibear™ and It's a dodl © bear are exclusive bears and available only from Daisa Original Designs.

● DAISY BEARS
Sonya Lancaster, 136 Westmead Road, Sutton, Surrey, SM1 4JL
☎ 020 8715 4274 Mob: 07910 433442
Handmade collectors bears and animals.

● DARI LAUT BEARS
Dari Laut, 25 De Chardin Drive, Hastings, East Sussex, TN34 2UD
☎ 01424 754418 email: pat@dari-laut-bears.co.uk
web: www.dari-laut-bears.co.uk
Traditional and character bears and animals designed and lovingly created by award winning artist Patricia Banks. Enquiries welcome. Photographs available.

● DAWDLE BEARS
26 Forge Close, Holmer Green, Bucks, HP15 6PY
☎ 01494 713250
email: dawn@dawdlebears.com
web: www.dawdlebears.com
Traditional and character collectors bears.

● DAWN, DUSK & MIDNIGHT
Dawn Slaughter, 18 Erlesmere Gardens, Ealing, London, W13 9TY
☎ 020 8579 0360
email: ddmbears@aol.com
web: www.ddmbears.co.uk
Small bears with big personalities. Handmade jointed mohair bears with a smile made at Dawn, Dusk and Midnight!

DEAN'S RAG BOOK COMPANY LTD
PO Box 217, Hereford, HR1 9AB
☎ 01981 240966 Fax: 01981 241076
email: teddies@deansbears.com
web: www.deansbears.com
Traditional jointed and collector bears.

DIANE HANLEY BEARS
64 Kepier Crescent, Gilesgate Moor, Durham, County Durham, DH1 1PQ
☎ 0191 386 7290
email: diane1964@supanet.com
Miniature and larger. Layaway service.

DO DO BEARS
27 Linden Close, Colchester, Essex, CO4 3LZ
☎ 01206 524261
email: dodo.bears@ntlworld.com
web: www.dodobears.com
Character bears made for you to treasure. One offs and small limited editions. Trade enquiries welcome. Visit our new website.

DOODLEBEARS
21 Churchill Avenue, Aylesbury, Buckinghamshire, HP21 8NF
☎ 01296 397082
email: doodlebears_uk@hotmail.com
web: www.doodlebears.co.uk
Smiley bears by Jane Martin.

DRAGONSLAIR BEARS
'Carmel', 11 Coronation Terrace, Ilfracombe, North Devon, EX34 9NN
☎ 01271 862180
email: dragonslairbears@tinyonline.co.uk
web: www.dragonslairbears.co.uk
Beautiful bears made by Jackie

DREAMTIME
Sue Woodhouse, 12 Yeoman Road, Northolt, Middlesex, UB5 5TJ
☎ 020 8842 2327 (Bear)
email: dreamtime@dsl.pipex.com
web: www.dreamtime.dsl.pipex.com
Handcrafted bears, dragons and furry friends. Collectors miniatures and micro's 1"-6" fully jointed. One-offs and special very small limited editions.

DRURY BEARS
85 Pembury Road, Tonbridge, Kent, TN9 2JF
☎ 01732 364042 Fax: As tel.
web: www.drury-bears.isom.com
Quality limited edition collectors bears.

DUSTYBEAR
South View, Parbrook, Somerset, BA6 8PD
☎ 01458 851404
email: penny@dustybear.co.uk
web: www.dustybear.co.uk
Lovingly handmade mohair collectors bears.

E. J. BEARS
8 Marsh Close, Waltham Cross, Hertfordshire, EN8 7JF
☎ 01992 714354
Traditional hand made bears.

EBOR GROWLERS
46 Wilstrop Farm Road, Copmanthorpe, York, North Yorkshire, YO23 3RY
☎ 01904 704966
Quality hand crafted collectors bears.

EDDY BEARS
3 Nayland Road, Felixstowe, Suffolk, IP11 2XJ
☎ 01394 670555
email: eddybears@btinternet.com
web: www.eddy-bears.co.uk
Original bears by Sharon Edwards. Made with quality mohair and hand sculpted features - very lovable.

EDWARD BEARS
444 Audenshaw Road, Audenshaw, Manchester, M34 5PJ
☎ 0161 217 0668
Special bears for special occasions.

MARK EGAN
3 Hermitage Close, Hythe, Kent, CT21 6HZ
☎ 01303 265248
email: in.fo@tesco.net
Hand made English teddy bears.

ELDERBEARS
20 Malmesbury Road, Shirley, Southampton, Hampshire, SO15 5FR
☎ 023 8077 2977 Fax: As tel.
email: gisela@kahler.freeserve.co.uk
Traditional small collectors bears.

'Mimosa'

'Cha Cha and Ching' bear 3.75 inches

Join the Deb Canham Collectors Club and receive Newsletters and a Free Club Pin (pictured, little bear with sunflower)

For more information on how to join our Club and for a store near you please check out our website

'Dottie and Dobbin' bear 3.75 inches

'Roll Up, Roll Up' bear 3.75 inches, elephant 4 inches

www.debcanham.com

UK Agent: Brian and Myrna Somers, Action Agents Ltd.,16 Station Parade, Whitchurch Lane, Edgware, Middlesex. HA8 6RW. Tel: 020 8954 5956 Fax: 020 8954 4606 Email: briansomers@actionagentsltd.com

● ELIZBET BEARS
128 Elm Drive, Risca, Newport, Gwent, NP11 6PA
☎ 01633 615208 email: aileen.terry@talk21.com
web: www.elizbet-bears.co.uk
Collector bears all one off.

● ELLIE-BEARS
272 Southend Road, Wickford, Essex, SS11 8PS
☎ 01268 762438 email: ellie@elliebears.com
web: www.elliebears.com
Lovable handmade collectable mohair bears.

● ENCHANTED PLACE BEARS
Demelia Cottage, Florence Place, Falmouth, Cornwall, TR11 3NJ
☎ 01326 210462
email: enquiries@demelia.freeserve.co.uk
At Enchanted Place Bears we endeavour to create individually designed, hand-made bears of the finest quality.

● PETER FAGAN
Castle Hills Lodge, Old Paxton Road, Berwick on Tweed, Northumberland, TD15 1UX
☎ 01289 330637
Teddy bear sculptures.

● FAIR BEARS
17 Athorpe Grove, Dinnington, Sheffield, South Yorkshire, S25 2LD
☎ 01909 564472
Quality bears for discerning collectors.

● FAIRYLAND BEARS
Unit 3, The Sloop Craft Market, St Ives, Cornwall, TR26 2TF
☎ 07720 957072 / 01736 799901
web: www.fairylandbears.co.uk
All of our collectable bears, fairies, wizards, dragons & gollies, really are a must have for all discerning collectors.

● FARNBOROUGH BEARS
78 West Heath Road, Farnborough, Hampshire, GU14 8QX
☎ 01252 543454
email: janettruin@ntlworld.com or farnborough-bears@ntlworld.com
Exclusive collectors mohair bears handmade and designed by Janet Truin. Small limited editions and one offs. Contact Janet as above.

● FENBEARS
Alyson Commons, Fulholme, 49 Seas End Road,
Moulton Seas End, Lincolnshire, PE12 6LD
☎ 01406 371509 Fax: As tel.
email: fenbears@aol.com
web: www.fenbears.co.uk
Limited edition miniature collectors bears.

● FINE AND DANDY BEARS
5 Manor Road, Burton Coggles, Grantham, Lincs,
NG33 4JR
☎ 01476 550079
email: finedandybears@yahoo.com
web: www.geocities.com/finedandybears
New business. Visit us online.

● FLORIDIAN BEARS
48 Grange Road, Gillingham, Kent, ME7 2PU
☎ 01634 570331
email: floridianbears@blueyonder.co.uk
web: www.floridianbears.co.uk
*Traditional handcrafted bears, folk art style
critters and other primitive items. Individual
characters with personality made by Kent
artist Ellen Johns.*

● FLUTTER-BY BEARS
by Ruth Bowman, 26 Ludford Close, Newcastle-under-
Lyme, Staffordshire, ST5 7SD
☎ 01782 560136
email: ruthbowman@tiscali.co.uk
web: www.geocities.com/fruib274
*Original miniature collectors' bears and
friends 1 to 3 inches sewn with loving attention to detail. Have a tiny hug!*

● FLYING HORSE ORIGINAL DESIGNS
39 Grove Road South, Southsea, Hampshire, PO5 3QS
☎ 023 9273 6634
*Traditional and character bears, designed
and handmade by artist Carol Ann Zawadzki.
Small limited editions and one-offs. Old
bears repaired.*

● FOLIE BEARS
8 Palmers Close, Maidenhead, Berkshire, SL6 3XF
☎ **01628 822323**
email: **laincar5@aol.com**
***Traditional and character bears hand
made for you to treasure. Exclusive and
limited editions. All enquiries welcome.***

● FOREST GLEN BEARS
1 Ditchbury, Lymington, Hampshire, SO41 9FJ
☎ 07967 972611
email: jo@forestglenbears.co.uk
web: www.forestglenbears.co.uk
Adorably cute limited edition bears.

● FURRIED TREASURES
4 Evelyn Terrace, Kilwinning, Ayrshire,Scotland, KA13 6JQ
☎ 01294 558792
Hand-held collectables. £2 for details.

● FUTCH BEARS
32 Hillside Walk, Brentwood, Essex, CM14 4RB
☎ 01277 219032
email: difutcher@dsl.pipex.com
web: www.futchbears.co.uk
Artist bears with antique accessories.

● G-RUMPY BEARS
4 Puller Road, Barnet, Herts, EN5 4HF
☎ 020 8275 0693 Fax: As tel.
email: jane@g-rumpy.demon.co.uk
web: www.g-rumpy.co.uk
Bears that bring a smile.

● GARRINGTON BEARS
16 Garrington Close, Vinters Park, Maidstone, Kent, ME14 5RP
☎ 01622 685194
Bears for loving and giving.

● GEMSTONE BEARS
Stepping Stones, 73 Pydar Close, Newquay, Cornwall, TR7 3BT
☎ 01637 877743
email: lesley@gemstonebears.fsnet.co.uk
web: www.gemstonebears.com
Unique limited collector's bears hand sewn with a real gemstone heart to add uplifting character to any hug. Commissions welcome.

● GERALDINE'S OF EDINBURGH
133-135 Canongate, Edinburgh, Lothian, EH8 8BP, Scotland
☎ 0131 556 4295 Fax: As tel.
email: geraldine.e@virgin.net
web: www.dollsandteddies.com
Creators of the 'Young at Heart' limited edition collection. New additions always available. Please send for details. Trade enquiries welcome.

When contacting advertisers please mention you saw their advertisement in the UK Teddy Bear Guide

● GINGERBREAD BEARS

by Vanessa Edwards
☎ mobile 07951 194177
Individually made bears.

● GLEVUM BEARS

11 Highfield Place, Gloucester, Gloucestershire,
GL4 4PB
☎ 01452 521672
email: jonesmargaret54@aol.com
Teddy Bears. 'Special only ones'.

● GOTOBED BEARS

94 High Street, Watton-At-Stone, Hertford,
Hertfordshire, SG14 3TA
email: pennydavis8@hotmail.com
web: www.gotobedbear.com
Unique collectable bears with character.

● GRACE DAISY BEARS

Lorraine Morris, 51 Gilbert Close, Basingstoke,
Hampshire, RG24 9PA
☎ 01256 476140
Traditional, individually made mohair bears.

● GRANVILLE BEARS

Granville, 5 Upper Howsell Road, Malvern,
Worcestershire
☎ 01684 565703
email: granvillebears@yahoo.co.uk
Mini bears and their friends.

● GREENLEAF BEARS

17 High Mount Street, Hednesford, Staffs, WS12 4BH
☎ 01543 877343
email: pjwarrington@email.com
Traditional bears with a twist.

● JO GREENO

**2 Woodhill Court, Woodhill, Send, Nr Woking,
Surrey, GU23 7JR**
☎ **01483 224312 Fax: 01483 223983**
email: **jo.greeno@freezone.co.uk**
*Now in sixteenth year. International artist
and designer, one-offs, limited editions
and shop exclusives. Show schedule and
stockists S.A.E. please.*

● GREGORY BEAR

5 Primrose Road, Walton-on-Thames, Surrey, KT12 5JD
☎ **01932 243263**
email: **gregory@hugoshouse.com**
web: **www.hugoshouse.com**
*Classic and character teddy bears
designed and made by Gregory
Gyllenship.*

● GUMDROP EDITIONS

Signals, Boswedden Terrace, St Just, Penzance,
Cornwall, TR19 7NF
☎ 01736 787370
email: gail.edwards1@talk21.com
web: www.gumdrop-editions.com
*Handstitched collector's bears. Restorations.
Pawtraits.*

● GUND (UK) LIMITED

**Gund House, Units 3-4 Carnfield Place, Walton
Summit Centre, Bamber Bridge, Preston,
Lancashire, PR5 8AQ**
☎ **01772 629292 Fax: 01772 627878**
email: **sales@gunduk.com**
web: **www.gund.com**
*Collector bears and premium soft toys from
the 2005 Gift Of The Year award winners.*

● GYLL'S BEARS

74 Kenilworth Crescent, Enfield, Middlesex, EN1 3RG
☎ 0208 366 1836 Fax: 0208 364 6234
Handmade mohair bears.

● H M BEARS

Greendales Hall, Mill Lane, Warton, Carnforth,
Lancashire, LA5 9NW
☎ 01524 733152 Fax: As tel.
web: www.interreach.com/bears
Original bears by Iris Chesney

● THE HAIRY BEARY COMPANY

Northlea, Longmoor Lane, Nateby, Preston,
Lancashire, PR3 0JB
☎ 01995 600912
Irresistable limited edition mohair bruins.

● HAMPTON BEARS

15 Bownham Mead, Rodborough Common, Stroud,
Gloucestershire, GL5 5DZ
☎ 01453 872615
email: ginnie.ebbrell@dsl.pipex.com
Bears for the discerning collector.

● HARDY BEARS

by June Kendall, 6 Clausen Way, Lymington, Hampshire, SO41 8BJ
☎ 01590 670615 Fax: As tel.
Handmade small collectable mohair bears by June Kendall. Also restoration of old bears. Trade enquiries welcome.

● HARMONY CRYSTAL BEARS

6 Cavendish Avenue, Newark, Nottinghamshire, NG24 4DP
☎ 01636 672147
email: JuliesNo1bears@aol.com
web: www.harmonycrystalbears.co.uk
Each bear individually handmade.

● HARTRICK BEAR COMPANY

Ty Newydd, Dinorwig, Caernarfon, Gwynedd, LL55 3ES, or Studio 1, Yr Hen Yogol, Brynrefail, Caernarfon, LL55 3NR, North Wales
☎ 01286 870761 Fax: As tel.
email: ruth@hartrickbear.co.uk
web: www.hartrickbear.co.uk
Original hand-made collectors bears.

● HAVEN BEARS

Newhaven, Hough Lane, Norley, Frodsham, Cheshire, WA6 8JZ
☎ 01928 788313 Fax: As tel.
email: info@havenbears.com
web: www.havenbears.com
Handmade mohair bears from the heart of Cheshire, made with love plus the cuddle factor! Send SAE for a catalogue.

● HAZELWOOD BEARS

11 Hazelwood Close, Crawley Down, West Sussex, RH10 4HF
☎ 01342 712413
email: christine.jenner@hazelwoodbears.com
web: www.hazelwoodbears.com
Exquisite bears by Christine Jenner.

● HEART 'N' SOUL BEARS

217 Holme Church Lane, Beverley, East Yorkshire, HU17 0QE
☎ 01482 871016
email: heartnsoulbears@yahoo.co.uk
Bears with heart 'n' soul.

● HEGARTY BEARS

75 Burley Road, Bockhampton, Christchurch, Dorset, BH23 7AJ
☎ 01425 672883
email: jenniferhegarty@beeb.net
Original bears and quality clothing.

● HELENS HUGGABLES

23 Purdy Meadow, Sawley, Long Eaton, Notts, NG10 3DJ
☎ 0789 981 5762
email: helen@helens-huggables.co.uk
web: www.helens-huggables.co.uk
Uniquely made bears with character.

● HEMBURY BEARS

Hockmoor Lodge, Buckfast West, Buckfastleigh, Devon, TQ11 0HN
☎ 01364 643758 Fax: 01364 643835
email: susantolcher@compuserve.com
Hembury Bears special one-of-a-kind bears by Sue Tolcher. For details please send £2 to above address.

● HERMANN TEDDY ORIGINAL

UK Main Agent Brian Somers, 1 Georgian Close, Stanmore, Middlesex, HA7 3QT
☎ 0208 954 5956
email: briansomers@actionagentsltd.freeserve.co.uk
web: www.teddy-hermann.de
Please see advertisement on page 155.

● HILDEGARD GUNZEL BEARS

c/o A M International Agencies Ltd., Digital House, Peak Business Park, Foxwood Rd, Chesterfield, Derbyshire, S41 9RF
☎ 01246 269723 Fax: 01246 269724
email: enquiries@AM-International-Agencies.com
web: www.hildegardguenzel.com
World famous award winning artist.

● HILLTOP TOYS / BON BEARS

Manor Cottage, Benn Lane, Farley, Wiltshire, SP5 1AF
☎ 01722 712265 Fax: As tel.
Quality mohair bears and accessories.

15141
Tansy™

15148
Slacker™

15090
Hiccup™

15210
McDougal™

15090
Hiccup™

15015
Manni®

15100
Butterscotch™

15157
Timber™

15032
Marmalade™

15229
Benson Jr.™

15237
Fleming™

15090
Hiccup™

14182
Mini Marmalade™

15256
Rodin™

Gotta
Getta
GUND®
The World's Most Huggable...Since 1898™

GUND UK LTD., GUND House, 3–4 Carnfield Place
Walton Summit Centre, Bamber Bridge, Preston PR5 8AQ
Tel: 01772 629292   Fax: 01772 627878   Email: sales@gunduk.com

HOBLINS

5 Byron Avenue, Warton, Preston, Lancashire, PR4 1YR

☎ 01772 635516

email: bears@hoblins.freeserve.co.uk

Lovely outfits or just bare, weighty mohair bears from four to twenty inches. All handmade in Lancashire by Linda Willetts.

GLENN HOLDEN

25 Boulton Road, West Bromwich, West Midlands, B70 6NW

☎ 0121 580 3423

email: glenn@panjandrum44.fsnet.co.uk

Unique marionette bears for sale.

HOLDINGHAM BEARS

Unit 6, Navigation Yard, Carre Street, Sleaford, Lincolnshire, NG34 7TR

☎ 01529 303266 Fax: 01529 307524

email: barbara@holdinghambears.com

web: www.holdinghambears.com

Limited edition and one of a kind quality mohair bears lovingly hand produced by Barbara Daughtrey. Commissions accepted. Enquiries welcome.

HOLLY BEARS

Rosebank Cottage, 70 Heath Road, Uttoxeter, Staffordshire, ST14 7LT

☎ 01889 568848

Handmade one-off bears, cats, rabbits.

HONEY HILL BEARS

Maureen Frost, 7 Honey Hill, Wimbotsham, King's Lynn, Norfolk, PE34 3QD

☎ 01366 383550

Happy bears from Honey Hill. Gollies and Pandas too. Small limited editions. Shop exclusives. Enquiries welcome.

HONEY POT BEARS

106 Purbrook Way, Havant, Hampshire, PO9 3SB

☎ 02392 472455/07881 644164

Beautiful handmade mohair collectors' bears by Melanie C. Willis. Please send sae for brochure. Loving homes needed for our cuddlesome bears.

H M Bears & Chesney Designs

– Lancashire & Cumbria –

Dressed and lifelike bears

Humorous cards and colour prints

Please send SAE to:

Greendales Hall, Mill Lane
Warton, Carnforth
Lancs, LA5 9NW
Tel/Fax: 01524 733152
www.interreach.com/bears

HONEYMEAD BEARS

5 Newmarket Road, Cheveley, Newmarket, Suffolk, CB8 9EQ

☎ 01638 730484 Fax: As tel.

email: ann@honeymeadbears.fsnet.co.uk

Individual, hand sewn collectors bears.

HOO BEARS

The Paddocks, Church Road, Crowle, Worcester, Worcestershire, WR7 4AT

☎ 01905 381456 Fax: 07092 228214

email: helen@hoobears.co.uk

web: www.hoobears.co.uk

Handcrafted mohair bears with character.

HORTY BEARS

'Valtos', 16 Parkway, Trentham, Stoke-on-Trent, Staffordshire, ST4 8AG

☎ 01782 642889

email: jacquie@hortybears.co.uk

web: www.hortybears.co.uk

Handmade bears created with love.

HUG-A-BOO BEARS

68 Hitchen, Merriott, Somerset, TA16 5RA

☎ 01460 72740

Handcrafted and adorable collectors bears.

HUGGLETS

PO Box 290, Brighton, East Sussex, BN2 1DR

☎ 01273 697974 Fax: 01273 626255

email: info@hugglets.co.uk

web: www.hugglets.co.uk

Thousands of artist bears available at the Winter BearFest and Teddies 2006. Organised by Hugglets, the publishers of the UK Teddy Bear Guide.

HUGGY BEARS UK BY GAYE PARKER

117 Diamond Avenue, Kirkby-in-Ashfield, Nottinghamshire, NG17 7LX

☎ 01623 458514

email: bonniray@yahoo.co.uk

Individual bears, clothes and gollies.

HUGS UNLIMITED

Dawn James, 212 Wilton Street, Glasgow, Strathclyde, G20 6BL
email: hugsunlimited@ntlworld.com
web: www.hugsunlimited.co.uk
Original Traditional Mohair Artist Bears dressed or undressed, by established Bear Artist, Dawn James, commissions undertaken, trade enquiries welcome.

HUMBLE-CRUMBLE COLLECTORS BEARS

by Victoria Allum, 78 Chalkwell Avenue, Westcliff-on-Sea, Essex, SS0 8NN
☎ 01702 715383
email: vkallum@hotmail.com
web: www.victoriaallum.co.uk
Award winning traditional mohair bears.

HUNI B'S

Walnut Cottage, Holyhead Road, Froncysyllte, Wrexham, LL20 7PU
☎ 01691 774070
email: huni-bs@fsmail.net
Take home a Huni-B's bear.

HUNTERSFIELD BEARS

57 Huntersfield, South Tehidy, Camborne, Cornwall, TR14 0HW
☎ 01209 711557
email: cfdell@clara.net
web: www.huntersfieldbears.com
Unique handcrafted bears with character.

HUTTON BEARS

1 Regents Court, Worple Road, Staines, Middlesex, TW18 1EB
☎ 01784 453037
email: huttonbears85@yahoo.com
web: www.geocities.com/huttonbears85
Hav'ta hav'a Hutton!

HYEFOLK

1 Ainsdale Close, Folkestone, Kent, CT19 5LU
☎ 01303 277925
Bears that make you smile!

Hugs Unlimited
Bears by Dawn James
www.hugsunlimited.co.uk

● **INEKE'S TEDDYBEARS**
Ineke Weber, 19 Crofts Lea Park, Ilfracombe, Devon,
EX34 9PN
☎ 01271 864689
email: inekeweber@yahoo.co.uk
Individual bears for bearlovers.

● **IRVINE BEARS**
53 Radcliffe Lane, Scawthorpe, Doncaster, South
Yorkshire, DN5 7XS
☎ 01302 782903
email: caren@irvinebears.com
web: www.irvinebears.com
Hand made limited edition bears.

● **J. C. W. BEARS & FURRY
FRIENDS**
11 Cockerell Close, Pitsea, Basildon, Essex,
SS13 1QR
☎ 01268 726558
email: jcwbears@blueyonder.co.uk
web: www.jcwbears.co.uk
Character bears & realistic dogs.

● **J R BEARS**
18 The Incline, Ilminster, Somerset, TA19 0HQ
☎ 01460 55461
*Unique bears from J. Ridge based in the
West Country. Made in English and German
mohair. For more details contact Janet.*

● **JABELOW BEARS**
Mrs Faye Low, 68 Alexander Chase, Ely,
Cambridgeshire, CB6 3SW
☎ 01353 659631 Fax: 01353 662195
email: faye@gundogs.freeserve.co.uk
web: www.jabelowbears.com
Miniature bears with big hearts.

● **JAC-Q-LYN BEARS**
1 Mere Cottage, School Lane, Marton, Macclesfield,
Cheshire, SK11 9HD
☎ 01260 224257
email: jacqui@jacqlynbears.fsbusiness.co.uk
web: www.jacqlynbears.com
Handmade limited edition collectable bears.

JAMMY BEARS
149A North East Road, Sholing, Southampton, Hampshire, SO19 8AW
☎ 023 8044 9797
email: jammybears@tiscali.co.uk
web: www.jammybears.co.uk
Bears with personality, commissions welcomed.

JAN'S TIDDY BEARS
75 The Street, Ashtead, Surrey, KT21 1AA
☎ 07889 794637
email: jannettysbears@aol.com
web: www.jannettysbears.co.uk
Award winning miniature bear artist. Lovingly designed and hand sewn miniatures by Jan. One to four inches. Commissions taken.

JANBU BEARS
13 Percival Drive, Stockton Brook, Stoke on Trent, Staffordshire, ST9 9PE
☎ 01782 251790
email: janbubears@ntlworld.com
Personal commissions welcome by telephone.

Jan's Tiddy Bears©

Prize winning quality miniature collectors bears, from 1" to 4" Call or see me at fairs.

Free catalogue available on request

T: 07889 794 637
E: jannettysbears@aol.com
W: jannettysbears.co.uk

JANET CLARK ORIGINALS
61 Park Road, Hemel Hempstead, Hertfordshire, HP1 1JS
☎ 01442 265944   Fax: As tel.
email: JCTeddystyle@aol.com
web: www.janetclark.com
Bears, dogs, dolls, animals, classes.

JANNETTY'S BEARS
16 Ormonde Avenue, Epsom, Surrey, KT19 9EP
☎ 01372 813558
email: jannettysbears@aol.com
web: www.jannettysbears.co.uk
Loveable, huggable, unique handsewn fully jointed quality collectors bears. From miniature 1 inch to 30 inches. See us at fairs. Commissions accepted.

JASCO BEARS
67 Talbot Street, Southport, Merseyside, PR8 1LU
☎ 01704 539324
email: jascobears@hotmail.com
Handmade quality mohair character bears.

JESTER BEARS
54 Treveneague Gardens, Manadon, Plymouth, Devon, PL2 3SX
☎ 01752 704625
Traditional creations by Wendy Patey.

JEWELFIRE BEARS
F. Warrington, 9 Dunbar Way, Ashby De La Zouch, Leicestershire, LE65 1AQ
☎ 07904 235821   email: fredamike@aol.com
web: http://members.aol.com/jewelfirecrafts/index.htm
Unique, lovingly made mohair bears.

JO BEARS BY JO NEVILL
Minster, Sheppey, Kent
☎ 01795 874557
email: jo.bears@tiscali.co.uk
Bears with sculpted porcelain faces.

JO-ANNE BEARS
20 Wilkin Drive, Tiptree, Essex, CO5 0QP
✉ 01621 815049
email: joanne@jo-annebears.co.uk
web: www.jo-annebears.co.uk
Award winning artist bears, original designs. One off bears, small editions. Modern and traditional, open mouthed, airbrushed, handpainted etc.

HERMANN *Teddy* ORIGINAL®

Limited to 300 pcs.
Design: Traudel Mischner-Hermann

Teddy Bear "J & N"
11100 9   36cm

The Teddy-Hermann Collectors' Club is in its 6th year now and unites more and more bear friends all over the world. Come and join the ever-growing family and enjoy the benefits and privileges that membership brings.

An exclusive gift awaits you: a high-quality **"HERMANN Teddy ORIGINAL"** Bear of 13 cm size. You have the right to acquire an Exclusive Club Edition which is only available to members of the Teddy-Hermann Collectors' Club and receive twice a year our newsletter called "Barenpost" as well as our latest catalogues and updates.

For further information please contact your shop and ask for an application form to join the Club.

Teddy-Hermann GmbH, Postfach 1207, D-96112 Hirschaid, Germany

UK Main Agent: Brian Somers, 1 Georgian Close, Stanmore, Middx, HA7 3QT
Tel: 0208 954 5956 email: briansomers@actionagentsltd.freeserve.co.uk

JODI BEARS
Lyngarth, Bowden Avenue, Pleasington, Blackburn, Lancs, BB2 5JJ
☎ 01254 201177
email: jo@reeve49.freeserve.co.uk
Marvellous creations just for you.

JOY BEARS
Joy Green, 67 Oak Road, Scarborough, North Yorkshire, YO12 4AP
☎ 01723 354419
email: joybears@joybears.co.uk
web: www.joybears.co.uk
Hand modelled ornaments. Free catalogue.

JOYBUNNYS ART DESIGNS
33 Trenholme Avenue, Woodside, Bradford, West Yorkshire, BD6 2NJ
☎ 07971 076259
email: hugs@revjoybunny.fsnet.co.uk
web: www.joybunnysartdesigns.co.uk
Handcrafted unique bears, novelties and gifts. All Joybunny originals with a little piece of nature's beauty in every creation.

JU-BEARY BEARS
Studio 3, Barleylands Craft Village, Barleylands Road, Billericay, Essex, CM11 2UD
☎ 01268 525775
Exclusively designed mohair collectors bears, pandas and cats by Betty and Julie Guiver. Small limited editions and one offs available.

JULZ BEARZ
6 Wilton Close, Kingsmead, Northwich, Cheshire, CW9 8WE
☎ 01606 810667 Fax: 08717 172142
email: julie@julzbearz.co.uk
web: www.julzbearz.co.uk
Handmade miniature collectors' bears, animals and birds by Julie Lawton.

JUST BEARS BY DENISE
Denise Bradnam, 47 Roman Way, Haverhill, Suffolk, CB9 0NG
☎ 01440 762847
Individually handmade traditional mohair bears.

K M BEARS
by Kerren Morris, 66 Kirklees Drive, Farsley, Pudsey, West Yorkshire, LS28 5TE
☎ 0113 2192651 Fax: As tel.
email: kerren@kmbears.co.uk
web: www.kmbears.co.uk
Beautiful handmade bears. Commissions undertaken.

KAYSBEARS BY KAY STREET
93 Singlewell Road, Gravesend, Kent, DA11 7PU
☎ 01474 351757 Fax: 01322 521746
Award winning miniature bears.

KAYTKINS
9 Ballantyne Road, Rushden, Northamptonshire, NN10 9FJ
☎ 01933 355782 mob: 07887 877181
email: kiles@totalise.co.uk
Affordable bears made with love.

KAZ BEARS
23 Whinbush Avenue, Allenton, Derby, Derbyshire, DE24 9DQ
☎ 01332 731948
email: kazbears@ntlworld.com
web: www.kazbears.com
Traditional and cute mohair bears.

KEEPSAKES
Old Market Hall (Fri/Sat), Scunthorpe, North Lincs
☎ 01724 851080 (home)
email: wljhn5@aol.com
'Keepsakes' limited edition mohair bears.

KERSHY BEARS
6 Kensington Close, Milnrow, Rochdale, Lancs, OL16 3HJ
☎ 01706 357652   email: kershybear@aol.com
web: www.kershybear.co.uk
Collectors hand made teddy bears.

KEVINTON BEARS
155 Hillbury Road, Warlingham, Surrey, CR6 9TG
☎ 07957 333044 email: kevintonbears@aol.com
Handmade Kevinton Bears :o)

KIMBEARLEYS
8 Barnmeadow Road, Newport, Shropshire, TF10 7NP
☎ 01952 825927
email: kim.stokes1@virgin.net
web: http://kimbearleys.tripod.com
Miniature bears and other characters.

KINGSTON BEARS
Pavane Cottage, 133 Hightown Road, Ringwood,
Hampshire, BH24 1NL   ☎ 01425 470422
email: kingstonbears@aol.com
web: www.kingstonbears.com
*One of a kind and small limited edition bears
in antique clothing. Please see display
advertisement.*

KNUTTY BEARS
30 Kingsdown Crescent, Dawlish, Devon, EX7 0HL
☎ 01626 863032
email: knuttybears@nutley30.freeserve.co.uk
*Mohair and alpaca bears with big feet and
cute faces. From 6" to 19" fully jointed.*

KÖSEN UK
10 Wood Pond Close, Seer Green, Beaconsfield,
Buckinghamshire, HP9 2XG
☎ 01494 674872 Fax: As tel.
email: Koesen@RaMarketing.co.uk
web: www.RaMarketing.co.uk
German hand-made life-like bears/animals.

L J BEARS
1 Mead Road, Lymington, Hampshire, SO41 8EP
☎ 01590 676517 Fax: As tel.
email: teddies@ljbears.co.uk
web: www.ljbears.co.uk
*Traditional 'hug tested' teddy bears. Bear
cats, bunnies and musical bears. Also christening bears and special commissions
undertaken. Established 1995.*

LAAL BEARS
59 Mounsey Road, Bamber Bridge, Nr Preston,
Lancashire, PR5 6LU   ☎ 01772 315342
email: ursula@thelaalbear.freeserve.co.uk
web: www.laalbear.co.uk
Handmade collectable mohair teddy bears.

LAVENDER BEARS
Hillhouse, 32 Heol Maelor, Coedpoeth, Wrexham,
Clwyd, LL11 3LU
☎ 07836 730719
*Traditional, Wild and Wacky Munchkins and
Heraldic bears. All original and limited editions
with partial lavender fillings. Commissions taken.*

LAWRENCE BEARS
10 Wren Close, Taunton, Somerset, TA1 5EZ
☎ 01823 257674 Fax: As tel.
email: lawrence@lawrencebears.com
web: www.lawrencebears.com
Artist bears of unique design.

ELIZABETH LEGGAT - BETH'S BEARS
9 Jamieson Drive, East Kilbride, Strathclyde, G74 3EA
☎ 01355 249674
email: elizabeth.leggat@btopenworld.com
Edwardian style miniature mohair bears.

LESLEY JANE BEARS
21 Hallaway, Carlisle, CA3 9RG
☎ 01228 380134 email: lesley@omne.uk.net
web: www.craftycrochet.co.uk
Please see website for details.

LI'L BEARS
7 Friar Road, Brighton, East Sussex, BN1 6NG
☎ 07931 479736
email: lilbears@hotmail.com
Handmade and jointed miniature bears. Original designs. Small limited editions and one-offs. Li'l Bears with big hearts!

LILLIAN TRIGG OF ROCHESTER
58 Tern Crescent, Strood, Rochester, Kent, ME2 2RG
☎ 01634 713131 email: linda@lilliantrigg.co.uk
web: www.lilliantrigg.co.uk
Finest quality collectors bears made for the discerning collector.

LINDAL BEARS
86 Cambridge Road, Girton, Cambridge, CB3 0PJ
☎ 01223 277118
email: lindal.perkins@ntlworld.com
web: www.lindalbears.com
Artist designed handmade mohair bears.

LITTLE ACORNS
24 Mansel Street, Newport, South Wales, NP19 8LA
☎ 01633 271010
email: orphan64@hotmail.com
web: www.littleacorns.info
Bears to treasure by bearsmith Jane Montgomery. Bears to make you smile and melt your heart. 3 to 14 inches.

LITTLE BLOOMERS
2 Witley Avenue, Halesowen, West Midlands, B63 4DN
☎ 0121 602 2090 / 07949 664 286
email: littlebloomers@blueyonder.co.uk
web: www.littlebloomersdollsandbears.com
Award-winning bears. Member BTM Guild.

LITTLE SCRUFFS OF EVESHAM
16-18 High Street, Evesham, Worcestershire, WR11 4HJ
☎ 01386 429002 or 07977 262163
email: little_scruffs@hotmail.com
web: www.littlescruffs.co.uk
Handmade mohair collectors bears. Small bears from 'oldies' to punks by Jean Grogan. Visitors welcome, please phone first.

THE LITTLE WORKSHOP
Fiona Campbell, c/o 6 Barony Terrace, Edinburgh, Lothian, EH12 8RE, Scotland
Scottish bears handmade with love.

LOTENI BEARS
Lindy Mullard, 3 Hillside Close, Ormesby St. Margaret, Gt. Yarmouth, Norfolk, NR29 3PY
☎ 01493 731401 (pm/weekend)
Mohair collector bears, fully jointed, lovingly made and each named after the picturesque Norfolk villages amongst which they are born.

LOULOU BEARS
9 Hollow Road, Derbyshire, DE73 1AU
☎ 01332 865715
Special bears for special people.

LOVE IS IN THE BEAR
72 Lynmere Road, Welling, Kent, DA16 1PA
☎ 020 8304 1412
Handmade traditional bears.

LYNDA BROWN BEARS
18 Sutton Way, Heston, Hounslow, Middlesex, TW5 0JA
☎ 020 8570 0095
Handmade traditional and realistic bears.

LYNDEE-LOU-BEARS
Farrysthie, Eleanora Drive, Douglas, Isle of Man, IM2 3NN
☎ 01624 616475
email: dee@lyndee-lou-bears.com
web: www.lyndee-lou-bears.com
Hand made collector bears.

LYNN'S LITTLE GEMS
9 Kirkstall Close, South Anston, Sheffield, South Yorkshire, S25 5BA
☎ 07776 483561
Exquisite handcrafted lovable character bears.

LYNTON TEDDY BEAR COMPANY
11 Lochy Drive, Linslade, Leighton Buzzard, Bedfordshire, LU7 2XY
☎ 01525 371329
email: lyntonteddybears@btinternet.com
Limited edition and one of a kind collectable mohair bears created by Lynette Wallace. Commissions accepted. Enquiries welcome.

M. G. BEARS
24 Keys Drive, Wroxham, Norfolk, NR12 8SS
☎ 01603 783936
Personally designed quality one-of-a-kind bears.

MABLEDON ROAD BEARS
64 Mabledon Road, Tonbridge, Kent, TN9 2TG
☎ 01732 356360
Individual handmade mohair collectors bears.

MAC BEARS BY CAROL DAVIDSON
36 Fairholme Road, Harrow, Middlesex, HA1 2TN
☎ 020 8863 6192 web: www.macbears.co.uk
email: carolscottie@hotmail.com
Loveable handstitched 5" bears, lead-shot filled.

MADABOUT BEARS
by Lynn Bowie, 18 West End, Dalry, Ayrshire, KA24 5DU
☎ 01294 835432
email: lynn@aldesign.freeserve.co.uk
web: www.aldesign.freeserve.co.uk
Cute bears, cats and rabbits.

MADDIE JANES CHARACTER BEARS
Caerau Bach, Croes Goch, St Davids, Haverfordwest, Pembrokeshire, SA62 5JY
☎ 01348 831792
email: maddie@maddiejanes.com
web: www.maddiejanes.com
Original handmade bears and animals.

MADELEY BEARS TM
25 Broad Lane, Upperthong, Holmfirth, West Yorkshire, HD9 3JS
☎ 01484 680143/mob: 077 367 07574
email: madeleybears@aol.com
web: www.madeleybears.com
Small and smaller contemporary bears.

MAJACABUS BEARS
Coldharbour Cottage, Back River Drove, Glastonbury, Somerset, BA6 9SZ
☎ 01458 832008
email: carol@majacabusbears.co.uk
web: www.majacabusbears.co.uk
Quality bears, friends, 8" upwards.

MAJENSIE TEDDIES & GIFTS
76 Ambleside Avenue, Telscombe Cliffs, East Sussex, BN10 7LH
☎ 01273 586890 Fax: As tel.
email: majensie@btconnect.com
web: www.majensie.com
Handcrafted mohair bears. Various sizes.

MALDOD BEARS
3 Dol y Coed, Dunvant, Swansea, West Glamorgan, SA2 7UG
☎ 01792 427053 Fax: As tel.
Born in Wales, these irresistable collectors bears of quality by Sue Jones created for you to love and cherish.

MARIGOLD BEARS
Susan Cane, 92 Wychwood Avenue, Knowle, Solihull, West Midlands, B93 9DQ ☎ 01564 776092
Character and olden days bears.

MARILYN PELLING BEARS

11 Cumberland Road, Preston Village, Brighton, BN1 6SL
☎ 01273 884268
email: marilyn.pelling@ntlworld.com
Hand made bears and dolls. Bears in acrylic and faux furs. Biker bears and large character bears. Cloth/rag dolls.

MAWKISH BEARS

1 Halves Lane, West Coker, Somerset
☎ 01935 862984
email: mawkishbear@tiscali.co.uk
Original mohair creations with character.

MAWSPAWS

The Belfry, 11 Blyth Close, Aylesbury, Buckinghamshire, HP21 8TA
☎ 01296 338338
email: keith@mawspaws.com
web: www.mawspaws.com
Collector bears by Maureen Batt.

MAYPOLE BEARS OF OFFENHAM BY JEAN

Janus Cote, Gibbs Lane, Offenham, Evesham, Hereford & Worcester, WR11 8RR
☎ 01386 48217
email: jean@maypolebears.co.uk
web: www.maypolebears.co.uk
Beautifully designed, much sought after.

MEADOWS TEDDY BEARS

26 Gloucester Avenue, Horwich, Bolton, Lancashire, BL6 6NH
☎ 01204 693087
web: www.bearshopbolton.co.uk
For quality and craftsmanship since 1990, traditionally made teddy bears in quality mohair. Lovingly created by Stephen Meadows, B.T.M.G. member.

MELDRUM BEARS

Trelawn Farm, Chapel Hill, Sticker, St. Austell, Cornwall, PL26 7HG
☎ 01726 74499 Fax: As tel.
email: lizmeldrum@fsmail.net
Traditional limited edition collectors bears. Individual commissions & shop exclusives available. For further details please contact Liz Meldrum as above.

MELISSA JAYNE BEARS

94 Chester Road, Castle, Northwich, Cheshire, CW8 1JH
☎ 01606 76313 or 07732 749352 (mob)
email: melissa@melissajaynebears.co.uk
web: www.melissajaynebears.co.uk
Handcrafted mohair teddybears and cats.

THE MEREDITH COLLECTION

89 Woodhorn Road, Ashington, Northumberland, NE63 9EX
☎ 01670 855448
Dressed mohair artist bears £15.

MERRYTHOUGHT LTD

Ironbridge, Telford, Shropshire, TF8 7NJ
☎ 01952 433116 Fax: 01952 432054
email: contact@merrythought.co.uk
web: www.merrythought.co.uk
Please see colour advertisement on back cover.

MICHA BEARS
35 Trevillis Park, Liskeard, Cornwall, PL14 4EG
☎ 01579 345832
email: micha@bearcats.freeserve.co.uk
web: www.bearcats.freeserve.co.uk
Established 1992. Please see website.

MINI COMPANIONS TEDDIES & CHARACTERS
22b Hawkinge Gdns, Ernesettle, Plymouth, Devon,
PL5 2RW ☎ 01752 350849
email: minicompanions@yahoo.co.uk
web: www.minicompanions.co.uk
Smiling miniteds and other characters.

MINIBUMS
73 Randalls Croft Road, Wilton, Salisbury, Wilts, SP2 0EY
☎ 01722 742463
email: bumpkinbears@hotmail.com
Unique handsewn miniatures for collectors.

MIRKWOOD BEARS
34 Southdown Road, Southdown, Bath, Somerset
☎ 01225 356505
email: sales@mirkwoodbears.co.uk
web: www.mirkwoodbears.co.uk
Hand made bears of distinction. Small limited editions and one off bears with character.

MISFIT BEARS
24 Hallam Grange Rise, Fulwood, Sheffield, South
Yorkshire, S10 4BG
☎ 0114 2304078
email: misfitbears@dogrough.plus.com
web: www.misfitbears.co.uk
Unique and adorable artist bears.

MISS B'S BEARS
The Old School Cottage, 4 Castle Court, School Lane,
Holt, Nr Wrexham, Clwyd, LL13 9YX
☎ 01829 271873 email: bev@missbeesbears.com
web: www.missbeesbears.com
Traditional bears, traditionally made.

MISTER BEAR
17 Lord Roberts Avenue, Leigh-on-Sea, Essex, SS9 1ND
☎ 01702 710733 Fax: As tel.
email: jennie@misterbear.net
web: www.misterbear.net
Classical character bears for collectors.

Melissa Jayne Bears
Hand Crafted Mohair Teddy Bears and Cats

www.melissajaynebears.co.uk
melissa@melissajaynebears.co.uk

MISTLEY WOODLAND BEARS
Bruins, Windmill Road, Bradfield, Manningtree, Essex,
CO11 2QR
☎ 01255 870729
Original handcrafted collectors bears.

MOONSTRUCK
30 Lapthorn Close, Gosport, Hampshire, PO13 0SR
☎ 01329 281718
email: christine.stobbs1@btinternet.com
Hand sewn with love.

MOOSEBERRY BEARS
30 Gooding Avenue, Leicester, Leics, LE3 1BQ
☎ 0116 2246803 / mob: 0770 8299303
email: mooseberry@ntlworld.com
Collectable hand made artist bears.

MY OLD TEDDY
45 Alexandra Road, Upper Penn, Wolverhampton,
West Midlands, WV4 5UB
☎ 01902 332782 Fax: As tel.
email: myoldteddy@tiscali.co.uk
Traditional mohair bears.

NAMTLOC BEARS

Lynne Coltman, 21 Grasmere Street, Hartlepool, Cleveland, TS26 9AT

☎ 01429 422997

email: namtlocbears@hotmail.com

Handmade collectors bears using quality mohair. Crochet clothes designed for bears and dolls of all sizes. Commission for crochet accepted.

NARNIE BEARS

by Christine Howe, 1 Taylors Croft, Main Road, Authorpe, Louth, Lincolnshire, LN11 8PQ

☎ 07903 082630 / 01507 451380

Hand sewn bears commissions welcome. Layaway available. Payment tailored to ability to pay. Let your treasure be designed to measure.

THE NAUGHTY BEAR CO

124 Priory Road, Anfield, Liverpool, Merseyside, L4 2SJ

☎ 0151 476 6740 Fax: As tel.

email: info@nbcbear.co.uk

web: www.nbcbear.co.uk

Artist Bears by Jacqueline Barker.

NETTY'S BEARS

16 Ormonde Avenue, Epsom, Surrey, KT19 9EP

☎ 01372 813558

email: netty.paterson@ntlworld.com

web: www.jannettysbears.co.uk

See entry under JanNetty's Bears.

NOBLE BEARS

by Lorna Hatton, 194-196 Millbrook Road East, Freemantle, Southampton, Hampshire, SO15 1JR

☎ 023 8022 6474

email: lorna@noblebears.co.uk

web: www.noblebears.co.uk

1½ - 12 inch bears with hand knitted lace plus accessories, in small limited editions. Pirates with turned legs being our speciality.

NORBEARY

14 Claymere Avenue, Norden, Rochdale, Lancashire, OL11 5WB

☎ 01706 659819 Fax: As tel.

email: norbeary@btinternet.com

web: www.norbeary.co.uk

Unmistakeable and irresistable teddy bears with lots of old world charm and more than a little flavour of humour.

OAKWOOD BEARS

9 Newton Village, Nr Kettering, Northamptonshire, NN14 1BW

☎ 01536 742843

Quality hand crafted traditional bears, hares, dogs and bags made in mohair. Small limited editions and one offs. In stock.

OCHILTREE BEARS

Ochiltree, 241 Salisbury Road, Winkton, Christchurch, Dorset, BH23 7AS

☎ 01425 672030

Traditional mohair bears. Bear workshops.

OGGIES ATTIC

29 Bartlett Close, Poplar, London, E14 6LH

☎ 0207 537 3146

email: oggiesattic@fsmail.net

web: www.pittypatspoppets.com

Artist bears. Send SAE or view web site. New range of patterns now available.

OLLIE BEARS BY KIM

Twin Oaks, 21 Acorn Drive, Oakenshaw, County Durham, DL15 0TF

☎ 01388 748366 / mob: 07801070876

email: chris.cawley2@virgin.net

Handsewn teddies, stuffed with love...

OOPS! PARDON ME, BEARS!

6 King Edward Road, Deal, Kent, CT14 6QL

☎ 01304 367653

email: eileen.wood@mail.bta.com

web: http://eileenwood.bta.com/oops

Artist bears by Eileen Woods.

ORCHARD BEARS

2 Old Heatherdene Cottages, Common Road, Great Kingshill, High Wycombe, Buckinghamshire, HP15 6EZ

☎ 01494 717501

email: hayley@orchardbears.com

web: www.orchardbears.com

Traditional mohair bears designed and made by Hayley Orchard. Mail order available, send sae for details or see website.

OUT 'N ABOUT BEARS

52 Danecourt Road, Parkstone, Poole, Dorset, BH14 0PQ

☎ 01202 744196

email: helen.c@fsmail.net

web: http://outnabout bears.mysite.wanadoo-members.co.uk

Hand made original teddy bears.

Pamela Ann Designs Tel/Fax: 01778 344152

Pam Howells
39 Frognall, Deeping St James
Peterborough, Cambs
England PE6 8RR

Paw Lines Bears
Unique creations by Joy Surgenor
tel: 028 2564 5130
email: pawlines@fsmail.net
www.pawlinesbears.co.uk

● OUT OF THE WOODS©
1 Colegate Barn Cottages, Coopers Hill Road, Nutfield, Surrey, RH1 4HX
☎ 01737 821218
email: samsalter1@aol.com
Award winning mohair bears each beautifully dressed. Send SAE for details.

● PADZ
Colachla, Ardlamont, Tighnabruaich, Argyll, Scotland, PA21 2AH
☎ 01700 811524
email: padzbears@yahoo.co.uk
Can e-mail details and photograph.

● PAMELA ANN DESIGNS
39 Frognall, Deeping St James, Peterborough, Cambridgeshire, PE6 8RR
☎ 01778 344152 Fax: As tel.
web: www.cambridgebears.co.uk
Quality traditional teddy bears. Hand crafted from the finest mohair. Limited edition collectors' bears and award winning exclusive soft toys.

● PANDA JAK BEARS
59 Rowelfield, Luton, Beds, LU2 9HL
☎ 01582 405490
email: amandaj.ellis@ntlworld.com
Loveable affordable bears by Amanda.

● JOSEPHINE PARNELL
16 Hardwick Estate, Kirton, Boston, Lincolnshire, PE20 1HG
☎ 01205 723637
email: josephineparnell@hotmail.com
web: www.dollshousebears.free-online.co.uk
Bears for doll's houses. Original design, fully poseable, 12th and 24th scale, period costume. Commissions undertaken, and miniatures $7/8$ - 3 inch.

● PAW LINES BEARS
☎ 028 2564 5130
email: pawlines@fsmail.net
web: www.pawlinesbears.co.uk
Unique Bears designed and created with distinctive paws and pads. Sizes range from 12 inches to 20 inches.

● PAW PRINTS OF STAFFORDSHIRE

57 Newford Crescent, Milton, Stoke on Trent, Staffordshire, ST2 7EB

☎ 01782 537315

email: cjkeen@pawprints.org.uk

web: www.pawprints.org.uk

Beautiful limited edition bears.

● PECULIAR PAL'S BEARS & OTHER ANIMALS

by Suzanne Hodder

email: peculiar.pals@btinternet.com

web: www.peculiar-pals.co.uk

Something a little less ordinary.

● LOUISE PEERS

2 The Lawns, Wilmslow, Cheshire, SK9 6EB

☎ 01625 527917 Fax: As tel.

email: louisepeers@minibears.fsnet.co.uk

Award winning miniature bears. Please send £2.50 for catalogue of new bears.

● PENNBEARY

23 Priors Walk, St Johns Priory, Lechlade, Gloucestershire, GL7 3HR

☎ 01367 252809

Award-winning mohair bears, hand stitched by Penny Roberts. One-offs and small limited editions. £1.50 for photographs and details.

● PENNY BUNN BEARS

Pathways, Middle Street, Eastington, Stonehouse, Gloucestershire, GL10 3BB

☎ 01453 828060 Fax: As tel.

email: bearsbyNKW@aol.com

Beautiful miniature bears for collectors.

● NICOLA PERKINS

Ivy Cottage, Leycet Lane, Madeley Heath, Crewe, Cheshire, CW3 9LS

☎ 01782 751148 Fax: As tel.

email: nicola@annlouiseperkins.freeserve.co.uk

Miniature bears for collectors.

AMY C

PORTOBEL

A BEAR F

"To love is to

to admire is

Theo

Friends
are
flo

DRICH
BEAR CO
OSOPHY

with the heart,
with the mind"
tier

More rare and
one of a kind characters available
from Peggotty.

PHRED'S FRIENDS

2 Beech Court, New Moat, Clarbeston Road, Pembrokeshire, SA63 4RH
☎ 01437 532279 Fax: As tel.   email: phred@phredsfriends.co.uk
web: www.phredsfriends.co.uk
A magical world awaits you.

PICKLEPUMPKIN BEARS

Sarah Stonehouse, 5 Southdown Road, Seaford, East Sussex, BN25 4PA
☎ 01323 892048
Old style bears made with love. Unique and very special.

PIPEDREAM BEARS

28 Chiltern Drive, Woodsmoor, Stockport, Cheshire, SK2 7BE
☎ 0161 285 8254
email: r.cardey@ntlworld.com
Magical fairy bears made from pipecleaners featuring handmade toadstools. Also miniature mohair bears handmade by Jan Cardey and Sue Heap.

PIPSQUEAK AND PEPE-JOE BEARS

320 Havant Road, Drayton, Portsmouth, Hampshire, PO6 1PG
☎ 023 9232 6400
email: dianelouisa@zoom.co.uk
web: http://pages.zoom.co.uk/dianelouisa
Miniature chenille bears. SAE details.

PITTYPATS POPPETS

29 Bartlett Close, Poplar, London, E14 6LH
☎ 0207 537 3146
email: pittypatspoppets@fsmail.net
web: www.pittypatspoppets.com
Visit the new home of Oggies Attic Bears.

PIXEL'S BEARS

The Coach House, Heath Cottages, Clungunford, Craven Arms, Shropshire, SY7 0QB
☎ 01547 530607
email: info@pixelsbears.com
web: www.pixelsbears.com
High quality handmade collectable artist bears, one off's and small limited editions. Commissions welcome. See website for full details.

POGMEAR BEARS

8 Duporth Bay, St Austell, Cornwall, PL26 6AG
☎ 07730 788581 Fax: 01726 76234
Handmade mohair bears for collectors.

PORTOBELLO BEAR COMPANY

Amy Goodrich's artistic creations
☎ **01723 376929**
email: portobellobearco@aol.com
web: www.portobellobearco.com
'Aristocratic amongst bears; The blue
blood in your collection'©. Email for news
on showdates and stockists information.

PUTTY DINK BEARS

by Elizabeth Drake, 5 The Avenue, North Woodchester,
Stroud, Gloucestershire, GL5 5NH
☎ 01453 872649
email: lizzie@puttydinkbears.fsworld.co.uk
Exceptional bears for discerning collectors.

PUZZLE BEARS

61 Send Road, Send, Nr Woking, Surrey, GU23 7EU
☎ **01483 224524**
email: anitaweller@puzzlebears.fsnet.co.uk
web: www.puzzlebears.com
Handmade collectors mohair bears,
designed by Anita Weller, traditional,
themed character and miniature bears
made to order.

PYWACKET TEDDIES

Lin Grant, 75 Froxfield Road, West Leigh, Havant,
Hampshire, PO9 5PW
☎ 023 9245 2266 Fax: As tel.
Quality bears and other animals.

SUE QUINN

Hunter House, 7 Hunter Street, Paisley, Renfrewshire,
PA1 1DN, Scotland
☎ 0141 887 9916 Fax: 01505 702163
email: sue@bearsbysuequinn.co.uk
web: www.bearsbysuequinn.co.uk
Bears by Sue Quinn. Limited edition tradi-
tional jointed bears, dressed or undressed,
in pure mohair and other quality fabrics.

R.E.R. BEARS

24 Hunters Forstal Road, Broomfield, Herne, Herne
Bay, Kent, CT6 7DN
☎ 01227 741352 Fax: As tel.
email: rolferachel@hotmail.com
web: www.elizabethrosecreations.co.uk
Uniquely original handcrafted collectors bears.

RAMSHACKLE BEARS

'Ramshackle Cottage', 14 West Street, Shoreham-by-
Sea, W Sussex, BN43 5WG
☎ 01273 454746
Handmade mohair bears and restorations.

'RASCALS' BY ANGELA HODGON

16 Bradham Lane, Exmouth, Devon, EX8 4BB
☎ 01395 264964
email: angela@hodgon.wanadoo.co.uk
Award winning affordable miniature mohair
handsewn Devonshire-born character bears,
friends. From 1 inch. Commissions speciality.
Featured on Gems TV. Sae details.

READY TEDI GO!

102 Priory Way, Haywards Heath, West Sussex,
RH16 3NP
☎ 01444 413487
Collectable bears by Irene Wright.

REMEM-BEAR ARTIST BEARS

Braeside, 3 Mineral Terrace, Foxdale, Isle of Man,
IM4 3EY
☎ 07624 482 403 Fax: 01624 801197
email: remembear@yahoo.com
web: www.remembear.com
Unusual, freaky but so cute single edition
mohair artist bears.

RHIW VALLEY BEARS

Ratagan House, 2 Trem Hirnant, Manafon, Welshpool,
Powys, SY21 8BX ☎ 01686 650883
email: margery.youden@virgin.net
Individual bears handmade by Marge.

● RIVERBANK BEARS

90 Risley Lane, Breaston, Derbyshire, DE72 3AU
☎ 07816 148597
email: grant.jl@btinternet.com
Hessian and mohair collectors bears.
Handstitched original dressed charac-
ters.

● ROBIN RIVE BEARS

PO Box 6035, Poole, Dorset, BH12 9AH
☎ 07961 950452/ +64 9 5278 857
Fax: +64 9 527 1550
email: briguk@robinrive.com
web: www.robinrive.com
International award-winning New Zealand
bear-artist Robin Rive designs nostalgic soft
collectibles including limited edition fully
jointed mohair teddys and gollys.

● ROSIE'S ATTIC

'Chelsea Morning Cottage', 39 Ditton Street, Ilminster,
Somerset, TA19 0BW
☎ 01460 57775
email: rosieintheattic@yahoo.co.uk
web: www.rosiesattic.co.uk
Handmade country bears and collectibles.

Dialling the UK from overseas?

See codes information on page 219

● ROSY POSY BEARS

Rosemary Nancarrow, 30 Meadow Halt, East Ogwell,
Newton Abbot, Devon, TQ12 6FA
email: rosy.posy@virgin.net
web: www.rosyposybears.co.uk
Adorable handmade miniature bears. In the
fur to fully dressed. Catalogue online or send
50p in stamps.

● ROWAN BEARS

147 Singleton Crescent, Ferring, Worthing, West
Sussex, BN12 5DJ
☎ 01903 240467   email: sap441@hotmail.com
Traditional handmade mohair teddy bears.

● RUBEN BEARS

164 Cutenhoe Road, Luton, Bedfordshire, LU1 3NF
☎ 01582 731544   email: rubenbears@aol.com
Lovable bears requiring loving homes.

● SACQUE BEARS

by Susan Anne Coulthard, Ebenezer House, Roes
Lane, Crich, Derbyshire, DE4 5DH
☎ 01773 853159 Fax: As tel.
email: sacoulthard@aol.com
Award Winning Bears. Limited edition and
commission bears available direct or through
selected stockists. Enquiries welcome.

● SALLY ANNE BEARS

19 Abingdon Avenue, Doddington Park, Lincoln, LN6 3LB
☎ 01522 509329
email: sanray@aof113b.freeserve.co.uk
web: www.sallyannebears.co.uk
Award-winning dressed and undressed
mohair bears by Sandra Hobbs.

● SALLY B BEARS

email: salandbaz@hotmail.com
web: www.sally-b-bears.co.uk
Quality collectable OOAK artist bears (main-
ly miniatures), designed and handmade with
great care and attention to detail by Sally
Mathew.

● SANDYKAY BEARS

214 Whitchurch Lane, Edgware, Middlesex, HA8 6QH
☎ 020 8952 2600
email: sandy.kaye@virgin.net
web: www.sandykaye.ws
Individually hand stitched collectable bears.

SARAH LOU BEARS
93 Rowans Lane, Bryncethin, Bridgend,
Mid Glamorgan, CF32 9LZ
☎ 01656 722075   email: phillips_99uk@yahoo.co.uk
Quality hand crafted mohair bears.

SARAH'S BRUINS
24 Victoria Road, Wisbech, Cambs, PE13 2QL
☎ **01945 461257**
email: **sarahsbruins@aol.com**
web: **www.sarahsbruins.co.uk**
Original, unique and loveable artist
bears. Mostly one of a kind in mohair and
alpaca. 4" and upwards. Commissions
welcome.

SCRUFFIE BEARS BY SUSAN PRYCE
19 Parkfield Road, Broughton, Nr Chester, Cheshire,
CH4 0SE
☎ 01244 534724   email: scruffiebears@aol.com
web: www.scruffiebears.com
Mohair artist bears, mostly one of a kind or
small editions.

SCRUFFY BEARS
Flat 6, 57 Norfolk Road, Littlehampton, West Sussex,
BN17 5HE
☎ 01903 734865
Big bears, small bears. Bears handsewn
with love just waiting to come home with you.

SEVENTH HEAVEN TEDDIES
11 Ferguson Road, Oldbury, West Midlands, B68 9SB
☎ 0121 532 7421 / 07960 952 874
web: www.seventhheaventeddies.com
by Ruth Parsons

SHANTOCK BEARS
22 Downside, Hemel Hempstead, Herts, HP2 5PY
☎ 01442 260486
email: shantockbears@tiscali.co.uk
web: www.shantockbears.com
Traditional, themed and pretty bears.

Scruffie Bears
by Susan Pryce

Tel: 01244 534724
scruffiebears@aol.com
www.scruffiebears.com

Sally B Bears

Miniature Collectable Bears

Designed and Handmade with
great care and attention to detail
by Sally Mathew

Website: www.sally-b-bears.co.uk

● **SHEBOB BEARS**
7 Cottage Place, Copthorne, Crawley, Sussex,
RH10 3LF
☎ 01342 714568
email: sheila.tester@tesco.net
Original design collector's bears lovingly handcrafted by Sheila Tester. Also lifelike breeds of dogs etc. available spring 2006.

● **SHELLYSBEARS**
6 Osprey Close, Eaglestone, Milton Keynes, Buckinghamshire, MK6 5BQ
☎ 01908 679098
email: shelly@shellysbears.co.uk
web: www.shellysbears.co.uk
Little bears made to love.

● **JULIE SHEPHERD**
The Old School Cottage, Woolbeding, Midhurst, West Sussex, GU29 0QB
☎ 01730 810878
email: julieanita@aol.com
Original designs beautifully crafted in the finest mohair. Attending most major fairs. Catalogue available. Please telephone for details.

● **SHOEBUTTON BEARS**
11 Southern Road, Sale, Cheshire, M33 6HP
☎ 0161 282 8636
email: sue_wilkes_uk@yahoo.com
web: www.shoebuttonbears.co.uk
Miniature bears, bunnies, cats, dogs and gollies. Exclusive designs available mail order.

● **SHULTZ CHARACTERS**
by Paula Strethill-Smith, 4 Little Park Mansions, Titchfield Lane, Wickham, Hants, PO17 5PD
☎ 01329 834681 Fax: As tel.
email: p.strethillsmith@btconnect.com
web: www.paulastrethill-smith.com
Created by Paula Strethill-Smith, international-al award winning artist. Miniature vintage looking teddy bears, dogs, pressed felt gollies and characters.

● **SMALL WONDERS BY ANA MARIA DIAZ**
'Vanni', Sandy Lane, Send, Surrey, GU23 7AP
☎ 01483 222889 Fax: As tel.
Original designs for discerning collectors.

● SOUTHSEA BEARS
5 Langstone Road, Milton, Portsmouth, Hants,
PO3 6BP ☎ 023 9234 8182
email: info@southseabears.com
web: www.southseabears.com
100% hand stitched artist bears.

● SOUTHWAY BEARS
11 Stephen Martin Gardens, Fordingbridge,
Hampshire, SP6 1RF
☎ 01425 654768 Fax: As tel.
email: southwaybears@hotmail.com
web: www.southwaybears.co.uk
Beautiful mohair bears. Commissions welcomed.

● SPRINGER BEARS
26 Devonshire Avenue, Ripley, Derbyshire, DE5 3SS
☎ 01773 748093
email: springerbears@aol.com
Original bears made with love.

● STARLITE BEARS
32 Robertson Avenue
☎ 07802 568685
email: starlite_bears@yahoo.co.uk
web: www.starlitebears.co.uk
Hand made, original small and miniature character bears. Individual personalities 2 $\frac{1}{2}$" to 6" and larger on request.

● STEIFF UK
PO Box 158, Cranleigh, Surrey, GU6 8ZW
☎ 01932 568230 Fax: 01932 563427
Visit www.steiff-club.de to find your nearest stockist.

● STRAWBEARY'S
119 Fennycroft Road, Hemel Hempstead,
Hertfordshire, HP1 3NS
☎ 01442 265023 Fax: As tel.
Unique designs. Available to order.

● STREETBROOKE BEAR
309F The Big Peg, 120 Vyse Street, Birmingham,
B18 6ND
☎ 0121 236 6953 Fax: As tel.
email: info@streetbrookebear.co.uk
web: www.streetbrookebear.co.uk
High quality teddy bear jewellery. Hand made jewellery in precious metals. Pendants, brooches, earrings, rings. All hallmarked.

● STUDIO 44
7 High Street, Donington, Spalding, Lincolnshire,
PE11 4TA
☎ 01775 820429
email: grottigrumps@donington75.freeserve.co.uk
Collectors bears by Dorothy Short. Individually designed characters hand crafted in traditional and modern materials.

● SU TEE
8 Eskdale Terrace, Lingdale, Saltburn, Cleveland, TS12 3EL
☎ 01287 659117
Hand made miniature collectors bears.

● SUE GIBSON BEARS
53 Causton Road, Colchester, Essex, CO1 1RT
☎ 01206 760257   email: s.gibson@freeuk.com
web: www.sue-gibson-teddy-bears.com
Unique handmade mohair bears.

SUE'S TEDS
Blackthorn Road, Worcester, WR4 9TD
☎ 01905 29043
email: susan@spowell73.wanadoo.co.uk
web: http://suesteddybears.mysite.wanadoo-members.co.uk
Smiling loveable handmade mohair bears.

SUFFOLK BEARS BY SHIRLEY
20 Glastonbury Close, Ipswich, Suffolk, IP2 9EE
☎ 01473 686312   email: ballitfc@aol.com
web: www.suffolkbears.com
Quality designs, individually hand made limited editions, all fully jointed, from 1" to 36". Quality mohair used. Free catalogue available.

SUN MOON BEARS
Fl 1, 15 Western Place, Worthing, West Sussex, BN11 3LU
☎ 01903 205392
email: info@sunmoonbears.co.uk
web: www.sunmoonbears.co.uk
Happy bears with big hearts.

SWANNBEARY BEARS
14 Robert Moffat, High Legh, Knutsford, Cheshire, WA16 6PS
☎ 07792 759558
email: karen@swannbearybears.co.uk
web: www.swannbearybears.co.uk
Traditional and funky bears, handstitched with care by Karen J Swann. Limited editions and one-offs. SAE for details, prices, photos.

SYCAMORE BEARS
8 Birdsnest Avenue, Leicester, LE3 9NB
☎ 0116 2997243/07903227675
email: nicky.bacon@ntlworld.com
web: www.sycamorebears.co.uk
Quality hand made mohair bears.

TAMERTON TEDDYS
44 Rollis Park Road, Oreston, Plymouth, Devon, PL9 7LY
☎ 01752 480656
email: berylwhite@eurobell.co.uk
Collectors bears by Beryl White.

TAYLOR'S TEDDY'S
Goring on Thames, Reading, Berkshire
☎ 01491 874033
Handmade character bears.

TEACHERS PETS
81 Queens Road, Bury St Edmunds, Suffolk, IP33 3EW
☎ 01284 704253
web: www.teacherspetsonline.co.uk
Handsewn collector's bears, all individuals. Made with care from mohair or alpaca. Each has a gold star for being good!

THE TEDDY BEAR GROUP
☎ 01125 350 408
email: sales@teddybg.com
Please see display advertisement.

TEDDYBEAR TRAVELLERS
11 Queens Gardens, St. Andrews, Fife, KY16 9TA, Scotland
☎ 01334 478751 Fax: 01334 479679
email: enquiries@11queensgardens.co.uk
Small edition bears with soul.

TEDDYSTYLE
61 Park Road, Hemel Hempstead, Hertfordshire, HP1 1JS
☎ 01442 265944 Fax: As tel.
email: JCTeddystyle@aol.com
web: www.teddystyle.com
Please visit new website for bears, dolls, animals, patterns available. Classes online and hands on. Always new original characters.

TEDI ENFYS
39 Keene Ave, Rogerstone, Newport, S Wales
☎ 01633 780247
Teddies with a smile. Handmade traditional and modern style originally designed bears. Wide variety of sizes and mohairs. Also gollies.

TEDI TY COED
Forest Lodge, Treherbert, Treorchy, R.C.T., CF42 5PH
☎ 01443 776031
web: www.teditycoed.co.uk
Quality original handmade mohair bears.

TEDS OF THE RIVERBANK
'Riverbank', 2 Bohemia Cottages, Stalybridge, Cheshire, SK15 1JY
☎ 0161 303 0011
email: tedsoftheriverbank@btopenworld.com
web: www.tedsoftheriverbank.com
Artist teds for all tastes.

TEENY BEARS
11 Sparsholt Road, Weston, Southampton, Hants, SO19 9NH
☎ 02380 446356
email: teenybears@hotmail.com
Hand-made bears by Tina Gunn.

TESLINGTON BEARS
16 Bowling Road, Ware, Hertfordshire, SG12 7EQ
☎ 01920 420419
email: tracey.nelson-turner@ntlworld.com
web: www.teslingtonbears.co.uk
Hand crafted, one of a kind artist bears and exclusive limited edition kits.

TEWIN'S BRUINS
16 Lower Green, Tewin, Welwyn, Hertfordshire, AL6 0LB
☎ 01438 718700 Fax: 01438 840411
email: tbrand@talk21.com
Terry Brand (BA) handmade collector bears, rabbits, dogs, cats, mice, gollies etc...

THISTLE BEARS
☎ 07929 713566
email: thejazzbear@btinternet.com
Original, affordable and lovable bears.

THISTLECRAFT BEARS
Mrs Theresa Jones, BA(Hons), 15 Thistlecroft, Sanderson Park, Wednesfield, Wolverhampton, WV11 3XD
☎ 01902 306807
Traditional and character artist bears. Single editions made from finest mohair and vintage materials. Enquiries welcome. SAE for CD Rom.

THISTLEDOWN BEARS
133 High Street, Brotton, Saltburn-by-the-sea, Cleveland, TS12 2PY
☎ 01287 676302 email: thistledown@ntlworld.com
web: www.thistledownbears.co.uk
Hand-crafted collectors teddy bears.

ELIZABETH THOMPSON
12 Briar Thicket, Woodstock, Oxfordshire, OX20 1NT
☎ 01993 811915
High quality mohair and synthetic bears. Stock or personalised to order. For collectors and children.

THORNBEARIES
Elmbrook, Patch Elm Lane, Rangeworthy, South Gloucestershire, BS37 7LU ☎ 01454 228167
email: jayne@theoldchinashop.com
web: www.geocities.com/thornbearies
Handmade mohair collectors teddy bears.

THREAD-BEARS
The Pebbles, 28 East Street, Titchfield, Fareham, Hampshire, PO14 4AD ☎ 01329 845427
email: threadbearsuk@aol.com
web: www.thread-bears.com
Rachael Wintle creates original and outstanding bears for discerning collectors. Latest designs available via website or catalogue. Requests/commissions welcomed.

THREE O'CLOCK BEARS
27 Knoll Drive, Styvechale, Coventry, West Midlands, CV3 5BU ☎ 024 7641 6654
Fax: As tel.   email: jenny@threeoclockbears.com
web: www.threeoclockbears.com
Sweet faced individually made bears designed and stitched by Jenny Johnson. Loveable little friends to grow old with. Enquiries most welcome.

three o'clock bears

by Jenny Johnson
02476 416654
www.threeoclockbears.com

● TILLINGTON BEARS
13 Hurdles Way, Duxford, Cambridge, CB2 4PA
☎ 01223 837701 email: tilly@tillingtonbears.co.uk
web: www.tillingtonbears.co.uk
Bears who dare.

● TINY TEDDIES BY ANN
3 Cheriton Drive, Thornhill, Cardiff, South Glamorgan,
CF14 9DF ☎ 029 2075 3133
email: ann@tinyteddies.freeserve.co.uk
web: www.tinyteddiesbyann.co.uk
Miniatures a speciality. One-off handsewn unique designs 1-14 ins in mohair, cashmere, knitted silk thread. Miniature kits, fabrics, accessories available.

● TOGGLE TEDDIES
25 Laund Avenue, Belper, Derbyshire, DE56 1FL
☎ 01773 824258
email: wendi@toggleteddies.co.uk
web: www.toggleteddies.co.uk
Original handcrafted mohair bears. Primitive raggedy dolls using traditional homespun fabrics. By Wendi Walker.

● TOP 'N' TAIL TEDDY BEARS
82 Downs Road, Walmer, Deal, Kent, CT14 7TB
☎ 01304 363040
email: info@topntail.com web: www.topntail.com
Traditional bears with nostalgic character. Made to a very high standard with much fine detail from 7" up to 24".

● TORQUAY TEDDIES
12 Wilverley Court, Higher Woodfield Road, Torquay, Devon, TQ1 2JZ
email: emma@woottons.f9.co.uk
Modern funky mohair collector's bears.

● TOWNHOUSE BEARS
71 Percy Road, Shepherds Bush, London, W12 9PX
☎ 020 8746 2961 mobile: 07799 564132
email: belinda_pearce@easy.com
Quality hand crafted collectors bears.

● TRENDLE INTERNATIONAL LTD
PO Box 3, Williton, Taunton, Somerset, TA4 4YU
☎ 01984 656825
email: info@trendle.com
web: www.trendle.com
Please see colour display advertisement.

● TRIBAL BEARS
Flat 6, 57 Leyland Road, Southport, Merseyside,
PR9 9JA ☎ 01704 539476
Handmade quality mohair character bears.

● TRUDY'S TEDDIES
33 Thornton Hill, Exeter, Dvon
☎ 01392 681760
email: trudymarsden@hotmail.com
Classic and character mohair bears.

● TRUFFLE TUM TEDDIES
'Moss Bank', Bambers Lane, Marton Moss, Blackpool, Lancs, FY4 5LQ ☎ 01253 761500
email: thebearsbits@aol.com
Lovingly made bears to cherish!

● TUGALOT AND SCRUFFBAGS
Diane Armer, The Mill House, Canal Bank, Slaithwaite, Huddersfield, West Yorkshire, HD7 5HB
☎ 07968 806633
email: dianearmer@orange.net
web: http://myweb.tiscali.co.uk/tugalotandscruffbags
Happy, cuddly, character mohair bears and wabbits with pawsonality, from 3" to 24". One-off, hand dyed bears a speciality.

● TWILIGHT TEDS
by Tracey James, 37 Roeburn Way, Penketh, Cheshire, WA5 2PF
☎ 01925 725084
email: twilight_teds@hotmail.com
web: www.twilight-teds.co.uk
British Bear Artist Awards finalist 2003 and 2004. Artist bears, pandas, bunnies and gollies. Entirely hand stitched, 'one-off' exclusives.

● V. B. BEARS
(Vicki Butler), 51 Sunderland Road, Cleadon Village, Tyne & Wear, SR6 7UW
☎ 0191 536 9683
email: vbbears536@aol.com
Handcrafted teddy bears. Classes available.

● VANDA BEARS
Downside, 107 Old Newtown Road, Newbury, Berkshire, RG14 7DE
☎ 01635 36285
email: vanda.giles@vanda-bears.freeserve.co.uk
Handmade collectors bears lovingly crafted from quality mohair. One offs and small limited editions. At affordable prices.

The Teddy Bear Group

Bearaffe

Shaggy

Felipe

Timmy

● WALNUT TREE CORNER BEARS

by Gail, Walnut Tree Corner, 51 Heasman Close, Newmarket, Suffolk, CB8 0GR
☎ 01638 601708
email: info@bearsbygail.co.uk
web: www.bearsbygail.co.uk
Miniature artist bears, commissions taken.

● WARREN BEARS

4 Goddington Lane, Orpington, Kent, BR6 9DS
☎ 01689 871420 or 07753 800621
email: melanie@warrenbears.co.uk
web: www.warrenbears.co.uk
Adorable alpaca/mohair collector's bears.

● WATTS NEW BEARS

181 Burnley Road East, Waterfoot, Rossendale, Lancashire, BB4 9DF ☎ 01706 215308
email: wattsnewbears@hotmail.com
web: www.mrbears.vze.com
Gorgeous bears by Morna Watts.

● WELLWOOD BEARS

Ruth Dickinson, 46 Wellwood, Llanedeyrn, Cardiff, South Glamorgan, CF23 9JQ
☎ 029 2073 6610
email: ruth@wellwoodbears.freeserve.co.uk
web: www.wellwoodbears.com
Collectors bears. One offs, small limited editions. Available at fairs, shops or direct. See my website for bears and information.

● WENDY BEARS

101 Clements Road, Yardley, Birmingham, B25 8TZ
☎ 07788 112466
email: wendy.bears@blueyonder.co.uk
Quality handmade mohair alpaca bears some dressed one-offs 4" to 18". Available fairs - shops - direct. Lovingly made by Wendy Young.

● WENDY-SUE BEARS

33 Worcester Close, Northampton, NN3 9GE
☎ 01604 785942
email: wilkinson.bear@virgin.net
Tiny teds and furry friends.

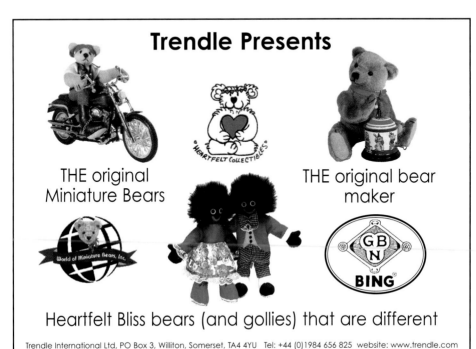

WESTIE BEARS

12 Norfolk Road, Horsham, West Sussex, RH12 1BZ
☎ 01403 241381 Fax: As tel.
email: andy@westiebears.com
web: www.westiebears.com
Wacky and punky mini bears, bunnies, monkeys and other critters. All one off pieces. Also bespoke work carried out.

WHISTY BEARS

51 Gordon Road, Whitstable, Kent, CT5 4NG
☎ 01227 770641
email: treclive@aol.com
web: www.whistycrafts.co.uk
Traditional bears by Pam Tress.

WHITTLE-LE-WOODS BEARS

23 Leinster Street, Farnworth, Bolton, Lancashire, BL4 9HS
☎ 01204 706831 Fax: As tel.
Traditional, limited edition collectors teddy bears, exclusively handcrafted and created by the artist, undressed and dressed. (View in Bear Gallery).

WICKENDEN BEARS

Base Lane Cottage, Base Lane, Sandhurst, Gloucestershire, GL2 9NJ
☎ 01452 502840 Fax: As tel.
Traditional teddy bears and realistic bruins.

WILLOW BEARS

Dawn Potter, 71 Rectory Lane North, Leybourne, West Malling, Kent, ME19 5HD
☎ 01732 871276   email: info@dawnpotter.com
web: www.dawnpotter.com
Designed to capture the appealing expressions and character of early teddies. Now made exclusively for The Old Playroom (see listing).

WINDY RIDGE BEARS

17 Heyworth Avenue, Blackburn, Lancashire, BB2 4SB
☎ 01254 696712 Fax: 01254 581958
email: mail@windyridgebears.co.uk
web: www.windyridgebears.co.uk
Award winning mohair artist bears.

Woodland Teddies
by Rita Harwood
Creative Editor
Teddy Bear Scene

VISA MasterCard

Original award winning handsewn & hand dyed realistic and wacky bears, cats, dogs and other furries
www.woodlandteddies.com
Beary Special Bearmaking Supplies
www.woodlandteddies.co.uk
5 Mildenhall Road, LE11 4SN 01509 267597
email rita@woodlandteddies.com

● WINKLEMOOR BEARS
11 Newport Road, Cwmcarn, Crosskeys, Newport, Gwent, NP11 7NE
☎ 01495 244528 mob: 07973 383128
email: elaine@winklemoor.co.uk
web: www.winklemoor.co.uk
Hand crafted collectors bears and friends. Nearly all one of a kind. A Winklemoor Bear always listens, never tells.

● WINTER BEARS
Columbine Cottage, Main Street, Spaldington, Near Goole, East Yorkshire, DN14 7NJ
☎ 01430 432120
Traditional bears aged and new, 12" to 26", mainly one-offs or very limited editions with real old style charm.

● WISDOM BEARS
2 Pladda Terrace, Broomlands, Irvine, Ayrshire, KA11 1DL, Scotland
☎ 01294 212822
email: wisdombears@aol.com
web: www.wisdombears.co.uk
Teddy bears and other critters.

● WOODGATE BEARS
8 Woodgate Meadow, Plumpton Green, Lewes, E. Sussex, BN7 3BD ☎ 01273 891665
email: sue@grasue.free-online.co.uk
web: www.woodgatebears.co.uk
Handmade mohair and alpaca bears.

● WOODLAND TEDDIES
Rita Harwood, 5 Mildenhall Road, Loughborough, Leicestershire, LE11 4SN
☎ 01509 267597 mob: 07973 821816
Fax: 01509 827389
email: rita@woodlandteddies.com
web: www.woodlandteddies.com
Beautiful handsewn originals. See display ad.

● WOODROW BEARS
19 Woodland View, Rogiet, Monmouthshire, NP26 3SY
☎ 01291 421369 email: beryl@stopgate.fslife.co.uk
web: www.woodrowbears.co.uk
Handmade dressed and natural bears.

● WOODVILLE BEARS
86 Bernard Street, Woodville, Swadlincote, Derbyshire, DE11 8BY
☎ 01283 221829 email: valbears@fsmail.net
Traditional handmade mohair collectors bears.

● WYNGARTH BEARS
62 Oakfield Road, Lobley Hill, Gateshead, Tyne & Wear, NE11 0AE
email: bears@wyngarth.com
web: www.wyngarth.com
Quality handmade miniature bears.

● YESTERDAY'S CHILDREN
Mill House, Mill Lane, St. Ive's Cross, Sutton St. James, Nr Spalding, Lincolnshire, PE12 0EJ
☎ 01945 440466
Individually designed, collectable, completely hand sewn, no order too small - maximum five of one design, many fabrics and sizes.

● ZENA ARTS
82 Kent Road, Mapperley, Nottingham, Nottinghamshire, NG3 6BN
☎ 0115 960 5820 Fax: As tel.
email: zena@zena-arts.com
web: www.zena-arts.com
Harris Tweed bears, gollies, dolls.

For information about telephoning abroad, please see page 219

● ADORABLE BEARS

Susan Bartlett, 1 Sturt Street, Shepparton, Victoria 3630, Australia
☎ +61 (0)3 5821 9979
email: sbart@bigpond.com
web: www.adorablebears.com.au
Collectable bears designed and handcrafted by Australian artist Susan Bartlett. View the Adorable Bears website at www.adorable-bears.com.au.

● ALICE BEARS

Hong Kong ☎ +(852) 9243 3326
email: alicebw@netvigator.com
web: www.alicebears.com
My teddies are made from finest mohair and are stuffed with poly and pellets. Size range from 3" to 24".

● ANNA KOETSE'S BEARS

Anna Koetse, Willem de Zwijgerlaan 8, 2012 SC, Haarlem, Netherlands
☎ +31 (0)23 5472048 Fax: +31 (0)23 5472034
email: koetse@xs4all.nl
web: www.annakoetse.com
Special, funny, inspiring, mostly dressed originals for collectors and museums. 100% handmade by artist. Many sizes. Visit gallery at website.

● ARTIG & FRECH

Danziger Str 64-66, 45145, Essen, Germany
☎ +49 (0)201 765 125 Fax: +49 (0)201 750 2408
email: schwarz@artigundfrech.de
web: www.artigundfrech.de
Classical and cheerful artist bears made with great care. Small limited editions and one-offs.

● BALU BEARS

Thomas Balke & Susanne Ludwig, Am Weissen Kamp 7d, D-38114 Braunschweig, Germany
☎ +49 (0)531 342690 Fax: As tel.
email: balubears@aol.com
web: www.balu-baer.de
Antique styled teddy bears with charm and appeal, irresistible bears with a real personality.

● BÄRENBANDE

Ostdeutsche Str. 2, 27619 Schiffdorf, Germany
☎ +49 (0)17 57 57 53 88
email: teddybaerenbande@t-online.de
web: www.teddybaerenbande.de
Teddys & Pandas jointed/unjointed, handcraft boxes and a pattern book, especially pandas - English translation available!

● BÄRENHÄUSL OSITOS®-BÄREN

Pfarrer-Braun-Str12, 83043 Bad Aibling, Germany
☎ +49 (0)80 61 34 33 10
Fax: +49 (0)80 61 34 33 11
email: ositos-teddys@web.de
web: www.ositos-baeren.de
Meet us at Hugglets Teddies Festival or ask for a shop near you!

BÄRENHÄUSL
Ositos®-Bären
handmade & designed by Angela Schulz
www.ositos-baeren.de   ositos-teddys@web.de
Phone +49 (0)8061-343310
Fax +49 (0)8061-343311

● BARKER BEARS

Saskatoon, USA
email: barkerbears@yahoo.com
web: www.barkerbears.com
A mother/daughter adventure of handmade creative one-of-a kind bears in vintage/mohair fur, we love an old looking teddy!

● BAYSIDE BEARS

72 Greenland Pond Road, Brewster, MA, USA
☎ +1 508 896 5350 Fax: +1 508 394 7062
email: baysidebr@aol.com
web: www.baysidebears.com
Mary Lou Foley of Bayside Bears is an award winning Artist specializing in Polar bears.

● BEAR MANIA

72 Main Road, 5252 Nairne, South Australia, Australia
☎ +61 (0)8 8188 0166 Fax: +61 (0)8 8188 0161
email: sk@bearmania.com.au
web: www.bearmania.com.au
Sandy-Kay Murphy designs original Artist bears and patterns. The studio also has bear making supplies and bears by other Artists.

● BEARABLE BEARS

Kortebeinstraat 3, 7311 RA Apeldoorn, Netherlands
☎ +31 (0)55 5788067
email: bearablebears@hotmail.com
web: www.bearablebears.nl
I hope my self designed bears can give you a little journey to the past.

● BEARGAMIN BEARS

20 Pickworth Drive, Mill Park, Melbourne, Victoria, Australia
☎ +61 (0)3 9436 6871 Fax: As tel.
email: wendybergamin@dodo.com.au
web: www.beargaminbears.com
Australian made original design bears in mohair or alpaca. Every bear is completely made by Wendy Bergamin.

● BEARKIDZ (TM)

by Marion Fraile USA
email: marion@bearkidz.com
web: www.bearkidz.com
One of a kind crocheted/felted mini artist bears, dressed baby & toddler bears.

● BEARS ABUNDANT

Ruth Fraser, 156 Shaughnessy Blvd, North York, Ontario, M2J 1J8, Canada
☎ +1 416 493 2944
Original old look bear designs, fully jointed 12" scale dollhouse bears, loving restoration, identification and evaluation of old bear friends.

● BEARS BY ARMELLA

PO Box 296, Marion, IA 52302, USA
☎ +1 319 377 5869
email: bearsbyarmella@mchsi.com
web: www.bearsbyarmella.net
Mohair character and historical bears and recycled fur (muskrat, mink, kangaroo, among others) bears 2" to 28" lovingly created.

● BEARS BY BEESLEY™

Box 83, Site 8, R.R. 2, Tofield, Alberta, T0B 4J0, Canada
☎ Toll free in Canada 1866 467 3494
email: teddybears@bearsbybeesley.com
web: www.bearsbybeesley.com
Husband and wife team. Artist designed, hand made mohair and alpaca OOAK teddy bears.

● BEARS BY ECE

Winnetka, CA, USA
email: ece@bearsbyece.com
web: www.bearsbyece.com
Miniature bears by Ece Hanson.

● BEAUT BEARS

Postbus 4058, 2980 GB Ridderkerk, Netherlands
☎ +31 (0)610 623 559
email: marianne@beautbears.nl
web: www.beautbears.nl
Colourful one-offs, designed and handmade by Marianne Risseeuw. All BeauT Bears are born and bred aboard a 19th-century sailing barge.

● BERENATELIER DUIMELOTJE

Marleen Poppe, Gontrode Heirweg 126, 9090 Melle, Belgium
☎ +32 (0)9 2314365 Fax: As tel.
email: duimelotje@skynet.be
web: www.duimelotje.be
Quality handcrafted character bears in mohair. All one of a kind. Kits for making adorable teddy bears. All materials.

● BEST DRESSED BEARS
2 Abelia Court, Hillside 3037, Victoria, Australia
☎ +61 (0)3 9449 0944
email: kerrie@bestdressedbears.com.au
web: www.bestdressedbears.com.au
Best Dressed Bears are created by award winning artist Kerrie Mouat. Uniquely costumed, hand made artist bears.

● BINE'S BÄRENAUSLESE
Sabine Hohmann, Jessener Str. 3b, 48308 Senden, Germany
☎ +49 (0)2597 98139
email: binesbaeren@aol.com
web: www.binesbaerenauslese.de
Handcrafted high quality artist bears. Winner of 'Ted Worldwide 2005', 'Old fashion teddy'. Feel free to contact me.

● BLACK FOREST BEARS
103 Dianne Avenue, Simpsonville, SC 29681, USA
☎ +1 864 228 0359
email: peppermint217@direcway.com
web: www.myblackforestbears.com

● BRENTWOOD BEARS
191 Dunlin Drive, Burleigh Waters, Queensland 4220, Australia
☎ +61 (0)7 5520 5191
email: judy@brentwoodbears.com
web: www.brentwoodbears.com

● BREWER'S BRUINS
Miniature Bears by Andrea Brewer, 2113 Yost Street, Salisbury, NC 28144, USA
☎ +1 704 637 3206
email: bearsbyandrea@aol.com
web: www.BrewersBruins.com
Specializing in one-of-a-kind character bears in miniature. Detailed pattern booklets, small edition kits and supplies.

● BRIDDY BEARS
Brigitta Hoffman, Auweg 7, 82234 Wessling, Germany
☎ +49 (0)8153 3714 Fax: As tel.
email: info@briddy-bears.de
web: www.briddy-bears.de
Wonderful handmade artist bears and friends of modern, classic and antique design - winners and nominations TOBY Award, BBAA, Ted Worldwide, TITA.

● BRIGIT'S BEARS
14 Carstairs Road, Darlington, WA 6070, Australia
☎ +61 (0)8 9572 4125 Fax: As tel.
email: bears@iinet.net.au
web: www.iinet.net.au/~bears
Handcrafted collectable teddybears recycling furgarments into family heirlooms from your fur or mine. Patterns for bears and other animals available.

● CALA BEAR DEN
18 Bibeau Bay, Winnipeg, Manitoba, R2J 2A7, Canada
☎ +1 204 257 6003
email: calabear02@yahoo.ca
web: www.calabear.ca
I create OOAK collectible bears out of mohair, synthetic and needle felting. Needle felting products available as well.

● CANNA BEAR PAINT
by Margaret Mount-Zimmerman & Kelly Zimmerman, USA
☎ +1 (585) 425 0567
email: cannabear@frontiernet.net
web: www.cannabearpaint.com
Artist bears, bunnies and other animals in real fur, mohair and quality synthetics. Designs from traditional teddies to realistic animals.

● CHANGLE BEARS
10 Cecil Lloyd Street, Stirling, East London 5241, South Africa
☎ +27 (0)43 735 4216 Fax: +27 (0)43 743 1130
email: footman@intekom.co.za
web: www.changlebears.homestead.com
Artist bears, one-off and small limited editions, air brushed detail. All enquiries welcome.

● CHANTAL'S BEARS CREATIONS
Canada
☎ +1 506 642 9788
email: chantal.giroux@gmail.com
web: www.mignonettestitch.com/chantalbears.htm
Miniature teddy bears designer, in thread, plush, faux fur, felting needle; I mix different styles - adding bobbin lace, tatting, beads.

● CHATHAM VILLAGE BEARS L.L.C.

Artist Art Rogers, 2722 Chatham Dr., Maryland Heights, MO 63043-1208, USA
☎ +1 314 739 8426 Fax: +1 314 291 1580
email: geoart1@swbell.net
web: www.chathamvillagebears.com
Handmade teddy bears and other animals by artist Art Rogers. These are really a nice addition to any collector's collection.

● CHINA CUPBOARD BEARS

519 S. Main Street, Marion, OH 43302, USA
☎ +1 740 387 7742 Fax: As tel.
email: chinacupboardbears@hotmail.com
web: www.teddybeargallery.com/cindymcguire.html
Made & designed by Cindy McGuire in traditional and Japanese styles. With fashion design background many are dressed in vintage clothing.

● CHRISTY'S BEARS

3701 Grapevine Mills Parkway #425, Grapevine, TX 76051, USA
email: bearsbyc@aol.com
web: http://christyfirmage.com/

● COLLECTOR'S BEARS BY HELGA TORFS

Veldstraat 74, 2450, Meerhout, Belgium
☎ +32 (0)14 30 32 08 Fax: As tel.
email: helga.torfs@pandora.be
web: www.collectorsbears.com
Handmade collectors bears by award-winning artist. Bears featured on stationery items worldwide. Specialized in theme bears - dwarfbears, eskimobears, clownbears etc..

● COONI BEARS

Ingrid Finck, Winsheimstr. 88, 58454 Witten, Germany
☎ +49 (0)23 02 89 407 Fax: +49 (0)23 02 59 211
email: ingrid.finck@cooni-bears.de
web: www.cooni-bears.de
Award winning classical character and miniature bears for collectors. Also scenes in 1:12 scale.

● CORNELIA BEARS - HOLLAND

Dedemsvaartweg 314, NL-2545 AJ, Den Haag, Netherlands
☎ +31 (0)70 32 95 857 Fax: As tel.
email: info@corneliabears.com
web: www.corneliabears.com
Miniature bears. Own design. Materials: mohair, upholstery and suede. Also crocheted bears. Accept PayPal, Visa and Mastercard. Handmade with love.

● ALINE COUSIN

70 Rue Du Docteur Sureau, F93160 Noisy Le Grand, France
☎ +33 (0)1 43 04 38 03
email: cousin.aline@free.fr
web: http://cousin.aline.free.fr
New bears, new designs, new web site by Aline Cousin - pioneer bear artist in France. Visit gallery at web site.

● DEB CANHAM ARTIST DESIGNS

1435 E Venice Ave, Unit 104 PMB 242, Venice, Florida 34292, USA
(UK Agent: Brian Somers, 1 Georgian Close, Gordon Ave, Stanmore, Middlesex, HA7 3QT tel: 020 8954 5956.)
☎ +1 941 480 1200 Fax: +1 941 480 1202
email: order@debcanham.com
Limited edition mohair bears, dragon, rabbits, mice and other animals. Miniature and mini sizes.

● DIE WUSCHELBÄREN

Silvia Gericke-Vieweg, Treskower Ring 48, 16816 Neuruppin, Germany
☎ +49 (0)3391 5052 72
email: silvia.gerickevs@t-online.de
web: www.wuschelbaer.com
Collectible mohair bears lovingly handcrafted with cute expressions, mostly with smiling faces. Usually made from German Schulte mohair.

● DRIFTWOOD BEARS

Australia
☎ +61 (0)7 4945 4245
email: jaccy@driftwoodbears.com
web: www.driftwoodbears.com
One of a kind collector bears by triple museum-listed artist Jaccy Thomas from Australia's tropical Whitsundays.

VÉRONIQUE DUBOSC

103 rue Abbé de l'épée, 33000 Bordeaux, France
☎ +33 (0)5 56 51 04 65
email: v_dubosc@yahoo.fr
web: www.foliesdours.com
Traditional collectors' bears in the finest mohairs. Dressed with a romantic French touch. One-offs.

DUFEU-BEAR

Muhrenkamp 31, 45468 Mülheim an der Ruhr, Germany
☎ +49 (0)208 3 23 88
email: dufeu-bear@gmx.de
web: www.dufeu-bear.de
Character bears, teddies, artist bears and stuffed animals for lovers and collectors.

DURRERBEARS AND MORE

South Perth, Western Australia, Australia
☎ +61 (0)8 9368 1557 Fax: As tel.
email: durrerbears@iinet.net.au
web: www.iinet.net.au/~durrerbears
durrerBears: Artist bears and gollies, all original designs and hand crafted by award winning artist. Patterns and workshops available.

ESKOLE NOOMBAS

11 Jalan Pergam, 488370, Singapore
☎ +65 6545 5904 Fax: +65 6542 2918
email: alicia@eskolenoombas.com
web: www.eskolenoombas.com
Playful and beautifully realistic bears plus other animals! Airbrushed, unique and very life-like. Please request photos or visit my website.

ESSENTIAL BEARS

Wendy & Megan Chamberlain, 20 Belmont Road, Mowbray, 7700 Cape Town, South Africa
☎ +27 (0)21 685 3487 Fax: +27 (0)21 68 53 487
email: ebears@iafrica.com
web: www.essentialbears.net
Award winning miniature bears and other animals. Patterns and kits available.

FOOL'S GOLD BEARS

6451 Elk River Road, Eureka, CA 95503, USA
☎ +1 707 442 2084 Fax: As tel.
email: lweltsch@cox.net
web: www.foolsgoldbears.com
Unique individuals by Laure Weltsch. Sweet, engaging faces and unusual use of color, in celebration of the Creator.

FRED-I-BEAR

Lynette Kennedy, PO Box 6502, Westgate, 1734, South Africa
☎ +27 (0) 83 2500378 Fax: +27 (0) 11 672 4008
email: lck@mweb.co.za
web: www.fred-i-bear.co.za
Limited edition artist bears made from the finest mohair with unique painted faces.

GERTIE WIGGINS

'Gerties', Tinnescart, Aglish, Waterford, Ireland
☎ +353 (0)24 96811 Mob: 0876 913318
email: gertieswiggins@eircom.net
Mostly pirates with leather noses.

GILLES BAEREN
by Silvia Gilles Germany
email: silvia.gilles@silviagilles.de
web: www.silviagilles.de
Lovely mohair and alpaca bears of own design, natural-looking, fully jointed with claws and leather pads.

GIZMO BEARS
Diane Bester, PO Box 22066, Glenashley, 4022, Durban, South Africa
☎ +27 (0)31 562 0709 Fax: As tel.
email: gizmo@sentechsa.com
web: www.gizmobears.homestead.com
Bears & critters with an attitude! One of a kind and small limited editions - 3" and larger made from quality mohair.

HEARTFELT BEARS
65 Old Warburton Highway, Seville East, Victoria 3139, Australia
☎ +61 (0)3 5964 7964 Fax: As tel.
email: ahe83230@bigpond.net.au
web: www.heartfeltbears.com
Old style bears, gollys, rabbits and cloth dolls from miniature to large.

HEIKES KRINGELBÄREN
Rotenbergstr.28, 64658 Fürth-Krumbach, Germany
☎ +49 (0)62 53 60 80 04
Fax: +49 (0)62 53 2 31 44
email: kringelbaeren@aol.com
web: www.kringelbaeren.de
Hand sewn character bears, lovingly made from best quality German materials.

HERMANN TEDDY ORIGINAL
Teddy-Hermann GmbH, Postfach 1207, D-96112 Hirschaid, Germany
☎ +49 (0)9543 84820 Fax: +49 (0)9543 848210
email: info@teddy-hermann.de
web: www.teddy-hermann.de
Traditional mohair bears in limited editions, miniatures, accessories etc. UK Main Agent: Brian Somers. Tel: 020 8954 5956. Please see advertisement on page 155.

HOMEBREWED BEARS
9 Tennyson St, Balmoral, Auckland 1004, New Zealand
☎ +64 (0)9 630 9232
email: hbbears@yahoo.co.nz
web: http://homebrewedbears.homestead.com
Unconventional, colourful hand-sewn bears from Middle Earth, brewed individually for collectors with a sense of humour!

HONEY TEDDY
Russia
☎ +7 3422 16 74 75
email: kataev@permonline.ru
web: www.honey-teddy.narod.ru
I've made Teddy Bears since 2000. Hand made, classic, aged, modern teddys, in clothes, with accessories and without.

HOVVIGS
Yvonne Graubaek, Hovvigvej 68, 4500 Nykoebing Sj, Denmark
☎ +45 5991 3494 or in UK: 07785 788307
email: hovvigs@post.tele.dk
My UK Agent: Round About Bears, Suffolk. Please ask for free colour list, or see www.roundaboutbears.co.uk

INGE BEARS
PO Box 392, Kleinmond 7192, South Africa
☎ +27 (0)721104273
email: ingebears@itec.co.za
web: www.ingebears.homestead.com
One-of-a-kind miniature bears, designed by Ingrid Els.

JODIE'S BEARS
Tomoko Suenaga, 3-28-1 Kataseyama, Fujisawa, Kanagawa, 251-0033, Japan
☎ +81 (0)466 25 1202 Fax: +81 (0)466 27 2260
email: jodie@axel.ocn.ne.jp
Enjoy the fantastic fairy bears.

KAREN ALDERSON ARTIST DESIGN
PO Box 224, Gembrook, VIC 3783, Australia
☎ +61 (0)3 5968 1100
email: karen@karensdolls.com
web: www.karenalderson.com/bears
Original artist bears, specialising in costumed miniatures, using the finest fabrics and trims. One of a kind and limited editions.

● KARIN KRONSTEINER BEARS
- ENVOYS OF MY SOUL
Krenngasse 8, A-8010, Graz, Austria
☎ +43 (0)316 83 91 82 Fax: As tel.
email: karin.kronsteiner@schule.at
web: www.karinkronsteiner.at.tt
Please see display advertisement.

● KAZUAL BEARS
3 Yarradaup St Ashmore, Gold Coast, 4214, Australia
☎ +61 (0)7 5539 2404
email: kazbears@optusnet.com.au
web: www.kazualbears.com
Goofy style to traditional aged bears, using recycled fur, mink, lappin, fox etc. Also teach bear making at the Kympatti studio.

● IRINA KULIKOVA
Rossija, B.Spasskay st., 31-118, Moscow, 129090, Russia
email: brayni@mail.ru
web: www.brayni.narod.ru
Professional artist who creates bears and other animals from antiquarian fabric - using 40-50 year old plush, velvet, silk, ribbon, laces.

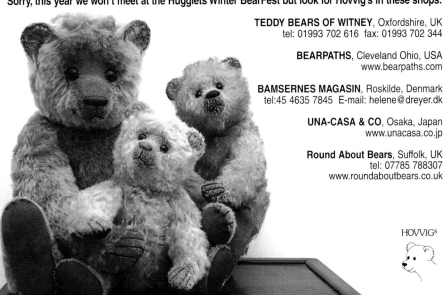

Lea Bears
Lenie Versteeg, Netherlands
www.leabears.com

Meister Bear

Josephine Meister,
PO Box 350, Sunninghill,
Sandton 2157, South Africa
Tel/Fax: 011 803 7189
email: pmeister@icon.co.za

Traditional bears from top quality mohair

● LEA-BEARS
Lenie Versteeg, Ysselstraat 42, 8303 LD Emmeloord, Netherlands
☎ +31 (0)527 616552 Fax: +31 (0)527 621320
email: lea.versteeg@zonnet.nl
web: www.leabears.com
Please see display advertisement

● LIEBHAB-BÄREN
Okko-ten-Broek-Str. 7, 26789 Leer, Germany
☎ +49 (0)491 3478
email: teddy4you@gmx.de
web: www.liebhab-baeren.de
Teddybears from the Bleeker-Twins are made with Love to make people happy. This is the best a Teddy can do.

● LORIS HANCOCK'S STUDIO 70
Suite 370, 80 The Pines, Elanora, Queensland 4221, Australia
☎ +61 (0)7 5598 2242 Fax: +61 (0)7 5525 6354
email: minibear@austarnet.com.au
web: www.lorishancock.com
Loris' award winning minibears are detailed and colourful. Her work often includes endangered animals. She also sells kits and takes workshops.

● LOVABLE FELLOWS
Karin Jehle, Uranusweg 1, 70565 Stuttgart, Germany
☎ +49 (0)711 748156
email: karin.jehle@tbears.de
web: www.tbears.de
Award winning designer bears with soul and character. See for yourself and visit my website at www.tbears.de

● MADELEINE'S MINI BEARS
Madeleine Nelken, 126 Avenue du Général de Gaulle, F-78500 Sartrouville, France
☎ +33 (0)1 39 14 50 86
email: mnelken@aol.com
web: www.madeleineminibears.com
Exquisite miniature bears designed and handcrafted with love $3/4$" to 5". One-offs and small limited editions.

● MAJA'S BEARS
by Maja Hansen, Ontvoogdingstraat 30, 2840 Terhagen, Belgium
☎ +32 (0)32 90 39 71
email: majasbears@telenet.be
web: www.majasbears.be
Adorable artist bears designed and created for the serious collector. Please visit my website to see different styles and sizes.

● MALU-BEAR
Marie-Luise Barwitzki, Max-Holder-Str. 8, D-73630 Remshalden, Germany
☎ +49 (0)7151 72769 Fax: As tel.
email: malu@malu-bear.de
web: www.malu-bear.de
Charming old fashioned and cuddly bears. Handmade with love from our own design. One-offs and small limited editions.

● MARIAN BEAR
Sloetsweg 131, 7556 HM Hengelo, Netherlands
☎ +31 (0)74 291 9115
email: marianbear@yahoo.com
web: www.marianbear.com
My minibears are colourful and sweet, made of different mohairs. Also mohair bears of 2". Visit my site.

● MARY GEORGE BEARS
6635 Poppleton Road, Canton, Michigan 48187, USA
☎ +1 734 453 6814
email: marygeorgebears@yahoo.com
web: www.marygeorgebears.com
One-of-a-kind antique style teddy bears, each with a sweet face and unique personality by artist Mary George.

● MEGELLES
679 Upper Brookfield Road, Upper Brookfield, Queensland 4069, Australia
☎ +61 7 3374 3373
email: dopking@bigpond.com web: www.megelles.com
Original bears designed and handmade by Lisa Dopking. Bear patterns and kits and stitchery kits featuring Lisa's designs also available.

● MEISTER BEAR
Josephine Meister, PO Box 350, Sunninghill, Sandton 2157, South Africa
☎ +27 (0)11 803 7189 Fax: As tel.
email: pmeister@icon.co.za
Please see display advertisement.

● MERRY BEARS BY ANNEI LEUNG
Flat D, 12th Floor, Mountain View, Discovery Bay, Hong Kong
☎ +852 8101 7923 Fax: +852 8100 6589
email: merrybears@merrygoround.com.hk
web: www.merrygoround.com.hk
Award winning artist from Hongkong. Love diverse design and unusual colours. Bears have their own character, not just my trademark.

Merry Bears
by Annei Leung

www.MerryGoRound.com.hk

MICK BEARS MAKERIJ

Marjolein Vos, Wilhelminastraat 104, 7001 GZ Doetinchem, Netherlands
☎ +31 (0)314 361 116
email: info@mickbears.com
web: www.mickbears.com
My bears look like real little children, ready to walk! Baby bears are weighted like real babies.

MINIKINS BY MAGGIE SPACK-MAN

711 Beverly Drive, Bridges of Summerville, Summerville, South Carolina 29485, USA
☎ +1 843 875 2565
email: minikins@sc.rr.com
web: www.maggiesminikins.com
Award winning miniature bears all hand-stitched and fully jointed. Small limited editions and one-offs. Original designs.

MLE-DESIGNS

1011 River Rd, Auburn, Michigan, USA
☎ +1 989 662 6598
email: marjorie450@charter.net
web: www.mle-designs.com
Miniature and small bears designed with attention to detail into who he or she was destined to become with love.

MOSSIE BEARS, SOUTH AFRICA

12 White Street, Parkdene, Boksburg 1459, Gauteng, South Africa
☎ +27 (0)11 965 1654 /+27 82 572 6969 (mobile)
email: cheryl@mossiebears.com
web: www.mossiebears.com
Realistic and traditional miniature creations handcrafted with love and attention to detail by Cheryl Moss.

NADINE MURAT THEVENOT, MABAWA THEMUR

20 rue Laurent Carle, 69008 Lyon, France
☎ +33 (0)4 78 75 54 68
Fax: +33 (0)4 78 69 57 13
email: themur@wanadoo.fr
web: www.themur.com
OOAK Creator of colourful whimsy BearsOfThreaD and traditional sewn mohair bears. From tiny to large. Unique art contemporary fantasy style.

NADJA BEARS

Monnikenhofstraat 120, 2040 Berendrecht-Antwerpen, Belgium
☎ +32 (0)3 568 15 15 Fax: As tel.
email: nadia.jacobs@pandora.be
web: www.nadjabears.be
Pre-loved bears who are looking for a good home. If you love those nostalgic feelings.

NORMANDY BEARS

Village de la Rivière, 50620 St Fromond, France
☎ +33 (0)2 33 55 98 61 Fax: As tel.
email: vicki.philip@wanadoo.fr
Collectors bears with French flair. Handcrafted by Vicki Philip in Normandy. One of a kind. Commissions welcome.

OKIDOKI ORIGINAL

Pistolvägen 6, 22649 Lund, Sweden
☎ +46 (0)46 142089 or (0)46 133820 Fax: +46 (0)46 133820
email: kajsa.lindstrom@telia.com
web: www.okidokioriginal.com
Colourful collection of one-off animals in washed wool. Bears, rabbits, duckies, pigs, dogs and more - all dressed up to go!

OLD TIME TEDDIES/ MARJOLEINE DIEMEL ORIGINALS

Zegge 16, 2631 DL Nootdorp, Netherlands
☎ +31 (0)15 310 8025 Fax: +31 (0)15310 9733
email: marjoleine1@wanadoo.nl
web: www.marjoleinediemel.nl
Antique styled Teddies and doggies.

ORIGINAL FELTED FOLKSIES

USA
☎ +1 203 729 7714
email: linda@originalfeltedfolksies.com
web: www.originalfeltedfolksies.com
Miniature needle felted wool vintage style teddy bears and animal friends! Come and see my Folksies!

● ORIGINAL HANNA BAEREN

Mühlweg 6, D-65618 Selters/Ts., Germany
☎ +49 (0)6483 3703 Fax: +49 (0)6483 3437
email: info@hanna-baeren.de
web: www.hanna-baeren.de
High-class artist bears designed and created by Hanne Leder, limited editions or one-off. Birth certificate, embroidered name. Established 1982.

● ORIGINAL RICA-BEAR®

Ulrike and Claude Charles, Friesenstr. 5, 32760 Detmold, Germany
☎ +49 (0)5231 59750 Fax: +49 (0)5231 580018
email: mail@rica-bear.de
web: www.rica-bear.de
Traditional collectors bears designed and handmade by Ulrike and Claude Charles. Small limited editions and one-offs.

● OZ MATILDA BEARS

PO Box 366, Crabbes Creek, NSW 2483, Australia
☎ +61 (0)2 6677 1388
email: ozmatilda@bigpond.com.au
web: www.ozmatilda.com.au
Lisa Rosenbaum - one of Australia's leading bear artisans - established 1994. International award winner. Specialising in historical themes, vintage & unique hand-painted oils.

● PENG PENG BEARS

Chicago, Illinois, USA
email: peng@peng-peng.com
web: www.peng-peng.com
Original handmade teddy bears by artist Peng Peng. Unconventional antiqued collector quality bears and original antiqued sock monkeys.

LISA ROSENBAUM
Oz Matilda Bear Co.
est. 1994

www.ozmatilda.com.au   ozmatilda@bigpond.com

Stine Birkeland, Denmark
www.stine-teddies.dk
Meet us at Hugglets Winter BearFest

● THE PIECE PARADE
7405 Laketree Drive, Raleigh, NC 27615, USA
☎ +1 919 870 1881
Fax: +1 919 870 6740
email: gbrame@pieceparade.com
web: www.pieceparade.com
3-12 inch teddies, scrapbook bears, 'bears&boxes' & one-offs created with care by Ginger Brame. Exclusive Internet shows semi-annually.

● PMBEARS
Patti Hendriks, RR#1 Brucefield, Ontario, Canada
☎ +1 519 522 0454
email: hendriks@tcc.on.ca
web: www.pmbears.com
100% mohair bears, lovingly distressed in the antique style, some traditional cuties, as well as funky folk bears. Award winning.

● POTBELLY BEARS
Chico, California, USA
email: info@potbellybears.com
web: www.potbellybears.com
Original, one of a kind, bearsonalities in mohair, real fur, and other fine fabrics, lovingly handcrafted by artist Shelli Heinemann.

● POTTERSHOUSE BEARS
27720 Jug Run Road, Frazeysburg, Ohio 43822, USA
☎ +1 740 668 4822
email: pottershousebears@hotmail.com
web: www.pottershousebears.com
Handmade OOAK mohair and real fur artist bears, bunnies and dogs with emphasis on antique style.

● PUCA BEARS
Schwalbengasse 29, Wald Michelbach, 69483, Germany
☎ +49 (0)6207 921461
email: maria.collin@t-online.de
web: www.puca-bears.de
Unique and original award-winning characters - completely hand crafted - big noses, big feet, fingers and, sometimes, even toes.

● R. JOHN WRIGHT DOLLS, INC.
2402 West Rd., Bennington, VT 05201, USA
☎ +1 802 447 7072
Fax: +1 802 447 7434
email: info@rjohnwright.com
web: www.rjohnwright.com
Fine and exquisitely crafted doll, bears, and animals for the discerning collector.

● RÊVES D'OURS
Pascale Nowicki, 3 rue Jean Baux, 62260, Auchel, France
email: contact@revesdours.com
web: www.revesdours.com
Creative Frenchwoman, artisanal creations, one-offs, traditional and equipped bears. I hand embroider my signature on the bear's leg.

● RUNNING BEAR COMPANY
Eisinghausener Str. 309, 26789 Leer, Germany
☎ +49 (0)491 912 1526
Fax: +49 (0)491 940 7264
email: runningbearco@aol.com
web: www.runningbearcompany.de
Bears to make you smile.

● SHARON GRACE'S BEARS
104 Manganese Point Road, Tamaterau, Whangarei, New Zealand
☎ +64 (0)9 436 0070
email: info@sharongrace.co.nz
web: www.sharongrace.co.nz
All original bears, fabric animals, gollies handmade by National Award winning artist (20 years experience). Recycled natural handcoloured fabrics, quality guaranteed.

● SHELINKA BEARS
55 Lyndhurst Rd, Kalamunda, Western Australia, 6076, Australia
☎ +61 (0)8 9293 3664
Fax: +61 (0)8 9293 0559
email: linton@iinet.net.au
web: www.shelinkabears.com
Offering a wide range of patterns for beginner to advanced bear makers, and an ever-changing range of edition bears.

● FABIAN SONG
Blk 8 Jalan Kukoh, # 03-33, 162008, Singapore
☎ +65 673 331 63 Fax: +65 67 33 31 63
email: fsong@singnet.com.sg
Unique & unusual creations.

● SPIELMITTEL
by Kristina Dietzel, Sonneberger Str. 11, Effelder, Thuringia, 96528, Germany
☎ +49 (0)36766 20632 Fax: As tel.
email: Kristina.Dietzel@bearsandtoys.de
web: www.bearsandtoys.de
My objects (bears, animals and dolls) should create a feeling of fantasy and affection, pleasure and playfulness.

● SPIELZEUGDESIGN
Annette Rauch, Neuhäuser Straße 42, 98701, Grossbreitenbach, Germany
☎ +49 (0)36781 40363 Fax: +49 (0)36781 29470
email: annette.rauch@t-online.de
web: www.annette-rauch.de
Handmade bears and animals from natural materials whose personal information will always be found on their bottoms.

● STANLEY BEARS
Rosengren Lane, Stanley, Victoria 3747, Australia
☎ +61 (0)3 5728 6623
email: eunice@stanleybears.com.au
web: www.stanleybears.com.au
I am Eunice Eiseman, a professional teddy bear artist (established 1990) specialising in exclusive teddies for discerning collectors worldwide.

● MARGARETE STEIFF GMBH
Richard Steiff Strasse 4, D-89537 Giengen/Brenz, Germany
☎ +49 (0)7322 131-1 Fax: +49 (0)7322 131-2 66
web: www.steiff-club.de
Richard Steiff invented the world's first Teddy bear in 1902.

● STINE-TEDDIES
Syrenstien 3, DK-8800 Viborg, Denmark
☎ +45 86 63 87 22 Fax: +45 86 63 87 99
email: stine@stine-teddies.dk
web: www.stine-teddies.dk
Beautiful bears designed and made by Stine Birkeland from the finest materials. Mostly one of a kind.

● TEDS FROM THREADS
201 Ridgeview Road, Sarver, PA 16055, USA
email: tedsfromthreads@connecttime.net
web: www.tedsfromthreads.com
Artist made Thread Crochet Bears/Animals. Large selection of supplies to make your own thread crochet animals plus patterns too!

● THEABÄR
Bergstrasse 47, 88267 Vogt, Germany
☎ +49 (0)7529913065
email: info@theabaer.de
web: www.theabaer.de
Ornamental antique style bears full of personality. Theabear is best known for its hand-embroidered, patented and internationally rewarded 'Rosenbären' (Rosebears).

THREADTEDS

De Braak 11, 5963 BA Horst, Netherlands
☎ +31 (0)77 3984960
email: threadteds@tiscali.nl
web: www.threadteds.com
Crochet, needle felted and fabric collectable mini bears, bigger bears too! Offering patterns and supplies for beginner to advanced crocheters.

TICKLE TEDS

44-5-503 Gonaka, Kagiya, Tokai, Aichi, 477-0032,
Japan ☎ +81 (0) 90 4087 6197
email: rei0101@hotmail.com
My bears will make you happy and cheerful. I hope to see you at the British Bear Awards in Hove.

TIN SOLDIERS STUDIO

South Africa
☎ +27 (0)83 305 5954 Fax: +27 (0)11 316 6166
email: soldier@lantic.net
web: www.tinsoldiers.co.za
One of a kind artist bears, specializing in miniature bears. Teddy bear kits and patterns. Polymer clay miniatures and accessories.

TOYS, STUFFED AND HANDMADE BY SUSAN

Proprietor: Susan Mansfield-Jones, 23 Sabrina Drive,
Toronto, Ontario, M9R 2J4, Canada
☎ +1 416 242 6446
Soft: mohair acrylic or polyfibres. Stuffed: buckshot, plastic pellets, foam limbs, polyester. Sculpture: 10cms-100cms height. Some sculpture includes growler or musicbox.

WINSOME & WILD ARTIST BEARS

11 Eclipse Drive, Albany, Western Australia, Australia
☎ +61 (0)8 9844 1956 Fax: +61 (0)8 9844 1956 (call first)
email: sallysimmons@westnet.com.au
web: www.winsomeandwild.com
Bears inspired by nostalgic times in early 1900's, always dressed using antique fabrics/accessories. Doleful faces 3" to 30".

END

PUBLISHING

This section is for gollies, dolls, animals and soft sculpture creations.

● ABCETA PLAYTHINGS LTD
19 Torkington Road, Stockport, SK7 4RG
☎ 0161 483 4500 Fax: 0161 456 6896
email: abceta.playthings@virgin.net
web: www.sashadolls.com
Please see display advertisement.

● ANTIQUE DOLLS & OLD BEARS
Tracie Lea Vallis, Central London NW6, appointments only.
☎ 0797 659 2898
email: tracie_l_vallis@btopenworld.com or teddy-bears87@hotmail.com
web: www.nadda.org
Antique Dolls are always available for sale. I buy early dolls (1700-1900). Insurance valuations given. By appointment, please call.

● BEDSPRING BEARS
6 Nottingham Place, Lee-On-Solent, Hampshire, PO13 9LZ
☎ 023 9260 2075 Fax: As tel.
email: bedspringbears@btopenworld.com
web: www.bedspringbears.com
Handcrafted artist bears, cats, gollies etc.

● JILL BENNETT
Mendip Lodge, 8 Bathwick Hill, Bath, Avon, BA2 6EW
☎ 01225 420828 Fax: 01225 427179
email: jill@bath-bennett.demon.co.uk
web: www.jillbennettdolls.co.uk
1/12th scale dolls and larger. Porcelain heads and wired to pose. Every character and historical periods. One-of-a-kind only.

● BURLINGTON BEARTIES
2 Ambergate Drive, Kingswinford, West Midlands, DY6 7HZ
☎ 01384 279731
email: bridgemark@bearties.freeserve.co.uk
Antique style realistic characters including cats, rabbits, foxes, rats, mice and pigs. All individually dressed in vintage clothing.

● CURTIS BRAE OF STRATFORD
32 Sheep Street, Stratford upon Avon, Warwickshire, CV37 6EE
☎ 01789 267277
email: sales@curtisbrae.co.uk
web: www.curtisbrae.co.uk
Collectable and traditional gollies and Russian dolls. Soft sculpture animals by Hansa Toys and Steiff. Beatrix Potter characters.

● DAY DREAM DOLLS & TEDDIES

142 - 144 Middlewich Road, Clive, Winsford, Cheshire, CW7 3NF

☎ 01606 592497

email: daydreamdolls@steggel.freeserve.co.uk

web: www.daydream-dolls.co.uk

Doll and teddy makers, hospital, courses. Stockists of Merrythought, Gund, Russ, Hansa. Plus own design bears, gollies, miniatures, limited editions.

● DIANE'S DOLLS! ANTIQUE & COLLECTABLE DOLLS

4 Dowland Gardens, High Green, Sheffield, South Yorkshire, S35 4GQ

☎ 0114 2846582

email: diane@dmcginley.com

web: www.dmcginley.com

Selling/buying antique/vintage dolls.

● DOLLS DESIGNS

Jane Woodbridge, 6 Newmans Gardens, Sompting, Lancing, West Sussex, BN15 0BD

☎ 01903 602988

email: dollywood@ntlworld.com

Dolls designs. 76 knitting patterns for dolls and teddies. Eight knitting books for dolls. Also fine needles.

● DOLLY DAYDREAMS

3 Titan House, Calleva Park, Aldermaston, Berkshire, RG7 8AA

☎ 0118 981 9924 Fax: 0118 981 9705

email: enquiries@dollydaydreams.net

web: www.dollydaydreams.net

Home to the largest stock of Artist Dolls in the South of England!

● FAIRYLAND BEARS

Unit 3, The Sloop Craft Market, St Ives, Cornwall, TR26 2TF

☎ 07720 957072 / 01736 799901

web: www.fairylandbears.co.uk

All of our collectable bears, fairies, wizards, dragons & gollies, really are a must have for all discerning collectors.

Your Business

can appear in

the next edition of the

UK Teddy Bear Guide

Contact Hugglets

Tel: +44 (0)1273 697974 Fax: +44 (0)1273 62 62 55

e.mail: info@hugglets.co.uk

Home to the largest selection of Artist Dolls in the South of England

www.dollydaydreams.net

3 Titan House, Calleva Park Aldermaston, Berkshire, RG7 8AA

Tel: 0118 981 9924

e-mail:
enquiries@dollydaydreams.net

● FLORIDIAN BEARS
48 Grange Road, Gillingham, Kent, ME7 2PU
☎ 01634 570331
email: ellen@floridianbears.co.uk
web: www.floridianbears.co.uk
Folkart style critters, primitive, grungy characters and seasonal treats to decorate your home handcrafted by Kent artist Ellen Johns.

● JUNE ROSE GALE
49 Cromwell Road, Beckenham, Kent, BR3 4LL
☎ 020 8658 1865
email: jr.gale@virgin.net
Original artists dolls. BDA member.

● GILL'S GOLLIES
101 Wainwright, Werrington, Peterborough, Cambridgeshire, PE4 5AH
☎ 01733 767202
email: gillsgollies@ntlworld.com
web: www.gillsgollies.co.uk
Tiny gollies with unique smiles!

● GOLLIES BY EVELYN MAY
'Hambledene', Brightlingsea Road, Thorrington, Colchester, Essex, CO7 8JH
☎ 01206 250341
email: evelynmay@freeuk.com
web: www.evesgollys.co.uk
Handmade character gollies for collectors.

● JANET CLARK ORIGINALS
61 Park Road, Hemel Hempstead, Hertfordshire, HP1 1JS
☎ 01442 265944 Fax: As tel.
email: JCTeddystyle@aol.com
web: www.janetclark.com
Please visit new website for bears, dolls, animals, patterns available. Classes online and hands on. Always new original characters.

Special Gollies

Handmade by Elaine Goodhand

www.petaloriginals.co.uk
email: elaine@petaloriginals.co.uk

Tel: 01372 724386

● JUST GOLLY COLLECTORS CLUB

60 Arundel Road, Littlehampton, West Sussex, BN17 7DF
☎ 01903 721070
email: justgolly@hotmail.com
Quarterly 24 page newsletter. News, views and information. Competitions with prizes. Covers all areas of golly collecting. SAE for details.

● LULLABYDOLLS

9 Chase Farm, Geddington, Kettering, Northamptonshire, NN14 1RA
☎ 01536 742325
email: carol@lullabydolls.co.uk
web: www.lullabydolls.co.uk
OOAK baby dolls sculpted modelene.

● LYNNE AND MICHAEL ROCHE

2 Lansdown Terrace, Lansdown Road, Bath, BA1 5EF
☎ 01225 318042 Fax: 01225 480723
email: lynne@roche-dolls.co.uk
web: www.roche-dolls.co.uk
Artist dolls - porcelain and wood.

● PETAL ORIGINALS

29 Lower Hill Road, Epsom, Surrey, KT19 8LS
☎ 01372 724386
email: elaine@petaloriginals.co.uk
web: www.petaloriginals.co.uk
Please see display advertisement.

● RECOLLECT - DOLLS & BEARS

17 Junction Road, Burgess Hill, West Sussex, RH15 0HR
☎ 01444 871052 Fax: As tel.
email: dollshopuk@aol.com
web: www.dollshospital.co.uk
All repairs to porcelain and composition dolls. Experienced 20 years. Old dolls bought & sold. Makers of dolls & moulds. Catalogue £3.

● SALLY B GOLLIES

12 Bridges Close, Wokingham, Berks, RG41 3XL
☎ 0118 9775464 Fax: 0118 9773228
email: zarir@btinternet.com
Snazzy jazzy funky crazy gollies.

● SHOEBUTTON BEARS

11 Southern Road, Sale, Cheshire, M33 6HP
☎ 0161 282 8636
email: sue_wilkes_uk@yahoo.com
web: www.shoebuttonbears.co.uk
Miniature bears, bunnies, cats, dogs and gollies. Exclusive designs available mail order.

● SNAZZY GOLLYS

60 Arundel Road, Littlehampton, West Sussex, BN17 7DF
☎ 01903 721070
email: gollyhouse@hotmail.com
Traditional and modern styles. One offs and small limited editions. Restoration service for overloved gollys. SAE or email for details.

● TEWIN'S BRUINS

16 Lower Green, Tewin, Welwyn, Hertfordshire, AL6 0LB
☎ 01438 718700 Fax: 01438 840411
email: tbrand@talk21.com
Terry Brand (BA) handmade collector bears, rabbits, dogs, cats, mice, gollies etc...

● **TOGGLE TEDDIES**
25 Laund Avenue, Belper, Derbyshire, DE56 1FL
☎ 01773 824258
email: wendi@toggleteddies.co.uk
web: www.toggleteddies.co.uk
Original handcrafted mohair bears. Primitive raggedy dolls using traditional homespun fabrics. By Wendi Walker.

● **WESTIE BEARS**
12 Norfolk Road, Horsham, West Sussex, RH12 1BZ
☎ 01403 241381 Fax: As tel.
email: andy@westiebears.com
web: www.westiebears.com
Wacky and punky mini bears, bunnies, monkeys and other critters. All one off pieces. Also bespoke work carried out.

● **GEORGINA WHALLEY**
Artist Signature Edition Dolls, 173 Allestree Lane, Allestree, Derby, DE22 2PG
☎ 01332 556880 Fax: As tel.
email: georgina.whalley@virgin.net
Artist Signature Edition porcelain dolls.

● **YESTERDAY CHILD**
David & Gisela Barrington, Paradise Cottage, 85 West Hill, Aspley Guise, Milton Keynes, MK17 8DU
☎ 01908 583403
email: djbarrington@btinternet.com
Antique dolls sold, bought, repaired.

● **ZENA ARTS**
82 Kent Road, Mapperley, Nottingham, Nottinghamshire, NG3 6BN
☎ 0115 960 5820 Fax: As tel.
email: zena@zena-arts.com
web: www.zena-arts.com
Harris Tweed bears, gollies, dolls, monkeys. Original designs, full of character. Fully jointed. New designs include cats and dolls.

END

www.hugglets.co.uk

You can discover a lot at the Hugglets website

 Welcome to the Hugglets World of Teddy Bears

Tell me about Hugglets Teddy Bear Festivals - including exhibitor lists

Tell me how to buy the Hugglets Teddy Bear Guide

Tell me about free electronic downloads of the Guide

Tell me about how my business can be in the Hugglets Teddy Bear Guide

Tell me how to contact Hugglets

Links to 2000 teddy bear sites   Secure ordering   Add or update contact details

 **Hugglets, PO Box 290, Brighton, BN2 1DR**

Tel: 01273 697974   Fax: 01273 62 62 55   Email: info@hugglets.co.uk

Website Index

Bayside Bears	- www.baysidebears.com
Bazil Bears	- www.bazilbears.co.uk
Beani Bears	- www.beanibears.com
Bear Bahoochie	- www.bearbahoochie.co.uk
Bear Basics	- www.bearbasics.co.uk
Bear Bits	- www.bearbits.com
Bear Bottoms	- www.bearbottoms.co.uk
Bear Bottoms	- www.bearsupplies.co.uk
Bear Corner	- www.bearcorner.co.uk
Bear Country	- www.bearcountryuk.com
Bear Crazee	- www.bearcrazee.com
Bear Cupboard	- www.thebearcupboard.co.uk
Bear Emporium	- www.bear-emporium.com
Bear Essentials	- www.bearessentials.co.nz
Bear Essentials (Ireland)	- www.irishbears.com
Bear Faced Cheek!®	- www.bearfacedcheek.co.uk
Bear Factory	- www.bearfactory.co.uk
Bear Gallery	- www.beargallery.co.uk
Bear Garden Company	- www.bear-garden.com
Bear Garden (Guildford), The	- www.beargarden.co.uk
Bear Huggery	- www.thebearhuggery.co.uk
Bear Leigh Made It©	- www.bearleigh.com
Bear Mania	- www.bearmania.com.au
Bear Museum, The	- www.bearmuseum.co.uk
Bear Necessities - Knarf-Bears	- www.thebearnecessities.be
Bear Paths	- www.bearpaths.com
Bear Shop Bolton	- www.bearshopbolton.co.uk
Bear Shop, Colchester, The	- www.bearshops.co.uk
Bear Shop, Totnes	- www.bearshop.co.uk
Bear Supplies Company	- www.bearsupplies.co.uk
Bear Today Shop	- www.beartoday.com
Bear Trading Company	- www.beartradingcompany.co.uk
Bear-a-thought	- www.bear-a-thought.co.uk
Bear-Faced Lies	- www.bear-faced-lies.com
Bearability by Kim	- www.bearability.co.uk
Bearable Bears	- www.bearablebears.nl
Bearable Friends	- www.bearablefriends.com
bearartistsofbritain.org	- www.bearartistsofbritain.org
Beargamin Bears	- www.beargaminbears.com
Bearhunt Bears	- www.bearhuntbears.co.uk
Bearitz	- www.bearitz.com
bearkidz	- www.bearkidz.com
Bearland Express	- www.dear-bears.com
Bearly Sane Bears	- www.bearlysanebears.com
Bearly There	- www.bearlythere.com
Bearly There Yorkshire	- www.bearlythere.co.uk
Bears 4 Hugs	- www.bears4hugs.com
Bears and Models Galore	- www.bearsandmodels.co.uk
Bears at the Real McCoy	- www.bearsattherealmccoy.co.uk
Bears at Wirk	- www.bearsatwirk.co.uk
Bears by Armella	- www.bearsbyarmella.net
bears by beesley TM	- www.bearsbybeesley.com
Bears by Design	- www.bears-by-design.com
Bears by Ece	- www.bearsbyece.com
Bears by Heather Jayne	- www.bearsbyheatherjayne.co.uk
Bears by Janet Steward	- www.janetsteward.co.uk
Bears by Maryke	- www.bearsbymaryke.co.uk
Bears by Susan Gam	- www.bearsbysusangam.com
Bears & Dolls (Miniatura)	- www.bearsdolls.com
Bears for Tea	- www.bears4t.com
Bears Galore	- www.bearsgalore.co.uk
Bears of my Heart	- www.bearsofmyheart.com
Bears of Rosehill	- www.bearsofrosehill.com

Bears of Windy Hill	- www.bearsofwindyhill.co.uk
Bears on the Square	- www.bearsonthesquare.com
Bears To Collect	- www.bearstocollect.co.uk
Bears upon Soar	- www.bearsuponsoar.co.uk
Bears Upon the River Nidd	- http://myweb.tiscali.co.uk/bearsuponrivernidd
bears4everyone	- www.bears4everyone.com
Bearsinc	- www.bearsinc.co.uk
BearsUwant Ltd	- www.bearsuwant.com
Bearwithlove.com	- www.bearwithlove.com
Beary Cheap Bear Supplies	- www.bearycheap.com
Beary Special Supplies	- www.woodlandteddies.co.uk
BearyWorks	- www.BearyWorks.com
Beatrix Bears	- www.beatrixbears.co.uk
BeauT Bears by Marianne	- www.beautbears.nl
Bebbin Bears	- www.bebbinbears.co.uk
Beckside Bears	- www.becksidebears.co.uk
Bedford Bears	- www.bedfordbears.co.uk
Bedspring Bears	- www.bedspringbears.com
Bee Antiques and Collectables	- www.oldteddybears.co.uk
Bees Knees Bears	- www.beeskneesbears.co.uk
Bel Air - Bournemouth	- www.belairgallery.co.uk
Benebears	- www.benebears.com
Benjamin Bears	- www.benjaminbears.org
Bennett, Jill	- www.jillbennettdolls.co.uk
Benthall Bears	- www.benthallbears.co.uk
Berenatelier Duimelotje	- www.duimelotje.be
Bertie Bear and Friends	- www.bertiebear.co.uk
Best Dressed Bears	- www.bestdressedbears.com.au
Beverley McKenzie Originals	- www.beverleymckenzie.com
Billy Buff Bears	- www.billybuffbears.com
Bine's Bärenauslese	- www.binesbaerenauslese.de
Bisson Bears	- www.bissonbears.com
Black Forest Bears	- www.myblackforestbears.com
Blossom Teddies	- www.blossomteddies.com
Bluebeary Bears	- www.bluebearybears.co.uk
Bluemoon Bears	- www.bluemoonbear-uk.com
Bobbys Bears	- www.bobbysbears.com
Bonhams	- www.bonhams.com/toys
Born Again Bears	- www.bornagainbears.co.uk
Bourton Bears	- www.bourtonbears.com
BowJangle Bears	- www.bowjanglebears.com
Box Bears	- www.boxbears.co.uk
Box Your Bears	- www.boxyourbears.co.uk
Bradgate Bears	- www.bradgatebears.co.uk
Bradley Bears	- www.bradleybears.co.uk
Brambly Bears	- www.bramblybears.co.uk
Bramley Bears	- www.bramleybears.co.uk
Braveheart Bears	- www.braveheartbears.co.uk
Brentwood Bears	- www.brentwoodbears.com
Brewers Bruins	- www.BrewersBruins.com
Briddy Bears	- www.briddy-bears.de
Bridget's Bears	- www.bridgetsbears.ukgateway.net
Bridon Bears & Friends	- www.bbears.fsnet.co.uk
Brigit's Bears	- www.iinet.net.au/~bears
British Bear Collection	- www.thebritishbearcollection.co.uk
British Bears on the Net	- www.britishbearsonthenet.co.uk
British Toymakers Guild	- www.toymakersguild.co.uk
Brodie Bears	- www.brodiebears.co.uk
Brotherwood Bears	- www.brotherwoodbears.com
Bryony Bears	- www.bryonybears.com
Brys Bruins Bears	- www.brysbruins.com
Buckie Bears	- www.buckiebears.co.uk
Buff 'n' Co. Bears	- www.buff-n-co.com

Bunky Bears - www.BunkyBears.co.uk
burlingtonbears.com - www.burlingtonbears.com
Burtonian Bears - www.burtonianbears.co.uk
C & M's Bearhugs - www.bearhugs.co.uk
Cala Bear Den - www.calabear.ca
Cameo Bears - www.cameobears.co.uk
Candi Bears - www.candibears.bravehost.com
Canna Bear Paint - www.cannabearpaint.com
Canterbury Bears - www.canterburybears.co.uk
Carmichael Bears - www.carmichaelbears.co.uk
Ce Gifts & Bears - www.cegifts.co.uk
Cees Bears - www.ceesbears.com
Celtic Companions - www.celtic-companions.co.uk
Changle Bears - www.changlebears.homestead.com
Channel Island Toys - www.channel-teddy.co.uk
Chantal's Bears Creations - www.mignonettestitch.com/chantalbears.htm
Character Bears - www.characterbears.co.uk
Charlie Bear - www.charliebear.co.uk
Charlie Bears Ltd - www.charliebears.com
Charnwood Bears - www.thehouseofbruin.co.uk
Chatham Village Bears L.L.C. - www.chathamvillagebears.com
Cheltenham Bears - www.cheltenhambears.co.uk
China Cupboard Bears - www.teddybeargallery.com/cindymcguire.html
Christie Bears Limited - www.christiebears.co.uk
Christie's - www.christies.com
Christine Pike Bears - www.christinepike.com
Christmas Angels - www.christmasangels.co.uk
Christy's Bears - http://christyfirmage.com/
Clayton Bears - www.claytonbears.co.uk
Clemens Bears of Germany - www.clemens.de
Collector's Bears by Helga Torfs - www.collectorsbears.com
Companion Bears - www.elainelonsdale.com
Conradi Creations - www.conradicreations.com
Cooni Bears - www.cooni-bears.de
Cornelia Bears - Holland - www.corneliabears.com
Cornwall and Devon Bear Fairs - www.emmarybears.co.uk
Cornwall Bear Shops - www.cornwallbearshop.co.uk
Cotswold Bear Company, The - www.thecotswoldbearco.com
Cousin, Aline - http://cousin.aline.free.fr
Cowslip Bear Company - www.cowslipbears.co.uk
Creations Past - www.dollshousewallpaper.co.uk
Crossfoot Bears - www.crossfootbears.co.uk
Cuddy Lugs - www.cuddylugs.com
Curio Bears by Debbie Robinson - www.curiobears.com
Curiosity Corner - www.curiosity-corner.com
Curtis Brae of Stratford - www.curtisbrae.co.uk
Cymruted Collectable Bears - www.cymruted.com
Daisa Original Designs Ltd - www.theoriginalreikibear.com
Daisa Original Designs Ltd - www.itsadodl.com
Dari Laut Bears - www.dari-laut-bears.co.uk
Dawdle Bears - www.dawdlebears.com
Dawn, Dusk & Midnight - www.ddmbears.co.uk
Day Dream Dolls & Teddies - www.daydream-dolls.co.uk
Dean's Rag Book Company Ltd - www.deansbears.com
der Bär - www.der-baer-stock.com
Diane's Dolls! Antique & Collectable Dolls - www.dmcginley.com
Die Wuschelbären - www.wuschelbaer.com
Do Do Bears - www.dodobears.com
Dolly Daydreams - www.dollydaydreams.net
Dolly Domain of South Shields - www.dollydomain.com
Dolly Land - www.dolly-land.co.uk
Dolly's Daydreams - www.dollysdaydreams.com

New England Country Store - www.newenglanddirect.co.uk
No 9 Paws for Thought - www.no9pawsforthought.com
Noble Bears - www.noblebears.co.uk
Norbeary - www.norbeary.co.uk
Nottingham Bear Fairs - www.nottinghambearfair.co.uk
Oakley Fabrics Ltd - www.oakleyfabrics.co.uk
Occasions Unlimited - www.occasions-unlimited.com
Oggie Bears - www.pittypatspoppets.com
Okidoki Original - www.okidokioriginal.com
Old Bear Company Ltd, The - www.oldbearcompany.com
Old Bears Network - www.oldbearsnetwork.co.uk
Old Playroom, The - www.dawnpotter.com
Old Time Teddies - www.marjoleinediemel.nl
Old Toys Vienna - www.oldtoys.info
Oldbearscene.com - www.oldbearscene.com
Olde Teddy Bear Shoppe - www.theoldeteddybearshoppe.com
Oldenbears - www.oldenbears.co.uk
Oops! Pardon me, Bears! - http://eileenwood.bta.com/oops
Orchard Bears - www.orchardbears.com
Original Felted Folksies - www.originalfeltedfolksies.com
Original Hanna Baeren - www.hanna-baeren.de
Original Rica-Bear - www.rica-bear.de
Out 'n About Bears - http://outnaboutbears.mysite.wanadoo-members.co.uk
Oz Matilda Bears - www.ozmatilda.com.au
Pamela Ann Designs - www.cambridgebears.co.uk
Parnell, Josephine - www.dollshousebears.free-online.co.uk
Paw Lines Bears - www.pawlinesbears.co.uk
Paw Prints of Staffordshire - www.pawprints.org.uk
Peacock Fibres Ltd - www.noblecraft.co.uk
Pearson, Sue - www.suepearson.co.uk
Pearson, Sue - www.sue-pearson.co.uk
Pebble Beach Bears - www.pebblebeachbears.co.uk
Peculiar Pal's Bears & other animals - www.peculiar-pals.co.uk
Peggotty – The Teddy House - www.peggotty.f9.co.uk
Peng Peng Bears - www.peng-peng.com
Petal Originals - www.petaloriginals.co.uk
Phred's Friends - www.phredsfriends.co.uk
Piece Parade, The - www.pieceparade.com
Pipsqueak and Pepe-Joe Bears - http://pages.zoom.co.uk/dianelouisa
PittyPats Poppets - www.pittypatspoppets.com
Pixel's Bears - www.pixelsbears.com
pmbears - www.pmbears.com
Pooh Corner - www.pooh-country.co.uk
Portobello Bear Company - www.portobellobearco.com
Postal Bears - www.postalbears.co.uk
Potbelly Bears - www.potbellybears.com
Pottershouse Bears - www.pottershousebears.com
Pottery Plus - www.members.aol.com/pottplus/index.html
Probär GmbH - www.probear.com
Puca Bears - www.puca-bears.de
Puppenhausmuseum - www.puppenhausmuseum.ch
Puzzle Bears - www.puzzlebears.com
Quinn, Sue - www.bearsbysuequinn.co.uk
QVC - www.qvcuk.com
R B Bear Supplies - www.bearsupplies.com
R.E.R. Bears - www.elizabethrosecreations.co.uk
R. John Wright Dolls, Inc. - www.rjohnwright.com
Raffles - www.rafflesgiftcollection.co.uk
Rainbow Dyes - www.rainbowdyes.ukart.com
Rainey Days - www.raineydays.biz
Recollect - www.dollshospital.co.uk
Remem-bear Artist Bears - www.remembear.com

Restoration - www.bear-hugs.co.uk
Rêves d'Ours - www.revesdours.com
Roberta Kasnick Ripperger... - www.beyond-basic-bears.com
Robyn's Bears & Bouquets - www.robyns-bears.com.au/repairs/index.php
Rosie's Attic - www.rosiesattic.co.uk
Rosy Posy Bears - www.rosyposybears.co.uk
Round About Bears - www.roundaboutbears.co.uk
Running Bear Company - www.runningbearcompany.de
Russian Teddy Bear - www.teddybear.ru
Sad Pads - www.sadpadbears.com
Sally Anne Bears - www.sallyannebears.co.uk
Sally B Bears - www.sally-b-bears.co.uk
Salon Gueules de Miel - www.salonagdm.com
Sandykay Bears - www.sandykaye.ws
Sarah's Bruins - www.sarahsbruins.co.uk
Scruffie Bears by Susan Pryce - www.scruffiebears.com
SelecTeds - www.selecteds.com
Serendipity - www.tedshop.com
Seventh Heaven Teddies - www.seventhheaventeddies.com
Shantock Bears - www.shantockbears.com
Sharon Grace's Bears - www.sharongrace.co.nz
Shelinka Bears - www.shelinkabears.com
Shellysbears - www.shellysbears.co.uk
Shoebutton Bears - www.shoebuttonbears.co.uk
Showcase - www.showcaseonline.co.uk
Shultz Characters - www.paulastrethill-smith.com
Sidmouth Bears - www.sidmouthbears.com
Snuff Box (est 1984) - www.snuffboxonline.co.uk
Southsea Bears - www.southseabears.com
Southway Bears - www.southwaybears.co.uk
Spielmittel - www.bearsandtoys.de
Spielzeugdesign - www.annette-rauch.com
St Ann's Dolls Hospital - www.dollshospital.freeserve.co.uk
St Martin's Gallery - www.stmartinsartandcraftcentre.com
Stanley Bears - www.stanleybears.com.au
Starlite Bears - www.starlitebears.co.uk
Steiff Club UK - www.steiff-club.de
Steiff Gallery - www.steiff-gallery.co.uk
Stine-Teddies - www.stine-teddies.dk
Streetbrooke Bear - www.streetbrookebear.co.uk
Sue Gibson Bears - www.sue-gibson-teddy-bears.com
Sue's Teds - http://suesteddybears.mysite.wanadoo-members.co.uk
Suffolk Bears by Shirley - www.suffolkbears.com
Sun Moon Bears - www.sunmoonbears.co.uk
Swannbeary Bears - www.swannbearybears.co.uk
Sycamore Bears - www.sycamorebears.co.uk
Talents of Windsor - www.etalents.com
Teachers Pets - www.teacherspetsonline.co.uk
Ted's Place - www.tpcollectable.com
Teddeez Bear Co - www.hugsters.com
Teddy Bear Club - www.teddybearclub.co.uk
Teddy Bear Club International - www.planet-teddybear.com
Teddy Bear House - www.teddybearhouse.co.uk
Teddy Bear Orphanage - www.teddybearorphanage.co.uk
Teddy Bear Scene - www.teddybearscene.co.uk
Teddy Bear Shop - www.teddybearshuddersfield.co.uk
Teddy Bear UK - www.teddy-bear-uk.com
Teddy Bears At Home - www.teddybearsathome.zoomshare.com
Teddy Bears Cottage - www.teddybearscottage.co.uk
Teddy Bears & Friends of Bourne - www.bournebears.co.uk
Teddy Bears of Witney - www.teddybears.co.uk
Teddy Bears' Picknick - www.teddybearspicknick.com
Teddy Bearsville - www.teddybearsville.info

END

PUBLISHING

Bear Business Phone Directory

A

A Better Class of Bear 01189 713182
A.C. Bears 01294 271389
A Hitchcock Bear 07773 296740
A Lanie Bears UK 01952 641643
Abbey Bears 01736 798586
Abceta Playthings Ltd 0161 483 4500
Rose Abdalla 020 7482 1911
Abelia Bears 01992 478229
Abracadabra Teddy Bears 01799 527222
Absolutely Bear.... . . . . 01622 691760
Actually Bears by Jackie. 01449 675951
Admiral Bears Supplies 01372 813558
Adorable Bears . . . . +61 (0)3 5821 9979
Alderson Bears 01773 850078
Alexander Bears 01322 337797
Alice Bears. . . . . +(852) 9243 3326
Alice's Bear Shop. 01297 444589
Alice's Wonderland. 01697 473025
Alicia's Zizbears 01932 854499
All Bear by Paula Carter. 01622 686970
All Occasions. 01684 566781
All Things Angelic 01252 690073
All Things Beary 0131 477 6970
All You Can Bear. 020 8368 5491
Allsorts of bears. 01263 514111
Always Bearing in Mind 01494 437238
Amber, Dolls, Bears... . . . . 01252 727722
AngieBears 01634 253165
Ann_Knits 4 Bears 02380 846987
Ann Made Bears. 020 8202 3165
Anna Koetse's Bears. . . . . +31 (0)23 5472048
Annie Davis 01531 634548
Antique Bear Collector . . . . +1 770 834 9599
Antique Dolls & Old Bears. 0797 659 2898
Apis Bears 0151 638 8079
Apple Pie House Ltd 01531 635290
Apples 'n' Bears 01553 765559
Appletree Bears 01925 263456
Arbury Bears. 024 7674 1453
Arctophilia 01795 597770
Arcturus Bears 0151 691 1297
Art2Heart. 01305 775597
Artig & frech . . . . +49 (0)201 765 125
Arundel Teddy Bears 01903 884458
Ashby Bears... . . . . 01530 564444
Ashway Bears 01604 889150
Asquiths. 01753 831200
Asquiths 01491 571978
Atlantic Bears 01445 712179
Aurorabearealis 01463 731470
Auscraft Publications 01488 649955
Avon Bearmakers. 01454 228167

B

B. A. Bears. 01782 318043
B.E.A.R. Fairs 07836 730719
B&B with Bear Bits. 01507 578360
Ba's Bears 01865 435314
Baba Bears. 0845 257 6091
Bacton Bears. 01449 781087
Baggaley Bears 0115 8757 031
Baggies Bears 020 8658 4093
Bagster Bears 01603 632085
Balfour Bears. 01382 624605
Balu Bears . . . . +49 (0)531 342690
Bamsernes Magasin. . . . . +45 46 35 78 45
Bar Street Bears 01723 353636
Bäradies . . . . +49 (0)8145 998 700
Barbara-Ann Bears 01303 269038
Bare Bears 01506 834233
BärenBande . . . . +49 (0)17 57 57 53 88
Bärenboutique . . . . +49 (0)7222 50 60 15
Bärenhäusl Ositos.... . . . . +49 (0)80 61 34 33 10
Barling Bears. 01732 845059
Barney Bears. 01702 472636
Barnwell Bears 01244 380422
Barricane Bears. 01271 866871
Barton Bears 0151 639 1236
Bay Bears 01524 824537
Bay Bears of Herne Bay. 01227 374034
Bayside Bears . . . . +1 508 896 5350
Bazil Bears 0208 3301193
Beani Bears of Lichfield 01543 444784
Bear Bahoochie 01324 411823
Bear Bits 01507 578360
Bear Bottoms 0191 383 2922
Bear Corner. 01733 252408
Bear Country 0114 287 9671
Bear Crazee 01226 725390
The Bear Cupboard 01376 563739
The Bear Emporium. 01142 482010
The Bear Emporium. 01142 482010
Bear Essentials . . . . +64 (0)9 630 8479
Bear Essentials (Ireland) . . . . . +353 (0)49 95 23461
Bear Faced Cheek!®. 020 8421 6507
The Bear Factory 0870 333 2458
Bear Friends 015395 68570
Bear Gallery 02870 831010
Bear Garden Company . . . . . . +886 (0)2 8866 5587
The Bear Garden. 01483 302581
The Bear Garden 020 8974 6177
Bear Huggery 01624 676333

Bear in Mind 01304 366234
Bear Lee Cottage. 01798 872707
Bear Mania . . . . +61 (0)8 8188 0166
The Bear Museum 01730 265108
Bear Necessities/Knarf.... . . . . +32 (0)5034 1027
The Bear Patch 01335 342391
Bear Paths. . . . . +1 216 566 1519
Bear Pawtraits 0780 3780050
Bear Shop Bolton. 01204 381937
Bear Shop 01206 577345
Bear Shop 01603 766866
Bear Shop (Totnes) 01803 866868
Bear Supplies Company 0191 383 2922
Bear Trading Company. 01323 491816
Bear-a-thought. 01207 563220
Bear-Faced Lies. 01398 324688
Bearability by Kim 01937 844030
Bearable Bears. . . . . +31 (0)55 5788067
Bearable Friends 01442 267328
bearartistsofbritain.org 07725 640179
Bearbury of London 020 8392 2625
Bearcraft Bear Company 0191 3711162
Beargamin Bears. . . . . +61 (0)3 9436 6871
Beargorrah! 01206 564472
Bearhunt Bears 07764 759703
Bearitz. 01828 670561
Bearland Express . . . . +1 604 872 2508
Bearly Sane Bears. 01752 403515
Bearly There 01384 236532
Bearly There Yorkshire 08700 272825
Bearly Trading of London. 0208 466 6696
Bearnard Bears 0208 655 7176
Bears 4 Hugs. 01967 421308
Bears Abundant. . . . . +1 416 493 2944
Bears and Models Galore. 01255 436195
Bears at the Real McCoy . . . . . +44 (0)28 2588 2262
Bears at Wirk 01629 822898
Bears by Armella . . . . +1 319 377 5869
bears by beesley™ . . . . +1866 467 3494
Bears by Bobbi 0141 554 7917
Bears by Design 01235 534536
Bears by Eunice 020 8205 6308
Bears by Hand. 01536 461159
Bears by Heather Jayne. 01526 860321
Bears by Janet Steward 01728 685743
Bears by Julia 01206 386654
Bears by Maryke. 077 0224 4922
Bears by Susan Gam. 01708 760021
Bears by Susan Jane. 01376 521230
The Bears Den 01709 828619
Bears & Dolls (Miniatura) 0121 783 9922
Bears Extraordinaire 01275 851999
Bears Galore 01797 223187
Bears in the Brambles 01709 815733
Bears of Grace 01480 385445
Bears of my Heart 01786 823344
Bears of Rosehill 01633 244554
Bears of Windy Hill. 01274 599175

Bears on the Square 01952 433924
Bears Paw Collectables. 0116 274 1441
Bears & Stitches 01394 388999
Bears To Collect. 01480 860376
Bears Unlimited 01590 670536
Bears upon Soar 01509 813203
Bears Upon the River Nidd. 01423 541366
Bears With Attitude 01332 865846
bears4everyone 01943 468444
Bearsinc 07710 465 168
BearsUwant Ltd 01793 706662
Beartifacts 07816 185707
Beary Cheap...Supplies . . . . . . +61 (0)7 5520 3455
Beary Special Supplies 01509 267597
Bearzone 01962 734524
Beatrix Bears. 01743 340276
Beau Bear 0208 7881052
BeauT Bears . . . . +31 (0)610 623 559
Bebbin Bears. 01296 423755
Bebes et Jouets 0131 332 5650
Beckside Bears 01526 323312
Bedford Bears 01767 318626
Bedraggle Bears™. 0117 9497389
Bedspring Bears 023 9260 2075
Bee Antiques... . . . . 01843 864040
Bees Knees Bears 01902 843124
Bel Air - Bournemouth 01202 298990
Bel Air - Meadowhall. 0114 256 9990
Bell Bears. 020 8778 0217
Belly Button Bears 01487 842538
Ben Design 01889 560195
Benebears. 01428 605972
Benjamin Bears 01634 832523
Benji's Bears 01782 320913
Jill Bennett. 01225 420828
Benthall Bears 01952 883779
Berenatelier Duimelotje. . . . . . . +32 (0)9 2314365
Bertie Bear and Friends 01873 880076
Bessy Bears 01931 716262
Best Dressed Bears. . . . . +61 (0)3 9449 0944
Best Friends 01384 897699
Beverley McKenzie... . . . . 01908 695430
Bexi Bears. 01622 884218
Big Softies 01943 600997
Big Tree Bears 0115 952 4022
Bilbo Bears. 0161 794 7931
Billy Buff Bears 01422 885059
Billy Bumpkin Bears 01244 534857
Bine's Bärenauslese . . . . +49 (0)2597 98139
Bisson Bears 01524 735014
BJ Bears 01452 547562
Black Forest Bears. . . . . +1 864 228 0359
Blakemere TB Festival 01606 888814
Blossom Teddies. 028 207 42927
Bluebeary Bears 01202 675735
Bluemoon Bears 0161 727 8170
Bobbys Bears 01257 232636
Bodkin Bears 01453 844551

Bolebridge Bears 01827 59097
Bonhams 08700 273627
Born Again Bears 01329 313786
Bourton Bears 01993 824756
Bowden's Bears 01925 268533
BowJangle Bears 01562 862892
Box Bears 07956 555230
Box Your Bears 01462 626567
Bracken Bears 01580 200306
Bradgate Bears 0116 287 0897
Bradley Bears 01406 373073
Brambly Bears 01829 770881
Bramley Bears 01622 843556
Brauronia Bears 01489 559318
Braveheart Bears 01379 678704
Brentwood Bears . . . . +61 (0)7 5520 5191
Brewer's Bruins . . . . +1 704 637 3206
Briddy Bears . . . . +49 (0)8153 3714
Bridget's Bears 020 8689 4091
Bridgwater Bears 01473 412066
Bridon Bears & Friends 01308 420796
Brigit's Bears . . . . +61 (0)8 9572 4125
British Bear Collection 01934 822263
British Bear Fair 01895 834348
British Toymakers Guild 01225 442440
Broadway Bears 01386 854645
Brodie Bears 01294 468532
Brooklyn Bears 01604 891585
Brotherwood Bears 01249 760284
Brow Bears 01229 467861
Bryony Bears 01245 264651
Brys Bruins Bears 01775 840916
Buckie Bears 01542 835639
Buff 'n' Co. Bears 01246 569393
Bumble Bears 023 80 326663
Bunky Bears 01636 678724
Bunty Bears 01392 851448
Burl's Bears 01606 888814
Burley Bears 01202 571867
Burlington Bearties 01384 279731
burlingtonbears.com 01243 602654
Burtonian Bears 01283 550074
Butlers Bears 01939 210672

C

C & M's Bearhugs 0115 916 3731
Cala Bear Den . . . . +1 204 257 6003
Cameo Bears 01772 627810
Candi Bears 01563 830729
Canna Bear Paint . . . . +1 (585) 425 0567
Canterbury Bears 01227 728630
Cariad Bears 01745 859487
Carmichael Bears 01928 563874
Causeway House Crafts 01433 620343
Ce Gifts & Bears 01629 814811
Cees Bears 01522 800942
Cejais Collectors Corner 024 76 633630
Celtic Companions 01294 471760

Chambears 01708 449370
Changle Bears . . . . +27 (0)43 735 4216
Channel Island Toys 01481 723871
Chantal's Bears Creations . . . . +1 506 642 9788
Chapple Bears 01736 755577
Character Bears 0870 241 3798
Charlie Bear 0870 760 7351
Charlie Bears Ltd 0113 2842742
Charlie's Furs & Features 01606 888814
Charnwood Bears 01509 844002
Chatham Village Bears . . . . +1 314 739 8426
Cheltenham Bears 07905 307859
Cherry's Chums 07885 710630
Chesney Designs 01524 733152
Chester Bears 01978 855604
China Cupboard Bears . . . . +1 740 387 7742
The Chocolate Box 01484 688222
Christie Bears Limited 01656 789054
Christie's 020 7752 3335
Christine Pike Bears 01983 403224
Christmas Angels 01904 639908
Chubby Cubs 01623 407988
Dawn Clarke 01455 230823
Clayton Bears 01765 608797
Clemens Bears of Germany 01246 269723
Collect-Teds 0113 286 7372
Collector's Bears by Helga Torfs . +32 (0)14 30 32 08
Companion Bears 0161 976 1877
Conradi Creations 020 8671 2794
Cooni Bears . . . . +49 (0)23 02 89 407
Cornelia Bears . . . . +31 (0)70 32 95 857
Cornwall & Devon...Fairs 01208 872251
Cornwall Bear Shops 01503 265441
Cornwall Bear Shops 01872 225545
Cotswold Bear Co 01684 564310
Aline Cousin . . . . +33 (0)1 43 04 38 03
Lizzie Cove 01603 717050
Coventry Bears 07947 066675
Cowslip Bear Company 01202 382073
Creations Past 01905 820792
Crossfoot Bears 01228 561892
Crotchety Bears 01562 752289
Cuddy Lugs 01837 840762
Curio Bears 01929 471225
Curiosity Corner 01787 248441
Curiosity of Dover 01304 202621
Curtis Brae... 01789 267277
Cymruted... . . . . 01745 336844
Cynnaman Restoration... . . . . 01268 754184
Cynnaman...Bears 01268 754184

D

Daisa Originals 01652 661881
Daisy Bears 020 8715 4274
Daphne Fraser's...Hospital 0141 776 1281
Dari Laut Bears 01424 754418
Dawdle Bears 01494 713250
Dawn, Dusk & Midnight 020 8579 0360

Day Dream Dolls & Teddies 01606 592497
Dean's Rag Book Company 01981 240966
Deb Canham . . . . +1 941 480 1200
der Bär . . . . +49 (0)2173 60428
Devon Bear Repairs 01803 782654
Diane Hanley Bears 0191 386 7290
Diane's Dolls! 0114 2846582
Anna Dickerson 01603 759647
Die Wuschelbären . . . . +49 (0)3391 5052 72
Do Do Bears 01206 524261
Doll & Teddy Fairs 01530 274377
Dolls, Bears & Bygones 01726 61392
Dolls Designs 01903 602988
Dolls House Plus 01424 432275
Dolly Daydreams 0118 981 9924
Dolly Domain 0191 42 40 400
Dolly Land 020 8360 1053
Dolly Mixtures 0121 422 6959
Dolly's Daydreams 01945 870160
Doodlebears 01296 397082
Dorset TB Museum 01305 266040
Dot Bird 01765 607131
Dragonslair Bears 01271 862180
Drawing the Web 01303 269038
Dreamtime . . . . 020 8842 2327 (Bear)
Driftwood Bears . . . . +61 (0)7 4945 4245
Drury Bears 01732 364042
Véronique Dubosc . . . . +33 (0)5 56 51 04 65
Duchess Court/Bear Island 01770 302831
Dufeu-Bears . . . . +49 (0)208 3 23 88
durrerBears and more . . . . +61 (0)8 9368 1557
DustyBear 01458 851404

E

E. J. Bears 01992 714354
East Midlands Doll Fairs 01477 534626
Ebor Growlers 01904 704966
Eddy Bears 01394 670555
Edward Bears 0161 217 0668
Mark Egan 01303 265248
Elderbears 023 8077 2977
Elizabeth Bears 01206 844598
Elizbet Bears 01633 615208
Ellie-Bears 01268 762438
Emmary Bears 01208 872251
Enchanted Place Bears 01326 210462
Eskole Noombas . . . . +65 6545 5904
Especially Bears Ltd 01622 690939
Essential Bears . . . . +27 (0)21 685 3487
Essex Bear Fair 01279 871110
Evolution Bears 0151 678 9452
Exmoor Teddy Bear Co 01643 821170
Exmoor Teddy Bear Co 01392 499044
Exmoor Teddy Bear Co 01278 450500
Exmoor Teddy Bear Co 01643 702333

F

Peter Fagan 01289 330637

Fair Bears 01909 564472
Fairyland Bears 07720 957072
FairyTales Inc . . . . +1 630 495 6909
Farnborough Bears 01252 543454
Fauds & Gibbles 01343 850609
Fenbears 01406 371509
Ferndown Gallery 01202 861186
Fine and Dandy Bears 01476 550079
Floridian Bears 01634 570331
Flutter-By Bears 01782 560136
Flying Horse Originals 023 9273 6634
Folie Bears 01628 822323
Fool's Gold Bears . . . . +1 707 442 2084
Forest Glen Bears 07967 972611
Fountain Fayres... . . . . 01454 414671
Fred-I-Bear . . . . +27 (0) 83 2500378
Furried Treasures 01294 558792
Futch Bears 01277 219032

G

G & T Evans Woodwool 01686 622100
G-Rumpy Bears 020 8275 0693
June Rose Gale 020 8658 1865
Gallery Fifty Five 020 8441 4920
Garrington Bears 01622 685194
Gazelle 01524 68765
Gemstone Bears 01637 877743
The Georgian Window 01249 750413
Geraldine's of Edinburgh 0131 556 4295
GermanBears.com . . . . +1 801 796 9888
Gertie Wiggins . . . . +353 (0)24 96811
Gift Concepts Ltd 020 7016 2713
Gift Shop @ Lochlorian 01241 852182
The Gift 01636 610075
Gill's Gollies 01733 767202
Gingerbread Bears 07951 194177
Gizmo Bears . . . . +27 (0)31 562 0709
The Glass Eye Co 01492 642220
Glevum Bears 01452 521672
Gold Teddy 01924 420272
Goldilocks 01425 403558
Gorge Bear Company 01934 743333
Grace Daisy Bears 01256 476140
Granville Bears 01684 565703
Greenleaf Bears 01543 877343
Jo Greeno 01483 224312
Gregory Bear 01932 243263
Greta May Antiques 01732 366730
Grizzly Business 01323 870836
Growlers Teddybears 01392 219917
Guernsey...Publications 01481 266223
Gumdrop Editions 01736 787370
Gund (UK) Limited 01772 629292
Gyll's Bears 0208 366 1836

H

H M Bears 01524 733152
Hairy Beary Company 01995 600912

Halcyon 01803 314958
Hamilton Toy Collection 018773 30004
Hamleys of London 020 7479 7308
Hampshire TB Fair 01279 871110
Hampton Bears 01453 872615
Hand Glass Craft 01384 573410
Hanna Bruce . . . . +1-877-7BEARMD
Hardy Bears 01590 670615
Harlequin Collectables 01244 325767
Harmony Crystal Bears 01636 672147
Hartrick Bear Company 01286 870761
Leanda Harwood 01529 300737
Hausser Marketing UK 01706 848670
Haven Bears 01928 788313
Hazelwood Bears 01342 712413
Heart 'n' Soul Bears 01482 871016
Heartfelt Bears . . . . +61 (0)3 5964 7964
Hegarty Bears 01425 672883
Heikes Kringelbären . . . . +49 (0)62 53 60 80 04
Helens Huggables 0789 981 5762
A Helmbold GmbH . . . . +49 (0)36946 22009
Hembury Bears 01364 643758
Hen Nest . . . . +1 334 696 3480
Heritage Bear Company 01556 690595
Hildegard Gunzel Bears 01246 269723
Hilltop Toys 01722 712265
Hoblins 01772 635516
Glenn Holden 0121 580 3423
Holdingham Bears 01529 303266
Holly Bears 01889 568848
Homebrewed Bears . . . . +64 (0)9 630 9232
Honey Hill Bears 01366 383550
Honey Pot Bears 02392 472455
Honey Teddy . . . . +7 3422 16 74 75
Honeymead Bears 01638 730484
Hoo Bears 01905 381456
Horty Bears 01782 642889
Hovvigs . . . . +45 5991 3494
Hug-A-Boo Bears 01460 72740
The Hugging Bear Inn . . . . +1 802 875 2412
Hugglets 01273 697974
Huggy Bears UK 01623 458514
Humble-Crumble 01702 715383
Huni B's 01691 774070
Huntersfield Bears 01209 711557
Hutton Bears 01784 453037
Hyefolk 01303 277925

I

ideenwerkstatt machl keg . . . . . . +43 (0)732 946159
Ineke's Teddybears 01271 864689
Inge Bears . . . . +27 (0)721104273
Ironbridge Gorge...shop 01952 433029
Irvine Bears 01302 782903

J

J. C. W. Bears... . . . . 01268 726558
J R Bears 01460 55461

Jabelow Bears 01353 659631
Jac-q-Lyn Bears 01260 224257
Jac-q-Lyn's...shop 01538 388831
Jammy Bears 023 8044 9797
Jan's Tiddy Bears 07889 794637
Janbu Bears 01782 251790
Janet Clark Originals 01442 265944
JanNetty's Bears 01372 813558
Japan TB Association . . . . +81 (0)3 5726 4484
Jarrold Department Store 01603 697253
Jasco Bears 01704 539324
Jaysart 01684 773333
Jeanne Toys 01204 495583
Jeannette - Teddies Galore 0208 958 6101
Jenny Scott's 015242 51122
Jester Bears 01752 704625
Jewelfire Bears 07904 235821
Jo Bears by Jo Nevill 01795 874557
Jo Jo Creations Ltd 01376 339080
Jo-Anne Bears 01621 815049
Jodi Bears 01254 201177
Jodie's Bears . . . . +81 (0)466 25 1202
Joy Bears 01723 354419
Joybunnys Art Designs 07971 076259
Ju-Beary Bears 01268 525775
Judy Bear Productions 01942 716367
Julz Bearz 01606 810667
Just Bears 01260 291188
Just Bears by Denise 01440 762847
Just Bears @ Inspirations 01792 472737
Just Bears Rubber Stamps 01302 743811

K

K M Bears 0113 2192651
Karen Alderson... . . . . +61 (0)3 5968 1100
Karin Kronsteiner . . . . +43 (0)316 83 91 82
Kay Turmeau 0118 978 6267
Kaysbears 01474 351757
Kaytkins 01933 355782
Kaz Bears 01332 731948
Kazual Bears . . . . +61 (0)7 5539 2404
Keepsakes 01724 851080
Kershy Bears 01706 357652
Kevinton Bears 07957 333044
Martin Kidman 01273 842938
Kieron James 01444 484870
Kikisams 01832 275314
Kimbearleys 01952 825927
Kindertruhe . . . . +43 (0)1 523 33 83
Kingston Bears 01425 470422
Kingswear Bears.. . . . . 01803 752632
Knutty Bears 01626 863032
Kösen UK 01494 674872

L

L J Bears 01590 676517
L'Ours du Marais . . . . +33 (0)1 42 77 60 43
Laal Bears 01772 315342

Latimer of Bewdley. 01299 404000	Mawspaws. 01296 338338
Lavender Bears 07836 730719	Mayfair Cards & Gifts 01255 674677
Lawrence Bears. 01823 257674	Maypole Bears. 01386 48217
Lazy Days. 07929 209233	Meadows Teddy Bears 01204 693087
Lea-Bears. . . . . +31 (0)527 616552	Meem's . . . . +61 (0)8 9325 2897
Leeds Doll & Teddy Fair 0191 42 40 400	Megelles . . . . +61 7 3374 3373
Elizabeth Leggat 01355 249674	Meister Bear . . . . +27 (0)11 803 7189
Leigh Toy Fair. 01702 473288	Meldrum Bears 01726 74499
Reinhold Lesch GmbH 020 7794 2377	Melissa Jayne Bears 01606 76313
Lesley Jane Bears 01228 380134	Memories . . . . +353 (0)64 34447
Let's Go Round Again! 01902 324141	Memory Lane. 01422 833223
Li'l Bears 07931 479736	Memory Lane 0208 288 0820
Liebhab-Bären . . . . +49 (0)491 3478	Memory Lane - Corfe 01929 480006
Lillian Trigg of Rochester 01634 713131	Meredith Collection 01670 855448
Lincoln Fairs 01522 510524	Merry Bears. . . . . +852 8101 7923
Lincrafts. 07050 245572	Merry Maidens. 01462 486734
Lindal Bears. 01223 277118	Merrythought Ltd 01952 433116
Little Acorns. 01633 271010	Micha Bears. 01579 345832
Little Bears 01279 816022	Mick Bears Makerij . . . . . . +31 (0)314 361 116
Little Bloomers 0121 602 2090	Midland Good Bears 0121 311 1723
Little Scruffs of Evesham 01386 429002	Midland TB Festival 01952 433924
Llangollen Teddy Bear Fair 07885 710630	Milford Models. 01590 642112
Lodge Cordell 01986 894482	Mini Companions... . . . . 01752 350849
London Teddy Bear Fair 01778 391123	Minibums. 01722 742463
Loris Hancock's Studio 70 . . . . . +61 (0)7 5598 2242	Minikins... . . . . +1 843 875 2565
Loteni Bears 01493 731401	Mirkwood Bears. 01225 356505
Loulou Bears 01332 865715	Misfit Bears 0114 2304078
Lovable Fellows . . . . +49 (0)711 748156	Miss B's Bears. 01829 271873
Love is in the Bear 020 8304 1412	Mister Bear 01702 710733
Lucky Bears Limited. 01702 204182	Mistley Woodland Bears. 01255 870729
Lullabydolls 01536 742325	MLE-Designs . . . . +1 989 662 6598
Lynda Brown Bears. 020 8570 0095	Moheart Teddybears. 01978 760700
Lyndee-Lou-Bears 01624 616475	Moonstruck 01329 281718
Lynn's Little Gems 07776 483561	Mooseberry Bears 0116 2246803
Lynne & Michael Roche 01225 318042	Jenny Morgan 01384 397033
Lynton Teddy Bear Co 01525 371329	Mossie Bears. . . . . +27 (0)11 965 1654
Lyrical Bears 01438 351651	Mr Punch's Old Toys 020 8878 0773
	The Mulberry Bush 01273 493781
M	Museum Of Childhood 0131 529 4142
	My Old Teddy. 01902 332782
M. G. Bears 01603 783936	N* Collection . . . . +7 238 0073
Mabledon Road Bears 01732 356360	
Mac Bears by Carol Davidson 020 8863 6192	**N**
Madabout Bears 01294 835432	
Maddie Janes Character Bears 01348 831792	Nadine Thevenot . . . . +33 (0)4 78 75 54 68
Madeleine's Mini Bears . . . . . . +33 (0)1 39 14 50 86	Nadja Bears . . . . +32 (0)3 568 15 15
Madeley Bears TM. 01484 680143	Namtloc Bears 01429 422997
Maja's Bears. . . . . +32 (0)32 90 39 71	Narnie Bears 07903 082630
Majacabus Bears 01458 832008	The Naughty Bear Co 0151 476 6740
Majensie Teddies.... . . . . 01273 586890	Netty's Bears 01372 813558
Maldod Bears 01792 427053	New England Country Store. 01905 723400
Malu-Bear. . . . . +49 (0)7151 72769	New Forest Bears 01590 673334
Marian Bear. . . . . +31 (0)74 291 9115	New Forest Doll Museum 012425 652450
Marigold Bears 01564 776092	No 9 Paws for Thought. 01522 510524
Marilyn Pelling Bears 01273 884268	Noble Bears 023 8022 6474
Mary George Bears . . . . +1 734 453 6814	Norbeary 01706 659819
Mary Shortle 01904 425168	Normandy Bears . . . . +33 (0)2 33 55 98 61
Mary Shortle 01132 456160	Nottingham Bear Fairs 0115 916 3731
Mawkish Bears 01935 862984	

O

Oakley Fabrics Ltd 01582 424828
Oakwood Bears 01536 742843
Occasions Unlimited 01491 833800
Ochiltree Bears 01425 672030
Oggies Attic 0207 537 3146
Okidoki Original . . . . +46 (0)46 142089
Old Bear Company Ltd. 01246 862387
Old Bears & Friends. 01795 410314
Old Bears Network. 01422 823079
The Old Playroom 01732 845582
Old Time Teddies . . . . +31 (0)15 310 8025
Old Toys Vienna. . . . . +43 (0)1 769 8901
Oldbearscene.com. 01892 521232
Olde Teddy Bear Shoppe . . . . +1 905 893 3590
Oldenbears. 020 8531 5061
Ollie Bears by Kim 01388 748366
Oops! Pardon me, Bears! 01304 367653
Orchard Bears 01494 717501
Original Felted Folksies . . . . +1 203 729 7714
Original Hanna Baeren . . . . +49 (0)6483 3703
Original Rica-Bear® . . . . +49 (0)5231 59750
Orphan Bears 01744 812274
Out 'n About Bears. 01202 744196
Out of the Woods© 01737 821218
Oz Matilda Bears. . . . . +61 (0)2 6677 1388

P

Padz 01700 811524
Pamela Ann Designs 01778 344152
Panda Jak Bears 01582 405490
Josephine Parnell 01205 723637
Party Bears 01225 446097
Past & Presents 015394 45417
Paw Lines Bears. 028 2564 5130
Paw Prints.... . . . . 01782 537315
Peacock Fibres Ltd 01274 633900
Sue Pearson 01273 774851
Pebble Beach Bears. 01273 277747
Louise Peers 01625 527917
Peggotty 01939 291328
Pennbeary. 01367 252809
Penny Bunn Bears 01453 828060
Nicola Perkins 01782 751148
Petal Originals 01372 724386
Phred's Friends 01437 532279
PicklePumpkin Bears 01323 892048
The Piece Parade . . . . +1 919 870 1881
Pipedream Bears 0161 285 8254
Pipsqueak and Pepe-Joe... . . . . 023 9232 6400
PittyPats Poppets 0207 537 3146
Pixel's Bears 01547 530607
pmbears . . . . +1 519 522 0454
Pogmear Bears 07730 788581
Pooh Corner 01892 770456
Portobello Bear Company 01723 376929
Postal Bears 01457 766650

Pottershouse Bears . . . . +1 740 668 4822
Pottery Plus. 01323 727430
The Potting Shed 01534 854203
Probär GmbH . . . . +49 (0)2562 7013 0
Puca Bears. . . . . +49 (0)6207 921461
Pam Pudvine 01244 347900
Puppenhausmuseum . . . . +41 (0)61 225 95 95
Putty Dink Bears 01453 872649
Puzzle Bears 01483 224524
Pywacket Teddies 023 9245 2266

Q

Sue Quinn 0141 887 9916
QVC. 020 7705 5600

R

R B Bear Supplies 07624 482 403
R.E.R. Bears 01227 741352
R. John Wright... . . . . +1 802 447 7072
Raffles. 01753 851325
Rainbow Dyes 01903 722078
Rainey Days.... . . . . 020 8647 6235
Ramshackle Bears. 01273 454746
Rascals.... 01395 264964
Razzle Dazzle 01179 614141
Ready Tedi Go! 01444 413487
Recollect. 01444 871052
Remem-bear... . . . . 07624 482 403
Restoration 01283 734147
Rhiw Valley Bears 01686 650883
Riverbank Bears 07816 148597
Robin Rive Bears 07961 950452
Robyn's Bears... . . . . +61 (0)3 9772 8330
Rochester Teddy Bear Fair 01279 871110
Rosemary's Doll's Hospital 01553 764474
Rosie's Attic. 01460 57775
Round About Bears 07785 788307
Rowan Bears 01903 240467
Royal Berkshire... Hospital. 0118 979 0228
Ruben Bears 01582 731544
Running Bear Company. . . . . . +49 (0)491 912 1526
Pat Rush. 01732 361994/07715 704025
Russian Teddy Bear . . . . +7 095 219 7094

S

Sacque Bears 01773 853159
Sad Pads. 01622 754441
Sally Anne Bears 01522 509329
Sally B Gollies 0118 9775464
Salon Gueules de Miel. . . . . . . +33 (0)1 42 00 64 27
Sandykay Bears 020 8952 2600
Sarah Lou Bears 01656 722075
Sarah's Bruins 01945 461257
Scruffie Bears... . . . . 01244 534724
Scruffy Bears. 01903 734865
SelecTeds 01702 390097
Serendipity. 01422 340097
Seventh Heaven Teddies 0121 532 7421

Shantock Bears 01442 260486
Sharon Grace's Bears . . . . +64 (0)9 436 0070
Shebob Bears 01342 714568
Shelinka Bears . . . . +61 (0)8 9293 3664
Shellysbears 01908 679098
Julie Shepherd. 01730 810878
Shoebutton Bears 0161 282 8636
Showcase 01242 224144
Shultz Characters 01329 834681
Sidmouth Bears 01395 512888
Small Wonders... . . . . 01483 222889
Snazzy Gollys 01903 721070
Snuff Box (est 1984) 01254 888550
Fabian Song . . . . +65 673 331 63
Southsea Bears 023 9234 8182
Southway Bears. 01425 654768
Spielmittel. . . . . +49 (0)36766 20632
Spielzeugdesign . . . . +49 (0)36781 40363
Springer Bears. 01773 748093
St Ann's Dolls Hospital 01494 890220
St Martin's Gallery 01425 489090
Stanley Bears . . . . +61 (0)3 5728 6623
Starlite Bears. 07802 568685
Margarete Steiff GmbH . . . . +49 (0)7322 131-1
Steiff Gallery. 0208 466 8444
Steiff UK 01932 568230
Stine-Teddies . . . . +45 86 63 87 22
Stonegate Teddy Bears 01904 641074
Stratford...Teddy Bear Fair 01279 871110
Strawbeary's 01442 265023
Streetbrooke Bear. 0121 236 6953
Studio 44. . . . . 01775 820429
Su Tee 01287 659117
Sue Gibson Bears 01206 760257
Sue's Teds 01905 29043
Suffolk Bears by Shirley 01473 686312
The Suffolk Doll Company 01473 827600
Sun Moon Bears 01903 205392
Swannbeary Bears. 07792 759558
Sycamore Bears 0116 2997243

T

Talents of Windsor 01753 831459
Tamerton Teddys 01752 480656
Taylor's Teddy's 01491 874033
Teachers Pets 01284 704253
Ted's Place 01606 888600
Teddeez Bear Co 01621 842752
Teddies 2006 . . . . 01273 697974
The Teddy Bear Club 01245 478578
Teddy Bear Club International 01206 505961
Teddy Bear House 01305 263200
The Teddy Bear Group 01125 350 408
The Teddy Bear Museum 01789 293160
The Teddy Bear Orphanage 01744 812274
Teddy Bear Scene Magazine 01778 391158
The Teddy Bear Shop. 01484 420999

Teddy Bear Times 01903 884988
Teddy Bear UK 0115 981 2013
Teddy Bears At Home 0191 2579541
Teddy Bears Cottage 01775 722523
Teddy Bears Downstairs . . . +61 (0)2 4933 1224
Teddy Bears & Friends of Bourne. . . . 01778 426898
Teddy Bears of Witney 01993 706616
Teddy Bears' Picknick . . . . +31 (0)343 577068
Teddy Bearsville 0121 559 9990
Teddy 'N' Friends 01300 348483
Teddy Traders. 01736 363143
Teddy Tricotts 0141 637 6306
Teddy's Room . . . . +49 (0)721 1517 809
Teddybear Travellers. 01334 478751
Teddysmiths. 07931 479736
Teddystyle 01442 265944
Teddytech . . . . +27 (0)31 312 7755
TedE-Guide 01273 697974
Tedi Enfys 01633 780247
Tedi Ty Coed 01443 776031
Teds of the Riverbank 0161 303 0011
Teeny Bears. 02380 446356
Terry's Teddy Hospital. 01438 718700
Teslington Bears 01920 420419
Tewin's Bruins 01438 718700
Theabär. . . . . +49 (0)7529913065
Prue Theobalds 01424 422306
Thistle Bears 07929 713566
Thistlecraft Bears. 01902 306807
Thistledown 023 9259 9932
Thistledown Bears 01287 676302
Elizabeth Thompson. 01993 811915
Thornbearies 01454 228167
Thread-Bears. 01329 845427
Threadteds . . . . +31 (0)77 3984960
Three O'Clock Bears. 024 7641 6654
Thumbelina's 01304 619802
Tickle Teds . . . . +81 (0) 90 4087 6197
Tillington Bears 01223 837701
Tin Soldiers Studio . . . . +27 (0)83 305 5954
Tiny Teddies by Ann 029 2075 3133
Tobilane Designs 01931 712077
Toffee Bears. 01323 449748
Toggle Teddies 01773 824258
Top 'n' Tail Teddy Bears. 01304 363040
Totally Teddies 01279 871110
Townhouse Bears 020 8746 2961
The Toy Chest 01768 891237
The Toy Emporium 01746 765134
Toy Gallery. 01482 864890
The Toy Store. . . . . +1 419 531 2839
Toys of Youth 01234 841649
Toys..Handmade by Susan. . . . . . . +1 416 242 6446
Traditional Toys Ltd. 01443 222693
Trafford Print & Design. 01933 229366
Travelling Teddies 01461 800587
Treasured Teddies 01295 690479
Trendle International Ltd. 01984 656825

Trevor Jenner...	01342 713858
Tribal Bears	01704 539476
Trudy's Teddies.	01392 681760
Truffle Tum Teddies.	01253 761500
Tugalot and Scruffbags	07968 806633
Twilight Teds.	01925 725084

U

Unique.	01284 723116

V

V and N Bear Supplies.	07971 213974
V. B. Bears	0191 536 9683
Vanda Bears	01635 36285
Vectis Auctions.	01642 750616
Village Bears	+1 941 366 2667

W

Walnut Tree Corner...	01638 601708
Warren Bears.	01689 871420
Watts New Bears	01706 215308
Wealden Manor Press.	0118 941 4000
Weaselpie Publishing.	01983 403224
Weavers Bears	01483 273708
Wellfield Bears.	02920 453045
Wellwood Bears	029 2073 6610
Wendy Bears.	07788 112466
Wendy-Sue Bears	01604 785942
Westie Bears	01403 241381

Westmead Teddies.	01983 840643
Georgina Whalley.	01332 556880
Whisty Bears	01227 770641
Whittle-Le-Woods Bears.	01204 706831
Wickenden Bears.	01452 502840
Wiggintons.	01992 505695
Wild Designs	01244 401856
Willow Bears	01732 871276
Windy Ridge Bears	01254 696712
Winklemoor Bears	01495 244528
Winsome & Wild...	+61 (0)8 9844 1956
The Winter BearFest	01273 697974
Winter Bears	01430 432120
Wisdom Bears	01294 212822
Woodgate Bears	01273 891665
Woodland Teddies	01509 267597
Woodrow Bears	01291 421369
Woodville Bears.	01283 221829
Wookey Hole...	01749 672243
World of Bears.	01823 332050

Y

Yesterday Child	01908 583403
Yesterday's Children.	01945 440466
Yorkshire Collectables	01756 797453

Z

Zena Arts	0115 960 5820

END

International Telephone Information

Dialling the UK from overseas

UK phone numbers in the Guide have been listed with their area dialling code, beginning with a zero. If dialling the UK from overseas please

- begin with your international dialling code
- then dial the UK dialling code – 44
- omit the zero from the start of the area code

Eg 01273 654321 should be dialled as:

Your international dialling code 44 1273 654321

Don't forget to check the time difference of the country you're phoning — to avoid calling in the middle of the night!

Dialling out from the UK - add 00

Internatinal phone numbers have been listed beginning with their country dialling code.

From the UK add the international dialling code –00– to the number. Eg +44 (0)987 12345 should be dialled as 00 44 987 12345, omiting the zero in brackets which only applies if within that country. Phone numbers in display advertisements have been included as supplied to us and so may need careful attention to ensure they are dialled correctly; check your phone book for details about phoning abroad under International Information.

Particularly note differences in ringing & engaged tones.

Europe	GMT	+ 1 hour	W. Australia	GMT	+ 7-8 hours	New Zealand	GMT	+12 hours
USA & Canada	GMT	– 6-8 hours	E. Australia	GMT	+ 10 hours	Japan	GMT	+ 9 hours

Advertiser Index

END

PUBLISHING

Hugglets

Your complimentary tickets are on page 225

Please see overleaf for floorplans

For exhibitor lists please see www.hugglets.co.uk

or send SAE to receive list by post 3 weeks prior to event

Venue – Kensington Town Hall
Hornton Street, London, W8.

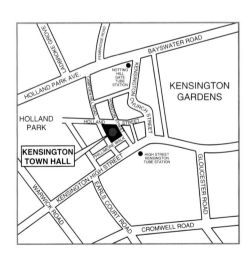

Entry times

11am - 4.30pm
Tickets at door:
£4 for adults,
£2 for children.

Parking is only £4
for the day.
400 spaces.
Nearest Tube is
High Street Kensington

Hugglets, PO Box 290, Brighton, BN2 1DR Tel: 01273 697974
Fax: 01273 62 62 55   Email: info@hugglets.co.uk www.hugglets.co.uk

Hugglets Festivals Floorplans

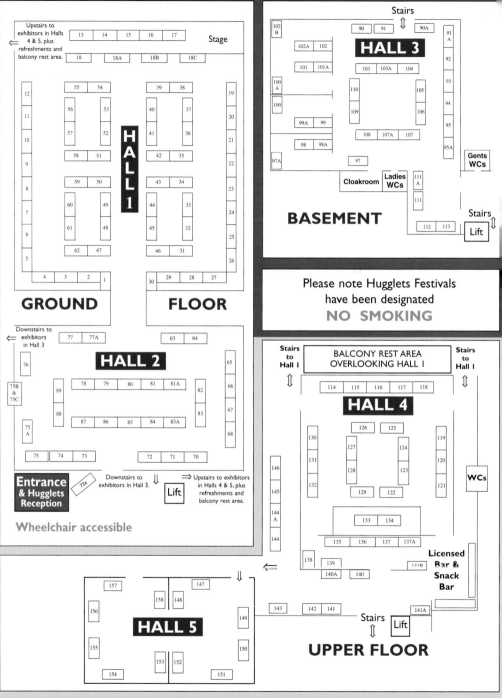

For exhibitor lists: www.hugglets.co.uk

WINTER BEARFEST

This entry ticket is valid for an adult or child from 11.00am – 4.30pm

26th February 2006

**Kensington Town Hall, Hornton St., London W8
Extra tickets on sale at reception**

TEDDIES 2006

NOW IN SEPTEMBER

This entry ticket is valid for an adult or child from 11.00am – 4.30pm

3rd September 2006

**Kensington Town Hall, Hornton St., London W8
Extra tickets on sale at reception**

WINTER BEARFEST

This entry ticket is valid for an adult
or child from 11.00am – 4.30pm

26th February 2006

**Kensington Town Hall, Hornton St., London W8
Extra tickets on sale at reception**

TEDDIES 2006

NOW IN SEPTEMBER

This entry ticket is valid for an adult
or child from 11.00am – 4.30pm

3rd September 2006

**Kensington Town Hall, Hornton St., London W8
Extra tickets on sale at reception**